The author

Len Markham has written many books
has dedicated much of his life to rec
greatest county in England. His outpu.   ...us
volumes on Hull. An adopted son of Hull th.   , ne has
a genuine passion for a city he knows is the r.   ...ting in the
county. Markham is a journalist and lives in   East Riding of
Yorkshire. He has two children.

Great Hull Stories

LEN MARKHAM

FORT PUBLISHING LTD

First published in 2003 by Fort Publishing Ltd, Old Belmont House,
12 Robsland Avenue, Ayr, KA7 2RW. (01292-880693)

Cover painting: *SS Fairy leaving Hull* by John Cooper, 43 St Hilda Street,
Bridlington, East Yorkshire, YO15 3EE (01262-676337)

Typeset by S. Fairgrieve (0131-658-1763)

Printed by Bell and Bain Ltd, Glasgow

ISBN 0-9536576-9-8

For Thomas Matthew and Chloë Elizabeth in memory of happy days in a great Yorkshire city.

CONTENTS

PREFACE

You can enunciate the name of the most interesting town in Yorkshire without moving your lips. Hull, or if you take lemon with your tea, Kingston-upon-Hull, is geographically aloof. Its comparative isolation has spawned a gruff, no-nonsense and independent breed of people who turned their backs on the rest of the county and looked seaward. It's no coincidence that the Beggars' Litany begins with the name of Hull: 'From Hull, Hell and Halifax, the Good Lord preserve us.' Beggars had good cause to seek divine preservation, for the burghers of Hull were renowned for their treatment of the idle. It was often said that neither beggar nor prince was allowed to trifle with its citizens, and their enterprise as merchant adventurers elevated the town to the position of the third port in England.

Over the centuries, the sea has dominated the life of Hull. Whaling, fishing, marine products and shipping have nurtured an incredibly hard working and close-knit community. Comprehensively blitzed during World War Two, Hull also saw its lifeblood industry largely destroyed after the Cod Wars of the 1970s. In consequence, whole fleets and several docks died with the extension of territorial fishing-limits and the introduction of quotas. For a while, the port looked doomed, and dereliction and unemployment created a mood of despair.

Hull's resilience and adaptability, however, brought about a renaissance in its economic fortunes. New motorway-links, the construction of the Humber Bridge and a programme of renewal that included the conversion of a former dock into a fashionable marina, have re-energised a thoroughly outward looking city that can offer you sherry on the sun deck or grog in some slightly nefarious alley.

Having comprehensively explored the place on foot, I can say without question that Hull is the most fascinating town in Yorkshire. A Leeds with fizz, its effervescent past is spiked with

Mickey Finns. Danger, disaster and dark deeds enliven a compelling history that will both captivate and entertain. In this book, I will offer you a personal selection of tales. They will tell you something about the idiosyncratic character of Hull, provide accounts of success and failure and relate the life stories of a number of remarkable individuals.

Despite its current cloak of modernity, Hull maintains its compelling air of intrigue and mystery. Take a wrong turn down one of its many old alleyways, and the pull of the tide at your feet will rouse the sea-soused soul. Visit Hull and you too will discover that there's something of the mariner in all of us.

I would like to thank the following people for their assistance. Shirley Streets and the late Douglas Streets for their unfailing help and inspiration. Irene Megginson. Chris Ketchell at Hull's Local History Unit. Staff at the Beverley and Hull Central and Local Studies Libraries. John Cooper for the excellent painting reproduced on the front cover.

Len Markham
April 2003

1

HULL'S FIRST SUPERSTAR

Although he is rarely heard today, a singer from a humble background in Hull was one of the biggest stars of the 1950s, not only in Britain but also in the United States. He had no less than twelve top-ten hits in this country, including two that went all the way to number one. In 1954 he became the first British act to have a major hit in America, an astonishing feat for that era. But, like many in his profession, life away from the world of show business would be tainted by controversy and scandal.

David Whitfield was born in February 1926 in a tiny house at 3 Albert Terrace, East Street, Hull, the third child of rulleyman James Whitfield and his wife Lillian who would go on to produce five more children. In the midst of an industrial area, dominated by the docks and the sprawling premises of the British Oil and Cake Mills and Rank's Flour Mills, their two up, two down, terraced property was cramped in the extreme. In common with many other houses in the area it lacked the facilities we take for granted today, including an indoor toilet and hot water.

Whitfield showed an early aptitude for singing. His recruitment into the ranks of St Peter's School choir by a perceptive choirmaster helped to develop his latent talents. Despite an impish nature that frequently lured him onto the dockside – one of his great delights was to launch himself into the full holds of grain ships – he did reasonably well at school. And frequent school concerts allowed him to develop a growing repertoire that included religious and operatic themes. At the age of 11, this precocious young man was sent out over the Christmas period to supplement the family's meagre income. Undaunted, he toured the local pubs and, with his little legs dangling over some convenient bar, entertained the customers with his songs. Frequenting such places, which undoubtedly would have greatly influenced a boy of his age, he was inculcated into the culture of drinking from an early age, and beer was always his favourite tipple. His subsequent life as a seaman which involved visiting strange ports, and his initial success as a singer entertaining in bars and clubs, gave him ample opportunity to indulge his appetite for alcohol.

By the time he was 13, the aspiring singer had moved home twice. After staying for a short time in a larger property in Harcourt Street, the Whitfield family eventually settled in a house in Beaumont Street, and the children beamed with joy at the sight of a postage-stamp front garden. With the advent of war in 1939 the threat of bombing initiated a programme of evacuation, particularly for the elderly residents of Hull and its schoolchildren. David Whitfield, along with three of his siblings, found himself for a short time in Scarborough. On returning home, the four youngsters adjusted to the rigours of wartime Britain. Whitfield by this time had left school and taken a job as a delivery boy for a Jewish baker. The baker supplied the bike!

During the blitz on Hull, the Whitfields' house in Beaumont Street was completely flattened by a bomb, causing the family to relocate again. This time they moved to 6 Florence Grove, off Lorraine Street, which was also damaged by the Luftwaffe. David gave up delivering bagels for a living and for a while he helped his ailing father in the carting business. Then, in 1942, he got his first break. A lady, who was married to the secretary of the Perth Street Club in Hull, recalled the event:

> One night when the club ran out of beer, it was rationed then, a party of us went to see a friend of ours, called Len Palen: he was compere at the Bowling Club in Stoneferry, just behind the Grapes public house. When we got there, they too had run out of beer, but we got some from the pub. During the evening, Len got a young boy up to sing. It was David. He was very shy and took a lot of persuading, but he sang really great; we all thought he would become a very good artiste. Before he left, my husband offered him a booking at the Perth Street Club. He refused at first as he was really shy, but an uncle offered to come with him, so it was arranged. This was, as far as I know, his first booking and he was paid seven and sixpence (37p) in the old money.
>
> On the said evening he sang so well. Arthur rang Fred Porter at the Dixon's Arms, Woodmansey and he gave him his second booking and that's how David started. I can remember two of the

songs he sang: 'Hear My Song Violetta' and 'Goodbye' from the musical *White Horse Inn*.

But this did not mean instant stardom. The aspiring singer had to keep his autograph pen sheathed for a while yet. With the country at war the 18-year-old volunteered for the Royal Navy. Whitfield was to stay in the navy for seven happy years. He saw action as a gunner on the battleship *Ramillies* on D-Day, and other duties took him aboard *Concorde, Belfast* and *Black Swan* with a final posting to HMS *Vernon*, the torpedo-ratings base, in Portsmouth. During his time afloat, the singing continued. He entertained his shipmates and took the opportunity of supplementing his naval pay by singing in bars and clubs from the Far East to the United States and beyond.

During 1947 and 1948, he found himself in Hong Kong where he took the opportunity of singing with Ken Cochrane's nine-piece dance-band. Exposure in venues like the Kowloon Cricket Club, the China Fleet Club and the Dockyard Social Club brought his talents to a cosmopolitan audience. At the time, he included such famous songs as 'Come Back to Sorrento' and 'I'll Take You Home Again Kathleen' in his repertoire. A regular slot on Radio Hong Kong followed, and his fine voice came to the attention of an American entertainer. She was so impressed by what she heard that she wrote to the British Admiral recommending that Able Seaman Whitfield be relieved of his duties as she felt 'he would give much more pleasure to servicemen and civilians by singing full time.' The Admiral's response has not been recorded but Whitfield's Divisional Officer did make one prophetic statement: 'Be patient, some day that voice of yours will make you famous.'

He spent most of his time abroad in Singapore, returning to England in 1949 to HMS *Vernon* in Portsmouth, where he again sang in local pubs. With an eye for the ladies, who adored his blond hair, blue eyes and svelte good looks, he naturally gravitated towards the Women's Royal Naval Service quarters, where one intuitive lady suggested he audition for a talent show. Heats for *Opportunity Knocks* were being held at the Theatre Royal, and Whitfield was reluctantly persuaded to try his luck. Only a last minute change of heart by its manager who had gruffly announced, 'Sorry but we're full right up with talent, and anyway you should have put his name down weeks ago', allowed the latecomer to enter. The 24-year-old lad from Hull belted out his version of 'Goodbye' and the audience went wild. Inevitably, the judges declared him the winner. The manager of the Theatre Royal was a chastened man. 'To think' he said, 'I nearly turned this young man away.'

The novice was through to the finals of the show. He won of course, and the legendary Hughie Green put him on the road to stardom in his Radio Luxembourg show *Opportunity Knocks*. After demobilisation in 1950, he toured Britain for eight months as an act with the *Opportunity Knocks* road show and he also became a regular singer on Radio Luxembourg. In the fifties this pioneering station did much to shape the youth culture of the post-war period. It was the preferred entertainment for the majority of the nation's young people, and his fine tenor voice garnered tens of thousands of fans. During the British tour, Whitfield's penchant for the company of young ladies brought him a lasting legacy. He appeared at the Metropolitan Theatre in London along with Doreen Sturgeon, who was part of a mind-reading act. The pair got together and the 16-year-old soon fell for his charms and became pregnant. Later, she ran away from home to join him on tour in Wales but her anxious relatives intervened and took her back home, quashing any thoughts of marriage. David's indiscretion led to the birth of a daughter, Madeleine, whom he subsequently supported for many years. When the tour came to an end, the bubble temporarily burst; the erstwhile heart-throb became a coalman and then a breeze-block maker in Hull.

Whitfield worked with the Hull Concrete Stone Company by day, and sang in Hull's extensive network of working-men's clubs by night, where he cheekily demanded a fee of a whole guinea. This made him a genuine celebrity in his native town, although the breakthrough into the big time that he dreamed of continued to elude him. He even found time to get married and continued with the day job, but his constant frustration at playing to local audiences made him consider giving up his showbiz ambitions forever.

Then Hughie Green contacted him again, asking if he would appear in a private concert in London's Criterion Theatre. David obliged and received his usual warm welcome. One applauding fan, an impresario called Cecil Landeau, offered him a short contract, worth £10 per week all found, singing at the capital's Washington

Hotel in January 1953. After the contract ended in March 1953 he once again returned, somewhat crestfallen, to Hull. With no income and an added mouth to feed – his son Lance had been born in May 1952 – there was no option but to return to the mundane business of making breeze blocks. Before he left London, he made a test recording at the request of the Decca Record Company's talent scout, Bunny Lewis, but this apparently came to naught and he went back to his breeze blocks and a wage of under £10 per week. His wife, who by this time had a young son to look after, settled back into Yorkshire life with some relief. Lewis, however, liked what he heard and contacted him after a few weeks, setting up a recording session with the backing of the Nat Temple Orchestra. The record, featuring two songs – 'Marta' and 'I'll Never Forget You' – was cut and released. Within a month, it had sold 20,000 copies.

Following this success, David Whitfield was groomed for stardom. He signed a personal management agreement with a publicity expert, revamped his image and moved, once again, to London. On 26 April 1953, he began his professional singing career with a performance at the Cine-Variety at the East Ham Granada. For that week's work, he earned an amazing £75. His shooting star was indeed in the ascendant.

The second disc 'I Believe' eventually sold 75,000 copies, and his third record 'Bridge of Sighs' reached the dizzy heights of number nine in the charts in October 1953. An even bigger chartbuster followed – the controversial 'Answer Me' – which despite being banned by the BBC, sold no less than 700,000 copies. During that amazing year, David's earnings rose to £500 per week and his popularity continued to soar. He toured the country giving sell-out performances, and his biggest ovation came in June when he appeared on home ground at the Tivoli Theatre in Hull.

Perennially the friendly and chipper Yorkshire lad, Whitfield really endeared himself to his army of fans when, between performances, he took time out to visit a female fan in Raywell Sanatorium near Hull. 'I was being nursed back to health from tuberculosis', she recalled, 'which only a short time before had killed my husband. David had only just turned professional and I wrote asking if he would come and see us at Raywell. At the time he was topping the bill at the Tivoli. We had a matron who was a bit of a Tartar and one day she asked me if I'd been writing to Mr Whitfield, and I said I had. Matron said, "He's here." '

In 1954, a car crash near Elvington nearly ended his meteoric rise, but he survived with only cuts and bruises. He then cut his greatest-ever record, a timeless rendition of 'Cara Mia', backed by the Mantovani Orchestra. It eventually sold more than one million copies and even entered the top ten in the United States. Of all his hits, this is the one that is most fondly remembered. It became a worldwide favourite, and Whitfield adopted it as his signature tune. He also splashed out on a white Cadillac and swooning, bobby-soxed female fans scrawled multiple kisses on its paintwork in lipstick!

In November 1954, Whitfield really knew he had hit the big time when he was asked to sing for the Queen at the London Palladium alongside Noel Coward, Bob Hope, Guy Mitchell, Howard Keel and Frankie Laine. This *Royal Variety Performance* was a great success, and even greater plaudits came his way after a surprise appearance on Ed Sullivan's *Toast of the Town* show in America. He received $4,000 for singing just two songs and, during his short stay in New York, met the legendary actor James Stewart and the great British film director, Alfred Hitchcock.

After returning to England, he took time out to recover from recurring bouts of laryngitis but resumed his punishing schedule of concerts in 1955. A string of hits followed. Massive sales of 'Beyond the Stars', 'Mama', 'When You Lose the One You Love' and 'Everywhere' ensured that he remained Britain's top male-recording-star of the period. However, away from the limelight his forthright style attracted some criticism. Together with his conductor, Ray Warburton, he would visit local pubs between shows and challenge all-comers to a game of darts. Whitfield was an excellent player and almost always won; legend has it he never paid for a pint. But his brashness and conceit in victory resulted in adverse publicity in the press. This blunt, yet modest, Yorkshireman hit back in typical style, emphasising the importance of his roots in Hull:

> A couple of years ago I worked with my hands loading concrete slabs onto lorries back home in Hull. Then my voice changed my fortunes. But, and this is important, it didn't change me and neither has the success and financial rewards that have come to me.

Apparently this is all wrong. I still speak with the accent of a son of Hull; I still say what I think because that honesty is worth more than well-chosen but insincere words.

The highlight of 1955 came in September with the presentation of a gold disc to mark the sale of one million copies of 'Cara Mia'. He capped off a momentous twelve months with further visits to the United States.

In 1956, three hit records – 'My September Love', 'My Son John' and 'My Unfinished Symphony' hit the charts. Whitfield's continued success allowed him to buy a smart new house in the fashionable Hull suburb of Kirkella. The house was named, of course, Cara Mia. Architect designed, it incorporated a raised dais for a grand piano. Outside, two replica records made of sheet metal were built into the property's wrought-iron gates and musical door-chimes played the singer's famous theme tune.

A record entitled 'The Adoration Waltz' opened his vocal account for 1957. This was the theme song in the film *Sea Wife* starring Richard Burton and Joan Collins. Later that year, he appeared in a show called *Five Past Eight* in Newcastle, and then moved on for the summer season to the King's Theatre in Southsea. The stage door of the theatre was besieged every night by frantic girl-fans, who would wait for hours for a chance to get their hero's autograph. Between shows, Whitfield would slip away from the bright lights 'to play darts and have a couple of pints.' A successful year was rounded off in fine style when he took the starring role, alongside Arthur Askey and Tommy Cooper, in the pantomime *Robinson Crusoe* at the London Palladium. The show, which received rave reviews, ran for over one hundred performances. As a tribute to his home town, its song sheets included an amusing ditty sung by Arthur Askey. It went by the rather catchy title of 'Hull, Hull Captivating, Fascinating Hull'.

The big chart successes of the following year were 'Cry My Heart' and 'On the Street Where You Live'. He made rare television appearances in 1958 on the now forgotten *Jack Jackson Show*, *Cool For Cats*, *The Dave King Show* and *Saturday Spectacular*. Although he didn't know it at the time, 1958 would be the year when his popularity began to wane. His ballad 'The Right to Love' reached only number thirty in a fast-changing music scene infiltrated by a new wave of stars that included Elvis Presley.

In 1959, he worked as hard as ever, and completed an exhausting programme of live performances. Realising that his style and voice were unsuited to the brave new world of rock and roll, he took the conscious decision to concentrate on operetta and musical shows. He also elected to take on a six-month tour of Australia in 1960. In Melbourne, he made an enduring impact and formed friendships that were to take him back repeatedly to that country over the next twenty years. Whitfield's contractual ties with the Decca Recording Company were severed in 1961, eight years and twenty-eight records after his first rise to fame. Although a three-year agreement was signed that year with rival company HMV, the lack of chart success brought on bouts of depression. The falling star also began drinking heavily, and his demeanour no doubt contributed to a series of bizarre personal injuries that included a broken foot, gashed head and damage to his hands and legs.

For the next few years he earned a respectable living, and his many loyal fans enjoyed seaside summer-shows, a pantomime in Leeds starring alongside newcomers Morecambe and Wise and performances in the touring musical *Desert Song*. At the beginning of 1963, he received a welcome offer that enabled him to renew his associations with the Royal Navy for a services tour that would take him to Kenya, Aden and the Persian Gulf.

A round of summer shows and Christmas pantomimes followed. He also accepted decidedly less glamorous bookings at working-men's clubs to supplement his dwindling income. With his career on a downward spiral this was undoubtedly when the rot set in, and two unfortunate incidents epitomise these twilight years. Whitfield had always been drawn to attractive women, especially when he had been drinking, and his amorous advances frequently aroused jealous comments from disgruntled husbands and boyfriends. In a Chesterfield club in 1965, he was serenading a woman when he was assaulted by her husband. He punched Whitfield in the face while he was belting out his rendition of 'A Spoonful of Sugar'. His assailant also grabbed him by the hair and cut him below the left eye, causing his face to become badly swollen. The assailant obviously thought the worse-for-wear Whitfield had pushed his luck. He had previously danced with the woman as part of his act, kissed her and escorted her back to her table. Insulted, and angered at the injury to his face, he consulted a solicitor and the case was heard by a Derbyshire court in March 1966. Although he won, and was awarded damages, the contention by the defence that the lady in question had been intimidated and embarrassed by the incident dented the singer's image. His perceived arrogance in court further eroded his popularity.

Then, just a year later, he was accused of something much worse – an indecent assault on an autograph hunter aged 11. At the time, he was performing a summer show in Llandudno, and living in a bungalow close to the theatre with his manager. Two sisters called at the house and asked him to autograph photographs. In the court case that followed it was alleged that Whitfield, who had been in bed at the time, told the girls to return in the afternoon when his manager had left. The court then heard evidence that on their return, Whitfield, who was wearing shorts, went outside 'and sat in the car with one leg outside, while he autographed the photographs'. The older sister said that, while in this position, he indecently exposed himself. Later, after receiving a present of some special 'David Whitfield rock', it was further alleged that one of the girls was indecently assaulted when Whitfield put his hand down the front of her dress. The alarm was raised when the distressed girls went home in tears and confided in their aunt, who immediately called the police.

The singer denied both charges, and called a surprise witness during the second day of the trial. A lady, referred to in court only as 'Miss W' for reasons of propriety, explained that she had been staying with Whitfield in the bungalow at the time of the incident and she had neither heard nor seen anything to substantiate the allegations. Interrogated by the prosecution barrister she explained that she had seen nothing untoward, suggesting that she had deliberately stayed out of sight for 'obvious reasons.' The defence counsel made more of her testimony by arguing, 'Is it likely that this man would choose to behave indecently with little girls when his girl friend is a few yards away to hear any outcry or complaint? You see that she is not an unattractive young lady. So is it likely that he would indulge himself with these young children?' At the end of the hearing, Whitfield was found guilty of indecent exposure and fined the maximum of £25 with costs, but he was acquitted on the more serious charge of indecent assault. He was naturally upset at the verdict, and suggested years later that he been framed. It has to be said that the star revelled in the adulation of female fans, and his practice of allowing adoring teenagers into his dressing room without chaperones drew much criticism over the years from many friends, including Hughie Green. But that was all part of his gregarious devil-may-care attitude.

In the mid 1960s, David Whitfield was regarded as something of a square and, compared with the raw, pulsating and often deliberately shocking music of the new pop idols, his songs came across as dated. He plied the clubs, drinking all the while, and made a repeat visit to Australia. He also tried his luck in New Zealand and Canada. His diehard fans continued to support him and he still had some notable nights. One particular appearance at the opening of the Northwood Club in Cottingham, where he enjoyed a rip-roaring session of repartee with Hull comic Norman Collier, stays in the memory. But despite the occasional triumph, the great days had gone forever.

By 1977, the ageing star had spent twenty-five years in show business. Billed as the 'Golden Boy of the Fifties' he could still pull in modest crowds and, among a certain age group, the old ballads had a timeless appeal. This was particularly true of Canada and Australia, and further trips to those countries reawakened a long-held desire to leave England for good.

David Whitfield died of a cerebral haemorrhage in Sydney on 15 February 1980, just days before his fifty-fourth birthday. A fellow entertainer summed him up thus: 'Gutsy, macho, very confident, almost to the point of arrogance. Couldn't give a damn about anything really. Kept the teenage hunger for wine, women and song all his life. Women got him into hot water, especially the young ones, and I think wine finally killed him.' His body was cremated and the ashes were flown back to England and taken to Hull, where a ship was waiting. A frigate, HMS *Sirius*, was charged with dropping them into the North Sea. The vessel took up her pre-arranged position five miles south-east of Spurn Point and, under the veil of a Union Jack, the casket was eased into the waves.

The next time you're leaving the Humber on the North Sea ferry, say a little prayer for David Whitfield. Or would that be 'Cara Mia'?

2

PUTTING ON THE RIX

Many people might find it hard to credit that an actor who dropped his trousers more than 12,000 times on stage would become not only a member of the House of Lords but also a highly influential campaigner and policy maker in the field of learning disability. Brian Rix was to the stage farce what Spike Milligan was to lunacy, and yet he was able to bridge the gap between performing and politics with ease, earning a CBE, a knighthood and a peerage along the way. His life has also been touched by a number of personal tragedies, all of which he has responded to with great fortitude and determination.

The youngest of four children, Brian Rix was born in 1924 in Cottingham, the so-called 'largest village in England'. His father, Herbert, was a wealthy shipowner in Hull, in partnership with his two brothers. The family later moved to a substantial house in Hornsea when Brian was 4 years old. Hornsea had become a fashionable location for successful Hull businessmen following the opening of the Hull and Hornsea railway in 1864, and a convenient service from Hull's Wilmington Station allowed passengers quickly to commute between home and office.

The young Brian Rix grew up under the watchful eyes of his parents and his nanny, Allie. His mother, Fanny, was very enthusiastic about amateur theatricals, and her love of the grease paint soon rubbed off on her son and a daughter, Sheila. An ebullient and influential lady, she encouraged her husband to create props and scenery for her productions. There was also a strong show-business tradition in Hornsea: for many years troupes of minstrels and actors, known as *pierrots*, had entertained the many thousands of visitors from Hull and elsewhere. Perhaps it is not surprising that both Brian and his sister – who much later would achieve fame as Annie Sugden in the television soap *Emmerdale* – took to the boards with such relish.

Rix did not relish his early education at St Bede's Preparatory School, which was located on Atwick Road to the north-west of Hornsea town centre (the building is no longer used for educational purposes and is to be converted into flats). This was despite its influential headmaster, Dr G. H. 'Bickie' Bickmore, who encouraged Rix to take up two activities in which he would later excel: cricket and drama. Then, from his point of view, it got even worse: he was sent to a prestigious boarding-school – Boothams, a Quaker establishment in York. Rix later confessed that he hated school in general, and boarding in particular, and used every trick in the book to get away. The advent of war in 1939 saved him from further academic tortures and he enrolled for the RAF. However, a deferment allowed him to cut his theatrical teeth and he joined the famous actor-manager Donald Wolfit on tour in 1942. This was followed by a season at the St James Theatre, six weeks of entertaining the troops for the Entertainments National Service Association (ENSA) – or Every Night Something Awful as it was more commonly known – and a short engagement with the White Rose Players repertory company in Harrogate. The experiences did not go to his head; shortly afterwards he became a 'Bevin Boy' and was sent down the pit to hew coal for a living. Then, almost as the last bullet was being fired, he got a call up from the RAF and served for a few months as a medical-orderly instructor.

Like millions of other young men after the war, he had to think about earning a living and he naturally turned to acting. His experiences with Wolfit, who combined performing with theatre management, gave him the encouragement to launch his own company at the age of only 24. With typical Yorkshire phlegm, he borrowed £900 and invested £1,000 of his own money in a show entitled *Nothing but the Truth*, which opened at the King's Hall, Ilkley on 29 March 1948. Despite the confidence of the budding impresario, it bombed and lost a farcical £3,000. Abashed but resilient, Rix licked his wounds and signed on for a winter season in pantomime at Bridlington where he coped admirably with repeated shouts of 'It's behind you!' And the production, *Babes in the Wood* at the Grand Pavilion, did at least make a little money, which allowed him to put the deposit down on a ring. He had met an aspiring actress, Elspet, in 1949 and after living together for a time asked her to marry him. Perhaps appropriately for someone who was to become the *farceur par excellence*, he popped the question while they were both in the bath! It was an excellent decision; unlike many show-business couples the marriage has endured and they celebrated their golden wedding in 1999.

With an eagle eye for a good script, he next turned his attention to a farce that had done the rounds with only a modicum of success. Noticing a potential that others failed to spot, he put on *Reluctant Heroes* in Bridlington's Spa Theatre, where its box-office takings broke the house record. Encouraged, he took the show to the Whitehall Theatre in London where it was to run for an amazing four years. The show's appeal was boosted when, in 1952, it became the first West End production to be televised. That pioneering excerpt on television also delivered an added bonus in the shape of a seventeen-year contract with the BBC starting with a full-length production, *Postman's Knock*. Seventy-six full-length farces and two series, *Dial Rix* and *Six of Rix*, followed. By his own admission these successes brought considerable material rewards. Rix was now a very wealthy man, and able to buy a substantial house in Roehampton.

But this success mattered little when, in 1951, there was an event that was to change his life forever. Elspet was pregnant and, like all expectant parents, they looked forward with great anticipation to the birth of a first child. When their baby girl, Shelley, was born they were ecstatic and, to their eyes, the child seemed perfectly normal. But a nursing sister told them that the consultant gynaecologist wanted to speak to Brian alone in his consulting rooms in London's prestigious Harley Street. Immediately, they both feared the worst. It is reported that the doctor spoke brusquely to Rix, 'Have you heard of mongolism?' he barked, 'Well your daughter is a mongol. Please tell your wife.' To add insult to injury, Rix was even asked if he had either venereal disease or a drink problem. Quite understandably, he later admitted that the memory of that fateful time still causes great pain.

In the 1950s even the name of the condition, which is today referred to as Down's Syndrome, stigmatised its unfortunate victims. Sadly, many people still found it a cause for shame: it is said that Rix's father, who had been brought up in the Victorian period, wept when he heard the news and never mentioned Shelley again. Knowledge of the debility was limited and sufferers were usually committed to an institution. Brian and Elspet Rix followed the accepted practice of the day and sent their daughter to specialist accommodation. She was there for five years, eventually transferring to a National Health Service establishment, Normansfield, in London. Although it was then operated by the National Health Service, Normansfield was the traditional home for the handicapped children of the upper classes and most of its residents still came from this background. But there was a humiliating experience to be faced before the girl was accepted by Normansfield: because Shelley was entering a state hospital she had to be certified. Thanks to pressure from parents this degrading practice has now been scrapped.

After the initial shock, Rix responded with characteristic determination. With great vigour, he and Elspet set about raising money to carry out research into the condition. They worked tirelessly for the Friends of Normansfield, so much so that Brian Rix eventually became the chairman. Indeed such was his devotion to the cause that he confessed in his autobiography, *Farce about Face* published in 1989, that he had difficulty in keeping his friends as he was always selling them raffle tickets.

But this was not the only misfortune to befall the Rix family. Around the start of the Second World War, Brian's elder sister, Sheila, then aged 20, was raped by an RAF officer and became pregnant. Her parents banned her from the family home and forced their daughter to give the baby up for adoption. This was a personal tragedy and induced in her a sense of loss that she was never able completely to overcome. But with typical Yorkshire grit she threw herself into her career and went on tour with Donald Wolfit's Shakespeare Company. Later she appeared with her brother in six Whitehall farces and two films. Then came the part she is best known for: under her married name of Mercier, she became a major television star playing Annie Sugden in the Yorkshire farming soap, *Emmerdale Farm* (later simply *Emmerdale*). She was the linchpin of the programme and appeared in the role from 1972–94 and from 1995–6. Eventually her character married the colourful pub landlord, Amos Brearly, and the fictional couple set off for a new life in Spain. Her private life also had a happy ending when her lost daughter, Janet, traced her and they began to build a relationship after so many years of enforced separation.

Away from the cameras there were further theatre successes for her younger brother, particularly with *Dry Rot, Simple Spymen, One for the Pot* and the last of the Whitehall farces, *Chase Me, Comrade*. Rix also found time to extend his family, and Louisa, Jamie and Jonathan were born healthy. By the sixties, their father had chalked up such a reputation that he was the subject of a *This Is Your Life* television programme, hosted by the legendary Eamonn Andrews, in which some of the distinguished guests hailed him as the greatest-ever exponent of farce. Perhaps the accolades went to his head for Brian Rix tried to buy the Whitehall Theatre, the scene of his finest performances, from its owner Felicity Cooper. He was unsuccessful in his attempts so he left for the Garrick Theatre.

At the new venue he tried to stimulate ticket sales by introducing a new formula – a repertoire of plays in short runs rather than a long run of a single play. This novel idea failed to excite the public who seemed to prefer single plays. So it was back to the old formula and a new play, *Let Sleeping Wives Lie*, did good box office (one of the stars was Andrew Sachs, later to achieve show-business immortality as the hapless Manuel in *Fawlty Towers*). This was followed in turn by *She's Done It Again*, about which one highly satisfied critic commented: 'The lark's on the wing; Brian Rix is in his element and all's right with the world.' An uproarious farce, *A Bit Between the Teeth*, came next in which Rix played a stammering jeweller who hides his business partner's naked wife in a closet. Get the picture? This was also a huge triumph. Then in 1976 came the swan song, when the king of farce hitched up his trousers, apparently for the last time, after another well-received show, *Fringe Benefits*.

A short time later, Rix was again hijacked by that beaming Irishman with the big red-book, when the guests lining up to pay tribute to him included his sister, Sheila, Leslie Crowther, Dickie Henderson and the great West Indian fast bowler, Wes Hall. Soon afterwards he began presenting *Let's Go* for BBC Television, a show devoted to literacy for the mentally handicapped. Fittingly, in 1977, he was honoured with the award of the CBE for his tireless voluntary work on behalf of those with disabilities.

Rix has often combined charity work with another of his passions: cricket. He had been an excellent schoolboy cricketer and represented Hull in the Yorkshire League. He also played for the

MCC and the Lords Taverners and, on another occasion, actually scored seventy-five runs at the Oval. Despite living in London for most of his professional life, he has never wavered in his support for Yorkshire County Cricket Club. Indeed one of his greatest regrets was that his son, Jonathan, was not qualified to play for Yorkshire as he had not been born in the county and had to turn out for Surrey instead!

Following his retirement from the stage Rix moved into theatre management but never seemed comfortable as an administrator. Then one day, quite by chance, he saw a job advert in the *Guardian* for a new Secretary General of the National Society for Mentally Handicapped Children (MENCAP). He decided to apply and became the Secretary General of MENCAP in 1980. At the time, there were many sceptics who doubted the suitability of a hare-brained actor for this challenging post. Yet there were others though who thought the candidate had the very best of qualifications: the patron of MENCAP, Queen Elizabeth the Queen Mother, spoke for many when she described his selection as 'a most imaginative appointment'.

In taking over an organisation that had nearly 100,000 members, 500 local societies and hundreds of specialist homes, Rix had a mighty challenge not least in changing the public perception of mentally handicapped people and integrating them into society. He set about the task with his customary vigour. He reorganised MENCAP and embarked on a sustained round of meetings with high-ranking politicians, business leaders and show-business personalities to raise awareness of the needs of those he represented. He travelled extensively, spoke at numerous functions, organised hundreds of charity events and helped to expose the indignities and cruelties of the old asylum-system. He also got involved in the political process, cajoling the legislators to bring about new laws to protect and enhance the interests of people like his daughter Shelley. The press cuttings of the day show him posing with the likes of Eamonn Andrews, Leslie Crowther, Bruce Forsyth, Queen Elizabeth the Queen Mother, the Duke of Edinburgh, Peter Bowles and Harold Wilson.

During his years at MENCAP, he received a number of awards. His knighthood at the end of his tenure was in some ways the most prestigious, although earlier he was given two honours that he perhaps treasured more. In 1981, he was given the Honorary Degree of Master of Arts from Hull University for services to mentally handicapped people. And in the same year, to use his own words, he received 'possibly the finest accolade of all: the Yorkshire Personality of the Year 1981.' But his organisation was helped, not hindered, by his personal accomplishments: Rix was able to bring MENCAP to national prominence and he saw it being designated as a Royal Society in 1981.

Brian Rix handed over the day-to-day management of MENCAP in 1987, although he remained as active as ever in promoting its interests as president of the organisation. He paused for breath and found time for a family holiday before returning to the stage for one last reprise of *Dry Rot* in 1988. Like most things he did in life, these last performances were executed in his own inimitable style, and one critic gleefully commented: 'I am relieved to be able to report that he drops his trousers and makes a right idiot of himself.'

In terms of his show-business career there can be no doubting Rix's popularity and influence. Indeed his name has almost become synonymous with the traditional English farce. Some highbrow critics have, from time to time, been less than kind about his work, a fact that clearly irritates him. In his autobiography he pointed out, with some justification, that the writers of farces had provided, 'more laughs for more people, than any other bunch of writers in history'. But they had never, he argued, received the critical plaudits they merited. Thankfully, the public simply ignored the critics, and turned out in their thousands over three decades. The *Sunday Express* perhaps summed it up best: 'Some trumped-up intellectuals . . . may have looked down on his farces. But the audiences who came by charabanc did not. Brian Rix brought pleasure to millions. He belonged to the ancient tradition on the English stage of healthy vulgarity.'

Rix continued to work tirelessly for MENCAP, even after an operation to replace his heart valves in 1992. He has a genuine commitment, amounting almost to a vocation, and has frequently called those suffering from a mental handicap 'our people'. One of his favourite causes was the restoration of the Normansfield Theatre, part of the hospital complex where his daughter had spent so many years of her life, and on whose behalf Rix had already raised substantial sums of money. Following two decades of frustration it was announced in March 2002 that a housing developer had agreed to meet the £1 million cost of renovating the derelict theatre, which will become an arts centre for the disabled. By this time, of course, Sir Brian Rix had become Lord Rix, an active member of the House of Lords where he used his new platform to speak up for more progressive attitudes to the disabled.

But there was another devastating personal blow to deal with. In 2001 his sixth grandchild, Robbie, was born, and it was soon discovered that the baby had Down's Syndrome (not, as some thought, a result of hereditary factors). There would be one consolation for the family: as a consequence of the successful campaigns waged by Brian Rix, Robbie will not encounter the level of discrimination and ignorance suffered by Shelley Rix in the 1950s. Despite the many triumphs in his show-business career this may indeed be his greatest legacy.

3

MISTRESS OF MIMICRY

A feast for the senses and an all-round good egg, Hull's best-known entertainer could be described as a female Lenny Henry with bagels. She is, of course the multi-talented actress, author and after-dinner speaker Maureen Lipman. Most successful show-business personalities who achieve lasting fame tend to mask their humble beginnings. Not so this daughter of a Jewish tailor. And any person who can entertain thousands of people with a one-woman show, become a household name with a ground-breaking television advert, bring up two children, recover from a life-threatening illness, write a succession of best-selling books and say, 'I still feel like a Hull girl. Coming from Hull is a bit like being Jewish. That's more than a religion and Hull is more than a place. It's a personality. I have the double whammy!' has to be a real Tyke.

Lipman grew up in Hull during the 1950s, living in a modest house in Northfield Road, off Anlaby Road. Her father Maurice, whose ancestors had come from Russia, was the chairman of the Park Street synagogue. An enterprising and hard-working man, he ran a little tailor's shop on the corner of Whitefriargate and Monument Bridge next to the dock. Her mother Zelma, irreverently christened 'The Humberside Oracle' by Maureen, took an early interest in her daughter's budding prowess as an actress. Legend has it that she was literally propelled into the profession by Zelma, when a persuasive elbow in the ribs during a pantomime intermission when boys and girls were invited onto the stage, began her career. In fact, Lipman attributes much of her comic talent to her parents. Her father, she has observed, had a very dry sense of humour, while her mother was a natural wit who never realised that she was funny.

By her own admission, it was a sheltered childhood in a comfortable middle class neighbourhood with few social problems. She enjoyed her youth, the excitement of the Jewish Social Club and films in the local cinema. On Saturday nights she took part in hectic dancing sessions at the Muriel Riley School of Ballroom Dancing in Anlaby Road. In the absence of male partners, she took it in turns with her friend Bernice to be the beau, learning the quickstep, foxtrot, waltz and samba in turn. Many years later she mused: 'No wonder I keep putting my arms around men's waists as soon as the band strikes up.' With Bernice and other female friends, she took great delight, after attending the synagogue on Saturday mornings, in 'ogling the local talent' at the nearby espresso bar followed by tours of Hull's department stores to buy American nylon stockings and Cliff Richard records. Eager to impress, the girls would dress like 45 year-olds, sporting two-piece suits with pleated skirts, blouses with lacy collars, fancy hats, white gloves and clutch bags. At the time, Lipman was a precocious teenager whose ambitions to become an actress were magnified with every successful school play. But, for a while at least, the grease paint would have to wait.

At the tender age of 15 she persuaded her reluctant parents to allow her to travel to Bridlington to become a waitress in an 'egg and chip' café. The wonderful descriptions of working at the seaside conjured up by her school mates led her to exchange a comfortable bedroom in Hull for a flat shared by two of her friends above a 'Greasy Joe's' on the outskirts of town. She left with high hopes and a suitcase full of vests and glamorous evening wear. However, the realities of the shabby café with its oilskin tablecloths and stench of chips dispelled all notions of going to the ball. She was cack-handed – her party pieces were dropping plates and putting brown sauce in the ketchup bottles – and hopeless with money. The manager of the establishment was none too pleased with the trainee's performance and she got short shrift, with an admonishment to her friends as they left for home: 'If you ever bring that bloody disaster here again, I'll sack the lot of you.' The salutary lessons learnt at the Bridlington café convinced Maureen that her future lay in acting. Her succinct reasoning is encapsulated in the immortal line: 'Because there was bugger all else.'

Elocution lessons at Newland High School For Girls honed her talent and she began competing in local music festivals. At the same time, her roles in school plays such as *The Lady's Not For Burning* and *The Importance of Being Earnest* drew critical acclaim. Her sensational performance in the title role of the play *Dr Faustus* really set her on the road to an acting career. So much so that, in 1964, suitably cautioned about talking to strangers and changing her knickers every day, she left Hull to join the London Academy of Music and Dramatic Art (LAMDA). Her anxious parents ran up astronomical phone bills and sent weekly Red Cross parcels to a rather untidy flat above a dentist's surgery. Meanwhile, the budding actress settled down to learn her craft. She engaged a theatrical agent who scanned his new commission and recommended a nose job. Wisely, she decided it would be less painful simply to find a new agent.

Lipman's acting career began with a three-year apprenticeship at the Old Vic. She then moved on to the National Theatre and the Royal Shakespeare Company. Countless West End appearances in shows like *Candida, Outside Edge, Messiah, See How They Run* and *Wonderful Town* brought her to prominence. Olivier and Variety Club Awards followed, and her acting prowess really came to the fore in a groundbreaking one-woman show entitled *Re–Joyce.* Running for three successful seasons in the West End, the play was based on the life and times of kindred spirit Joyce Grenfell. Lipman readily identified with this rather anarchic and militant comedienne, playing the role with wit and panache. She later explained that the show was ideally suited to her talents: 'I like to see something character-driven where the comedy comes as a result of character, where I can disguise myself and use my qualities . . . That's why I went for someone like Joyce Grenfell.'

Success in the theatre inevitably led to opportunities in television. Her appearances on the small screen included parts in *All at No. 20* and in two series of *About Face* for Central Television. Perhaps her greatest triumph on the small screen was in the hit comedy *Agony* in which she played Jane Lucas, an agony aunt with a radio phone-in show . . . and more problems than her clients. Her co-star was Simon Williams, who had previously starred in one of the biggest television shows of all time, *Upstairs Downstairs.* In an interview for *The Observer* in 2001, Williams paid tribute to Lipman's great professionalism, noting how she would insist on the cast and crew working on until everything was just right. But he also remembered her great warmth and humanity, and how she had come to his aid during a personal crisis: 'During the filming I was going through a tricky time because my marriage had broken down. But Maureen was always really there for me.'

On the big screen, her credits rolled in films such as *Up the Junction, Gumshoe* and *Carry on Columbus*. Her acting abilities were recognised with a best-supporting actress award for her portrayal of hairdresser Trish in the 1983 hit movie *Educating Rita*, in which she co-starred with Michael Caine and Julie Walters.

In landing the part of Sylvie in *Up the Junction*, Lipman used her talent for mimicry to good effect. In presenting herself for audition she faced a seemingly impossible task. The producers had stipulated in their advertisement that they were seeking only genuine cockneys to lend authenticity to the part. Undaunted, she spent days before her audition talking to Londoners and absorbing their nuances of dialect and language. Dressed appropriately in a dirty coat and scuffed shoes, and topped by a peaked cap, she presented herself somewhat cheekily before two flabbergasted producers who invited her to take her coat off. This cockney sparrow refused with the words: 'I got me ruddy party dress on under this ain' I?' And she went on to chastise the men for staring: 'Wot's a matter wiv you two then – I gotta smut on me nose or sumfing?' Next day, she was recalled for a second interview, at which one producer asked suspiciously: 'Is that accent of yours real?' Abashed, she replied: 'Well you don't fink I'd put this on if I could 'elp it do you mate?' 'Didn't they mind at LAMDA?' asked the producer. 'Nah', responded the girl born within the sound of the Hull trawler-sirens: 'I can talk posh as you if I want to mate. Want to 'ear me do some Shakespeare, eh?' Uneasily, with a growing sense of guilt, Lipman continued with the pretence until she was offered the part. Eventually, much relieved, she admitted her subterfuge to the astonished and delighted producers.

Like all natural mimics and comedians, Maureen Lipman played her parts with innate and seamless timing. With an optimistic and self-deprecating character she turned adversity to her advantage to reveal the humour in the pompous and the mundane. She readily admits, in her numerous interviews for the media, to possessing a child-like enthusiasm for life: 'I was a teenager until I was 26 . . . my mother did everything for me', and to using the inadequacies in her own life to get laughs.

But her talents are certainly not confined to stage and screen. Lipman has also had a second, highly successful career as a writer. In books such as *How Was It For You?, Something to Fall Back On, You*

Got an 'Ology?, *Thank You For Having Me* and *When's It Coming Out?* *(The Thoughts of Chairperson Mo)* she has demonstrated considerable prowess as a writer of humorous prose. The books have been phenomenally successful, selling no less than six million copies worldwide.

Ironically, it was not to be books, films, television or the stage that elevated her to the heady realms of national stardom. What really made her into an icon, and brought a smile to everyone's lips, was her portrayal of an archetypal Jewish grandmother, Beattie Bellman, in a national advertising campaign for British Telecom. 'Well, at least you got an 'ology' she famously said in frequent phone calls to her hapless grandson. The advert ran between 1989 and 1992, fifty-five commercials that were described by professionals in the advertising industry as the campaign of the decade. Lipman looks back on the adverts with affection and, in one interview, revealed an unexpected, yet pleasant, bonus: 'people are quite surprised by how young I look. They all expect this elderly lady to walk in.'

Lipman is married to Jack Rosenthal the distinguished playwright (and has appeared in a number of his plays). They have two children, Amy and Adam, and their family life is inspired by the Jewish ethic that gives the institution an importance that is sadly lacking from many modern partnerships. This has helped to create a rock that fires much of her life and work. In 1994, after being taken ill on stage, her roots sustained her during a dark period. She was diagnosed with life-threatening neuro-fibroma, and surgeons had delicately to remove a benign tumour from the top of her spinal chord during a six-hour operation. Happily she survived, and details of the near tragedy later surfaced in typically jocular comments and prose. Indeed, despite the time lost during this illness she has missed only four months of work in her thirty-year career. The actress was given a CBE in 1999, and her native Hull honoured her with an even more prestigious tribute shortly thereafter. She was immensely flattered when a beautiful and lithe 236-ton boring machine – it would spend years digging out earth to accommodate Hull sewers – was named Maureen!

As ever Lipman has refused to rest on her laurels, and in recent years has been busier than ever. Like many other actresses she was desperate to appear in the controversial play by Eve Ensler, *The*

Vagina Monologues, and achieved her ambition in 2001 when it opened at the New Ambassadors theatre in London. An important part of the role was to get the audience to shout out the naughty four-letter word beginning with the letter 'c', a task that Lipman thought more than a little risqué. Nevertheless, the drama critic of *The Guardian* was able to report that she did so divinely, kicking her legs in the air as the audience chorused the expletive. Her recent stage work included another first: her Proms debut at the Royal Albert Hall. In August 2002, she reprised her highly successful role as Aunt Eller in *Oklahoma* to mark the centenary of the birth of Richard Rodgers, the show's composer.

There has also been a part in the acclaimed film *The Pianist*, directed by the great Polish film-maker Roman Polanski. The film deals with the persecution of Jews in Warsaw by the Nazis and, in particular, with the attempts of a young musician to hide from the Germans in the apartments of sympathetic Poles. Lipman plays the musician's mother, who is shipped off to the death camp at Treblinka with her husband. *The Pianist* won the prestigious Palme d'Or at the Cannes film festival in 2002 and collected the best actor and best director Oscars in 2003.

But the part that caused the biggest stir was her appearance in that great British institution, *Coronation Street*. In July 2002 she joined the cast as relief pub-manageress Lillian, fresh from a stint at the Majestic Hotel in Cleethorpes, and complete with mynah bird and an 'overabundance of airs and graces', to quote one critic. During her short stay at the legendary Rover's Return, Lillian managed not only to capture the heart of owner Fred Elliott, but also set about raising the tone of the Rover's. She was delighted to get the part. In an interview with the *Sunday Express*, she said that, 'It was a dream really. All these years and I had never been in a soap! I found it the most extraordinary experience, with the papers calling me up.' There was also a family connection; her husband Jack Rosenthal wrote more than 130 episodes of the programmes in its early days.

The connection with the north of England is also important to her. Lipman is genuinely proud of her home city despite the fact that, for the sake of her career, she has lived for many years in London's Muswell Hill. In 2000, she said of Hull: 'It's a place you never leave. There's something very, very odd in the water. People from Hull are even more proud of the place than Liverpudlians are of their city . . . Hull has a history of putting its seat in the mud and refusing to budge – from the days of William Wilberforce. It's rather beautiful in the sense of beauty being functional.' She also believes that Hull has been important to her comedy: 'Comedy does fit with us rather well. I think that is because, being a port, it brings in lots of different people, and it's working class and poor. It's tight, and it can be regarded as mean, but it isn't. It's just excessively dry, like a fine wine.'

Reading all the literature on Maureen Lipman, you cannot fail to be impressed by the torrent of talent that pours effortlessly from her lips and her books. And yet she is an immensely modest and genuine person, reminding us frequently of the famous dying words of legendary actor Edmund Kean: 'Dying is easy; comedy is hard.' In trying to learn something about the inner character of the woman, I scanned her own quotations and was hypnotically drawn to the following: 'What life is about is getting through from seven in the morning until eleven at night without hurting your fellow human beings.'

4

CITY OF STARS

Hull can boast a plethora of famous people: Andrew Marvell, William Wilberforce, John Prescott, Alan Plater, Roland Gift and Tom Courtenay to name but a few. Then, of course, there are Brian Rix, Maureen Lipman and David Whitfield who are discussed elsewhere in this book. To this list can be added two more sons of the Humber, actors who became firm and enduring favourites, although from different generations. They had one thing in common: both had a real talent for comedy. They are Ian Carmichael and John Alderton.

The name Carmichael was as synonymous with Hull as cod and chips . . . served albeit with fish knives and cruets. And where would any self-respecting Hull housewife buy her posh cutlery? Why, at Carmichael's of course. The Yorkshire Harrods still evokes fond memories years after it closed down. When he was born on 18 June 1920, Ian Carmichael seemed destined to join a family business founded by his three uncles. They established a jeweller's shop, and the enterprise eventually moved to its well-known base in George Street, where his father joined the business after qualifying as an optician in 1914. Ian Carmichael may have been born with a silver-plated spoon in his mouth but fate had a golden future in mind for this rather sickly boy. In his own inimitable way, this great character-actor went on to match the achievements of immortals like American John Wayne in personifying the national character. He was the archetypal Englishman: debonair, solid, frightfully dependable and with an innate sense of fair play. These qualities were epitomised in his memorable role as Bertie Wooster when he played opposite Denis Price's Jeeves in the 1970s television series based on the P. G. Wodehouse novels. Equally memorable was his portrayal of aristocratic super-sleuth Lord Peter Wimsey in the successful television series inspired by the stories of Dorothy L. Sayers.

Ian Carmichael spent the first two years of his life in a pleasant terraced house at 114 Sunnybank in Hull. The house, his parents' first, was rented and enjoyed a pleasant aspect with uninterrupted views of Hymers College playing fields. From there the family moved to 32 Westbourne Avenue, and Ian began his education in 1924 in the nearby Froebel House School in Marlborough Avenue. He spent only a few months there; his concerned parents withdrew him after only one term because of the newly acquired bad language that the lad was practising over the breakfast table! Lodge School in Pearson Park had more moderate vocabulary and he remained there until the age of 7 when he was despatched to Scarborough College, a boarding school. He completed his education with a spell at Bromsgrove School in Worcester.

Carmichael remembered his Hull childhood with affection, and wrote warmly about his time at Westbourne Avenue in his book, *Will the Real Ian Carmichael*, which was published in 1979. One of his earliest memories was having his tonsils and adenoids removed on the nursery table. He also recalled another occasion when the men with black bags called at the house. Alarmed at what he described as 'a heavy thumping' head pain, the doctors poked and prodded, and finally concluded that their young patient was suffering from an engorged heart. They prescribed six weeks of total rest and the use of bedpans. During his confinement, he had little to do but peer out of the window at the comings and goings of residents and tradesmen. This enabled him to leave us with an appealing picture of suburban life in pre-war Hull. He wrote of the corporation dustcart pulled by an elegant shire-horse, the Eldorado ice cream vendor with his tricycle, the street entertainer and his barrel organ and, regular as clockwork, the daily rounds of the lamplighter. Eventually, Carmichael was allowed to get out of bed but his movements were strictly controlled and he was provided with an old-fashioned basketwork Bath chair more suitable for geriatrics than a young boy. In this contraption, he was pushed along the street, and neighbours often wondered if the wan little boy would make it through the week.

In these early years, the seed of an acting career was sown, although given his family's solid commercial background no one is quite sure where the spark came from. He instinctively knew, however, that he wanted to be a performer in either music or acting. In fact it was in music that he first made his mark, running a juvenile dance band in the Hull area with a great deal more enthusiasm than skill. Then, in 1939, came a place at the prestigious Royal Academy of Dramatic Art in London. Carmichael later admitted that he felt very much the 'unsophisticate, an innocent abroad'. While at RADA he started his professional career rather inauspiciously with a part as a robot in a play called *RUR* by Karel and Josef Capek at Stepney People's Palace. But he faced an uncertain future, and the looming war in Europe restricted his acting opportunities in 1940 to a ten-week engagement in a travelling review called *Nine Sharp* directed by impresario Herbert Farjeon. He made his first stage appearance alongside Hermione Baddeley and gained valuable experience on a tour of the provinces. His penchant for glamour and light-hearted banter gave him a strong indication of the route he should follow in his future career. But on the last week of the tour, he received his call-up papers in Glasgow and his fledgling career was suspended for the duration of the war. But every cloud has a silver lining and his stint in the army provided further inspiration.

The young soldier came back to his native Yorkshire as Trooper Carmichael in the Royal Armoured Corps at Catterick. He later trained at Sandhurst and a commission in the Dragoons soon followed. The move took him to Helmsley and Whitby, and his initiation into the elevated world of the officers' mess as a Second Lieutenant proved exhilarating: 'My first night in the mess was a bit awe-inspiring. Most of the senior officers wore blues, clanked about in spurs, referred to girls as fillies, drank large pinks and kept saying 'don'tcha know' with monotonous regularity. All of which was to provide me with great background material for later life.' During this period, Carmichael spent two rather dank years under canvas in the woods of Duncombe Park near Helmsley. But this was made more bearable by romance. While attending a dance at Whitby Spa Ballroom, he met Pym Maclean, an 18-year-old blonde with sensational good looks, who hailed from nearby Sleights. The pair fell in love and were married in Sleights in 1943. They eventually had two daughters. During the war he was in the thick of the action in northern France and was part of the drive into Germany between and 1944 and 1945. At the end of hostilities he finished up organising army entertainment in Germany.

After the war, with hardly any acting credits to his name, Carmichael had to start at the bottom of the ladder, taking any work he could find. He began by appearing in revues and light-hearted comedies such as *She Wanted a Cream Front Door* with Robertson Hare. Occasional work came through the recommendation of Leonard Sachs who organised shows at the Players Theatre in London and there were also minor sessions in television. The journeyman actor soldiered on, making a niche for himself in London as one of the most promising new talents in revue for years. At the Hammersmith Theatre in 1954, again with Baddeley and an up-and-coming actress called Dora Bryan, he performed in a hilarious burlesque entitled *At the Lyric*. His prowess on the saxophone during the performance added to his growing reputation. However, stereotyping hampered his quest for a broader career and, for a while, a succession of appearances in West End reviews, a small part in the epic film *The Colditz Story* and a play called *Simon and Laura* seemed to mark the limit of his ambitions. But fate was about to change his life forever.

The famous Boulting Brothers had been impressed with the young actor's performance in the Globe Review. Although they had some initial trouble discovering his name, he was finally contacted through his agent who broke the astonishing news of a telephone call he had received: 'We want to make Ian into a film star; we've got two parts all ready for him.' Carmichael was an immediate success. The comedy *Private's Progress*, released in 1955, received rave reviews: 'It was a tremendous feeling,' he enthused. 'Suddenly my own name and photograph were being featured in those movie magazines that I used to buy and study so avidly as a stage-struck boy.' A string of popular films such as *Brothers-in-Law*, *Lucky Jim*, *I'm All Right Jack*, *School for Scoundrels*, *Heavens Above* and *Left Right and Centre* followed. He was now a fully fledged movie-star and a household name.

His success continued into the 1960s with starring roles in *Heaven's Above* and *The Lady Vanishes*. Then, in succession, came the television parts that he made his own: Bertie Wooster and Lord Peter Wimsey. Strangely, the prospect of playing the part of the upper-class clot in the BBC's *World of Wooster* was at first unappealing. His reasoning was that the 1920s background to the series would make him appear rather passé. For over a year he remained determined not to commit himself to the part, until the producer persuaded him to change his mind. Luckily he did and the series became an immense hit. But so utterly convincing was his rendition of Wooster that, for a time, he again became stereotyped, and the producers of the series *Lord Peter Wimsey* doubted his ability to adapt to the new role. He persevered, however, and eventually convinced doubters of his versatility. And again the viewers loved him, although the BBC took the strange decision to withdraw the series at the height of its popularity, apparently for financial reasons.

He had by now achieved nearly all of his ambitions, although he confided later that he would have liked 'the lush romantic parts'. He and his wife were somewhat disillusioned with life in London and had become homesick for Yorkshire. They bought a large flat in a former hotel on Whitby's North Promenade, bolting there for holidays and weekends. In 1976, the pull of Yorkshire became irresistible. They sold their flat in London's Mill Hill for £100,000 and the holiday home in Whitby and bought a two hundred year-old farmhouse in the Esk Valley only walking distance from Sleights where they had been married more than three decades earlier. 'I had no desire to spend the rest of my life going through a stage door at 7 p.m.,' he admitted, 'I just didn't want to work as hard, the bloom had gone off it a bit.' Extended and modernised, the couple's idyllic retreat was to be their Yorkshire Shangri-La until February 1983 when fate snatched away everything Ian held dear. Cruelly, Pym fell ill with cancer. Just four months later she was dead.

Carmichael was devastated and admitted that he suffered black depressions and intense grief for two years. 'Eventually', he confided, 'the crying stops and the grief becomes a dull pain.' In 1984 though, he met someone who lifted his spirits. Kate Fenton, a BBC producer, commissioned him for readings on Radio Four. Five months later, she engaged him again and the friendship flourished. So much so that, in 1985, the couple decided to live together in his Yorkshire home. In a subsequent interview with a reporter from the *Yorkshire Post*, Carmichael acknowledged that the feeling of betraying his deceased wife, and the thought of becoming happy again, preyed on his mind. In this remarkably frank interview, he spoke of his loneliness and the complexities in his own character. He pointed to his ambition yet his deep distaste for ruthlessness; his sociability but his desire for privacy; his desire for peace and serenity but perennial restlessness;

and his immense appetite for work and a striving for perfection in everything he did. But he also alluded to his inherent laziness. Clearly impressed by the frankness of his host, the reporter wrote: 'The man and the mask are distinct entities, a quality rare in actors.'

Gradually this likeable, generous and self-deprecating man who, incidentally, had been a regular cricketer along with Lord Rix and John Alderton in the Lord's Taverners team, rose above his grief. Later, in honour of his achievements, he received an honorary Doctor of Letters degree from Hull University. A year later, he returned to his old stomping ground in Duncombe Park to play the role of a butler in a film entitled *Diamond Skulls* alongside Gabriel Byrne, Judy Parfitt, Amanda Donohoe and Sir Michael Horden. And then, in 1992, he returned to the genre he loved best when he starred as the Honourable Galahad Threewood in a Radio Four adaptation of the P. G. Wodehouse classic, *Galahad at Blandings*. In that busy year, he married for the second time.

In previous years, he may have confessed to a certain indolence. But there was no sign of it in April 1992 when the 72-year-old actor returned to the BBC in a ten-part period-piece called *Strathblair*, which was set in the 1950s. In this series he played the part of the laird, Sir James Menzies. He enjoyed the role, which was made more memorable because of its Scottish roots. His paternal grandfather had been an insurance man in Greenock before moving south to England.

Now an octogenarian, Ian Carmichael continues to live in his beloved Yorkshire home. But age has proved no barrier to his acting career and in 2003, at the age of 82, he appeared in *The Royal*, a Sunday night drama series in the *Heartbeat* mould and, like that programme, set in Yorkshire. He has also outlived his famous namesake on George Street. The once glamorous store is now a nightclub, although its elegant portico, monogrammed tympanum and two mosaic pavement-signs spelling out the single word 'Carmichael's' still survive.

*

John Alderton, the son of Gordon and Ivy Alderton, was born on 27 November 1940 in Gainsborough, Lincolnshire. He was the youngest of three children. Good humour, it seems ran in the family. So much so that his grandparents, between them, produced twenty-nine kids! The family moved to Hull where Alderton senior opened a fish-and-chip shop on Essex Street. He later went on to run an off-licence and a grocery shop. A funny, ebullient and generous man, Gordon Alderton regularly entertained his customers with non-stop banter. He always had a humorous word for the exploits of Hull City. Indeed, on one famous occasion, so confident was he of another mediocre season that alongside 'Frying Tonight', he painted the following promise on his shop window: 'I promise to give away 500 free fish-and-chip dinners if Hull City get promotion.' That year, of course, the forwards just rattled in the goals and according to John, his dad honoured his bet but became bankrupt. He managed to scrape together just enough money to open an off-licence in the city soon afterwards.

As a boy, John Alderton regularly helped out behind the counter and remembers the non-stop, ever-changing performance of his father who adapted his witticisms to every customer. Taking a cue from his wise-cracking dad, the boy joined in the fun, and unconsciously developed the easy-going demeanour that was to hold him in such good stead in later years.

The young man went to Kingston Grammar School with no thoughts of an eventual career in show business. He had aspirations to take his A levels, go on to university and become an architect. Then, in 1956, he was commandeered by English teacher Josh Large to appear in a Restoration comedy being produced by the school, called *Viceroy Sarah*. Large had specially written the play and believed that the confident Alderton would excel in his role. How right he proved. Looking back, he remembers being very comfortable and relaxed on stage. In fact, he relished the experience so much that he began actively to consider an acting career. This was despite the opposition of his headmaster, Cameron Walker, who 'went potty' at his student for daring to follow in the footsteps of another Kingston renegade, Tom Courtenay, who had left the school to pursue a theatrical career two years earlier. No shrinking violets, Alderton's parents put in their own 'two-pennyworth' and urged their son to get a proper job. But he persevered, encouraged by his champion, Josh Large, who saw the boy's potential. In 1959, for 'a bit of a lark', he left Hull with a school friend for an audition with the Royal Academy of Dramatic Art in London. To his surprise and delight he beat off the competition from 140 other young hopefuls and spent the next few years learning the craft of acting.

Back home in Hull, Gordon Alderton still cracked a few dubious jokes across the counter about his son's learning to talk with a plum in his mouth. But father's scepticism vanished when, in 1961, the young actor landed his first part in a weekly repertory-theatre production in York's Theatre Royal. En masse, the Alderton clan descended to enjoy the play, *Badger's Green*, and took up the two front rows at every performance. His real breakthrough came in 1962 when, to the delight of his family, he landed the part of Dr Richard Moone in the hit television series *Emergency Ward 10*. The star's excited father toasted the success by handing out free glasses of sherry to regular customers at the Hessle High Road off-licence. For years afterwards press cuttings, publicity photographs and posters about John's career were proudly displayed on the shop walls.

On the set of the pioneering medical soap, Alderton met fellow actor Jill Brown and the pair married. But it was an ill-starred union and the marriage ran into trouble. By 1969, the romance was over, and he married the new love of his life, Pauline Collins. The couple went on to forge one of the best known and most enduring marriages in the history of show business and had three children. Collins had previously experienced emotional turmoil of her own. After a brief and passionate affair with actor Tony Rohr in the 1960s she gave birth to a child, Louise, who was given up for adoption. Mother and daughter were parted for more than twenty years. In 1988, the ever-predatory tabloid press published articles about the 'secret love child' but the revelations failed to weaken the Aldertons' marriage. In 1993, Collins revealed the full facts about the affair and the relationship with her estranged daughter in a book, *Letter to Louise*.

For nearly five years between 1968 and 1972, John Alderton played the role that most people identify him with: as a teacher, Bernard Hedges, in *Please Sir!* The scripts were written by one of the great partnerships in British television comedy, John Esmonde and Bob Larbey, who would go on to pen ratings' winners such as *The Good Life* and *Ever Decreasing Circles*. With this pedigree it is hardly surprising that *Please Sir!* became a huge hit and made Alderton one of the best-known actors in the country. The premise was very simple. An idealistic young teacher, Hedges, arrives at a tough inner-city school, Fenn Street, and attempts to clean it up. He is put in charge of the rowdiest class, the dreaded 5C, which is full of no-hopers not much younger than himself. At first, the pupils take advantage of his naivety and inexperience but are gradually won over by his obvious sincerity. The comic possibilities were fully exploited by a talented cast that included Deryck Guyler, Joan Sanderson and Peter Cleall, as well as Alderton. Such was the impact made by *Please Sir!* that it was copied by American television, and the version set in New York starred no less a luminary than John Travolta.

With this success under his belt Alderton won a role in the classic London Weekend Television series *Upstairs Downstairs*, one of the most acclaimed programmes in the history of the small screen. Co-starring with Collins, the duo also found success in programmes such as *Thomas and Sarah*, *No Honestly* and *Forever Green*. They appeared together in a number of films including *Unpleasantness at Bludleigh Court* and *The Rise of Minna Nordstrom*. Alderton also starred in the *Upchat Line* in 1977 and in *Father's Day* between 1983 and 1984.

Life on the screen blissfully mirrored that at home, but there was a danger that both actors were becoming so stereotyped that only joint offers of work would come their way. So they branched out and agreed, in career terms, to go their separate ways. Alderton broke the mould by appearing in *Keeping Tom Nice*, a thought-provoking play that explored the often desperate and violent relationship between a father and his handicapped son. Suddenly, to critical acclaim, he was seen as a serious actor and a plethora of opportunities came along including roles in a series of Noel Coward plays. John's rise to stardom was steady and measured. His wife's ascendancy though was meteoric, and her appearance in 1988 in the single-character play *Shirley Valentine* by Willy Russell earned her a coveted BAFTA award and rave reviews on both sides of the Atlantic. With a Best Actress Oscar nomination for the reprise of her role in the feature film starring Tom Conti, Julia McKenzie and Sylvia Sims, she made even more of an international name for herself. In 1991, she starred with sex symbol Patrick Swayzee in the movie *City of Joy* and continued to flourish with appearances in *My Mother's Courage* in 1995. Then, in 1997, she starred in the World War Two drama, *Paradise Road*, about a group of women imprisoned by the Japanese on the island of Sumatra. Her down-to-earth husband meanwhile, who has confided in numerous interviews that he is not the ambitious type, 'Hollywood doesn't interest me', continued his own successful, but less glitzy career and also devoted a great deal of time to bringing up his children. 'Pauline and I have always had a system where one stays at home while the other works away,' he explained. 'People seemed surprised that I should be the one to stay at home, but why is it so extraordinary to find men washing pots and cooking meals?' Away from the kitchen, he also found time in the early years to take the crease alongside those other two Yorkshire stalwarts mentioned in this book – Lord Rix and Ian Carmichael – for the Lords Taverners cricket team.

5

'MURDER WILL OUT'

The lock burst open, the door of 97 Hodgson Street rocked back on its hinges and Constable Ridsdale stumbled on the threshold. Aghast at the smell, he recoiled, and the murmuring, expectant crowd outside wondered about the fate of their 60-year-old neighbour Sarah Hebden. They would not wonder long. The policeman discovered her crumpled, bloodstained body at the foot of a narrow flight of stairs. She had been brutally murdered, and the post-mortem revealed that she had died around 6 a.m. that day from a frenzied attack, sustaining around twenty blows to the head.

The constabulary-surgeon, Doctor Slater, was summoned to examine the corpse, whose head had been bashed in. The signs of a desperate struggle that had left one finger hanging from a hand by a thread, and another dislocated, showed there had been a frantic fight for life. Beside the body was a twisted pair of fire tongs covered in blood. A broken fragment of the implement was found under the corpse.

Why was this quiet, lonely widow killed so savagely in her own home on that dark November day in 1901, and who had committed such a heinous crime? The answers lay all around. Detectives soon established that the industrious Sarah Hebden, one of three sisters, earned a modest living as an agent for the Royal Liver Friendly Society. This was a common practice in those days. Local fishermen's families, who lived in the tight-knit huddle of terraced housing near the river, put modest sums aside each week to pay for annuities and funeral expenses.

Sarah Hebden collected her dues every Thursday but, on that fateful 28 November, she never left home. She was last seen alive some hours earlier on the eve of a planned trip to Elloughton. A young girl named Jackson called at her house that morning to pay over the family insurance premiums and, although she knocked at the door repeatedly, received no answer. Worried by the lack of a response, the girl inquired at the next-door home of one of Sarah's sisters, Mrs Bower, who also became agitated. After some time had elapsed, the anxious sister contacted the local offices of the Friendly Society to determine whether Sarah had been there to pay over the insurance monies. Finding that the society was as mystified as she was about the break in the routine of the invariably methodical collector, she sent her daughter Florence to investigate. The young girl used a candle to probe the gloom in the eerily silent 97 Hodgson Street. She found her aunt slumped on the floor at the foot of the stairs and immediately raised the alarm.

Robbery was the obvious motive for the crime. Rumours in the neighbourhood suggested that the murderer had been lured by the prospect of stealing up to £10 from the premiums Sarah had collected. A well-respected member of the local community, the thrifty widow was known to own her modest home and have a healthy bank balance. The police immediately suspected members of her own family and neighbours. On searching the house, detectives found a cache of insurance books hidden upstairs. Nearby, were two purses. One was empty. The other contained £3 12s 2d. Two more empty purses were discovered in a tea-caddy that Sarah had used as a makeshift money box. This had normally been kept locked on a downstairs shelf but it was found with its lid smashed under the victim's bed. Detectives concluded that it had been forced open with the murder weapon. Something else was inside the tea caddy; a newspaper cutting about the trial and imprisonment of a Brigg thief named Arthur Richardson. This was a promising lead.

The head of Hull CID, Detective Superintendent Chapman, directed two of his colleagues – Cherry and Proctor – to find out more about the intriguing Mr Richardson. Their enquiries uncovered two illuminating facts. The governor of Lincoln prison told them he had been imprisoned for robbing another of the dead woman's sisters and was released from custody on 20 November 1901. Surprising in itself, this remarkable fact was topped by another. Richardson, it would seem, was the illegitimate son of the same sister.

Further information on the suspect was obtained from prison records. Richardson, a joiner by trade, had been cashiered out of the Indian Army for dishonesty and was described as a calculating and ruthless criminal. Detectives launched an intensive manhunt, and their enquiries revealed the full background to his sojourn in Lincoln jail. The story was that, after he had returned from the sub-continent in disgrace, Richardson married and separated within a few months. He then took temporary accommodation with his aunt in Brigg, where the theft of £26 from the lady's purse led to his conviction. Penniless after his release, he returned to Hull with the intention of seeing his wife, taking lodgings with a family called Skelton in Faith Terrace, Walker Street.

Richardson was an out-an-out villain but he was certainly not a man of any great intelligence. Shortly after the murder of Sarah Hebden, his lack of guile took him back to the lodging house in Faith Terrace, which was only a few miles from police headquarters. Cherry and Proctor apprehended him there two days after the murder and asked him to turn out his pockets. They contained £10 in cash, a gold watch and a brooch. The detectives also searched Richardson's room and took away several bloodstained items of clothing that had recently been washed, a bank book belonging to the deceased, together with a woman's brooch and a gore-splattered silk handkerchief.

Under interrogation, he claimed that the £10 was his own money. He protested that the note had been concealed about his person while in Lincoln jail. He also told police that he had pawned the gold watch before his prison sentence and redeemed it after his release. As far as the damning evidence of the clothing was concerned, this was put down either to a nosebleed or the outcome of a fight before he went to prison. Richardson also insisted that he had bought the brooch legitimately, and blamed the sullied state of the silk handkerchief on a shaving accident.

His arguments, though, failed to remove the mounting suspicions. The testimony of Mr and Mrs Skelton, the proprietors of the lodging house, further implicated him in the murder. Richardson had told his landlord that he worked at the local Reckitt factory in Hull, but subsequent enquiries proved this was a lie. In his first week at Faith Terrace he left every day at five o'clock in the morning, ostensibly to begin his shift, so that no doubts about his veracity were raised. However, when just a day after the murder, he arrived at his lodgings in a new suit and requested the loan of a key to wind a gold watch, his landlord became suspicious. Alarmed, Mrs Skelton admitted to the police that she asked her guest point-blank if he had committed the murder. There was stony silence.

The detectives expanded the lines of enquiry, and publicity about the case drew out a number of other witnesses who had met Richardson shortly after the grim discovery in Hodgson Street. One of these was rulleyman William Fenton, who referred to a meeting he had with the accused on Hedon Road on the morning of the murder. Fenton told the police that, at the time, Richardson openly talked about having a large amount of cash on his person, crediting his new-found wealth to luck with a bet. Mrs Lakin, the landlady of the Trafalgar Inn on Blackfriargate, also assisted the police. She recounted how the prisoner had openly talked about the crime, loudly lamenting the loss of his aunt and suggesting that, like many other homicides in Hull, it would remain undetected.

It is interesting to observe that had the facilities of modern forensic science been around in 1901, a simple DNA test would have identified the blood on Richardson's clothing as that of Sarah Hebden and he would have been charged with her murder within days. But such tests were not available at the turn of the twentieth century and Detective Superintendent Chapman needed to widen the search for evidence still further. All efforts were channelled into discovering the provenance of the gold watch, and teams of detectives visited every jeweller in Hull. The enquiries proved immensely rewarding. A watchmaker by the name of William Morely confirmed that he had regularly repaired the timepiece for a customer – Sarah Hebden. Faced with this compelling evidence, Richardson might have been expected to admit his guilt, but he resolutely continued to plead his innocence. He admitted lying about visiting the murdered woman, but said that his aunt had asked him to take the watch to a jeweller for repair. Chapman decided that he now had enough evidence to charge the suspect with the murder of Sarah Hebden. His recommendations were passed to Hull's Chief Constable, Captain Gurney, for endorsement. Gurney concurred with the detective's findings and Richardson was duly charged and committed to York Assizes for trial.

According to the transcripts of the trial, Richardson was remarkably relaxed, even nonchalant, about the catalogue of evidence presented against him. On one occasion the trial judge, Mr Justice Lawrence, even rebuked the accused for levity. During the trail, the accused repeatedly passed scribbled messages to his bemused counsel on prison notepaper and, when he did take the stand, his own contradictory evidence sealed his fate. He had initially explained to the police that he left his lodgings at 7 a.m. on the day of the murder. However, in court, he admitted he that he had lied, and claimed he was confused about his movements on the day in question. He also altered his testimony about the gold watch, suggesting that his aunt had given the timepiece to him two days before her murder for repair. The damning bloodstains on his clothing he put down to nosebleeds and a fight with a stranger shortly before his arrest. He also acknowledged that he had never worked at the Reckitt's factory, asserting that this was a ruse to convince his landlord that he had the resources to pay his rent. Ironically, one of the jurors who listened attentively to this evidence was none other than the owner of the famous Hull firm, Sir James Reckitt. When questioned about the proposition that his largesse was attributable to a winning bet, Richardson infuriated the judge by casually commenting that his previous testimony had been meant as a joke. The irate Justice Lawrence remarked: 'For heaven's sake, think of what you are saying. Do think what position you are standing in!'

Convinced of his guilt, the jury took just twenty minutes to reach a guilty verdict. Even now though, Richardson, it has to be acknowledged, displayed a high degree of *sang froid*. After the judge solemnly asked him if he had anything to say in response to the verdict he replied: 'All I have to say is that I am innocent and that any punishment I receive will be an unjust punishment.' This valedictory statement was delivered with such self-assurance that some observers noted that the body language of certain jurors suggested unease. But the verdict had been given. Mr Justice Lawrence put on his black headpiece and delivered the sentence of death. Richardson was delivered back to Hull Prison for execution. At Paragon Station, flanked by two prison officers, he flashed a smile at the small crowd that had gathered to greet his arrival.

In the interval between his confinement in the condemned cell and the date set for the hanging, the prisoner received a tearful visit from his mother. The meeting prompted him to write a letter seeking a reprieve. The missive read: 'Grant me a reprieve that my life may be spared, not only for my own sake but for my dear wife's and my mother's who are so laid up on account of this sentence that has been passed upon me and more so that my innocence of this crime maybe brought to light which I am certain will be sooner or later.' The gallows that awaited him had been constructed to accommodate three convicted men and had been built the year before for the execution of John Walker, who stabbed his drunken father to death. Walker escaped the noose after an appeal to the Home Secretary, who took the view that the death penalty for the 21-year-old was too severe.

The authorities in Hull, together with most of the population, were disturbed about the prospect of the first execution of one of its citizens in more than a hundred years. The responsibility for organising the macabre event fell on the shoulders of the reluctant Under-Sheriff, Alderman Arthur Rollit, who refused the press access to the execution. There was also deep concern amongst the ranks of the magistracy, as one of them was obliged to attend the hanging. The magistrates convened a special meeting to discuss the issue and, when no volunteer came forward, they resolved to hold a secret ballot. Only the brave intervention of Dr George Lilley, JP, prevented the drawing of straws.

The hangman recruited to carry out the sentence was William Billington, who was to be assisted by his younger brother John. These men were the sons of a barber from Bolton and had taken up the profession simply to earn extra money. The duo arrived in Hull the day before the execution and went about their tasks in a methodical manner. They spent the night in Hull Prison and measured Richardson's height and weight in order to calculate the optimum drop. The condemned man was slightly built, so a ten feet drop was agreed upon and the gallows were duly tested by attaching sandbags equivalent to his weight to the rope.

After a sound night's sleep, Richardson ate a good breakfast around 6 a.m., and the prison chaplain offered him Holy Communion before the executioners arrived. They strapped his arms together and led him just ten paces from his cell to the scaffold. His legs were tied together, the noose placed around his neck and a white hood pulled over his head. The onlookers, who included the prison governor and the Deputy-Sheriff, heard Richardson say his final words: 'I have made my peace with God and I believe I am forgiven and ask for the forgiveness of my fellow men.'

Meanwhile, outside the prison, a large crowd had gathered and the police guarded the main gate. Nearby, an equally grim knot of prison officers barred the entrance to a cemetery, thus preventing some of the more ghoulish spectators from climbing trees in order to secure a better vantage point. All the onlookers were listening for the tell-tale sounding of the prison bell and the raising of the black flag that would signal the end of Arthur Richardson.

Inside the prison, William Billington pulled the bolt and Richardson disappeared into the void. He died instantly and his body danced just once on the rope. From the moment that Richardson left the cell, the entire proceedings had taken less than sixty seconds. The bell duly sounded and the awful black flag was raised. Many of the spectators silently recited prayers before they dispersed.

Arthur Richardson duly paid the price for his crime. But the evidence against the murderer judged in today's terms, and even taking into account his final words, was inconclusive. So was he guilty? The answer would emerge a few days after his execution. Before he walked to the gallows he dictated a letter to the prison's acting chaplain in the following terms:

> I Arthur Richardson, did wilfully murder my aunt Sarah Hebden, my motive in entering her house was not theft but murder. I trusted to chance to provide me with this weapon and I took nothing with me for the purpose. I entered her house at 7.30 on the morning of the murder and I remained there an hour and a half, leaving about 9 o'clock making my escape across the Groves allotments. When I entered the house my aunt had some words and in trying to avoid me tripped over something and fell, in which attitude I struck her a blow. She then reached the tongs and rattled behind the fire grate to arouse the neighbours; I took the tongs from her and struck her with them on the head; she then arose and staggered towards the

door behind which her body was found. Whilst there and to silence her screams for a knock at the door frightened me, I struck her with the tongs until she died. The most horrible part of the murder for me was some words my aunt uttered just as she was dying; taking my hand in both hers she said, 'I forgive you all Arthur' and then died. At the same moment I heard a voice close behind me, which said audibly, 'murder will out'. It was the voice of my conscience.

Thus, one of Hull's vilest murderers got his just deserts and any mystery surrounding the death of Sarah Hebden was cleared up. But was it? If Richardson's motive was murder rather than theft, the apparent motive for the crime, what had inspired such a desperate deed? And what did his aunt mean by the words, 'I forgive you all Arthur'? And, focusing on the word 'all', was anybody else implicated in the dreadful affair?

All Hull was shocked by the flying of that black flag on that desperate day of 25 March 1902. But there was more communal anguish to come. The death bell sounded a further nine times in the city during the next thirty-two years.

6

THE FIRE STARTER

It is no coincidence that our view of hell is wreathed in flames. There can be no more agonising end than death by burning. It is therefore hard to imagine why anyone, particularly a young man in the late twentieth century, would want to set himself up as a modern Torquemada, the much feared Grand Inquisitor of the Spanish Inquisition? Indeed, the psychiatrists are still debating this question more than two decades after Bruce George Peter Lee from Hull admitted starting eleven separate fires and killing twenty-six people. During his six years of arson attacks, the victims included a baby aged only six months and a 95-year-old man. On 20 January 1981 Lee, a self-confessed pyromaniac and misanthropist, was sentenced to an indefinite period of detention at a special hospital. At the time, he had the unenviable distinction of being the most prolific mass murderer in modern British criminal history.

Lee had an ignominious start in life. His mother, Doreen, was a prostitute who never knew the identity of her baby's father. She worked the city streets, and frequently left her son and his younger sister in the care of relatives. Doreen endured two volatile marriages, and the turbulent, often violent, atmosphere of the marital home badly affected both children. Identified by the social services as vulnerable, they were consigned to care homes. In one of these, the impressionable Lee was introduced to the pervasive influences of homosexuals. Categorised as educationally subnormal, he was then sent to a special school. He dreamt of a romantic life as a trawlerman, but even the job of a deckie-learner was beyond him. His physical disabilities, which included a limp and a withered arm, also severely restricted his chances of finding employment ashore.

With few prospects the teenager roamed the streets of Hull

dissolute and dispirited. He developed a psychopathic urge to make his mark, and was often driven to rage by petty insults. These factors seem to have led him to begin a reign of terror. During six years of mayhem, surprisingly attributed by the authorities and the coroner to accidental causes, Lee killed his victims indiscriminately and without mercy. He later admitted that, on one occasion, he had doused a man with paraffin and set him alight after an argument about racing pigeons.

Only the opportunities afforded by a number of local training schemes offered Lee a chance of life beyond the dole. But he drifted, hiding his dark secrets, unsupervised, uncared for and unloved. Occasionally, he would earn a little extra money by taking menial jobs at the speedway track and at Hull Football Club's Boulevard stadium. Now 19, and already with several murders to his name, he lived with his mother in a shabby and crumbling council maisonette off Cavill Place. A dirty and disturbing figure, mutilated with self-inflicted tattoos, he wandered between the amusement arcades and pubs of Hull city centre causing a mixture of fear, derision and mirth, not least because of his change of name. Born Peter Dinsdale he took the name of his hero, the film star Bruce Lee, by deed poll. A poster of the kung-fu legend adorned his wall, but this image was the nearest Lee would ever come to the martial arts.

Frequently drunk and intimidating, Lee would curse people of his own age who had the nerve to mock him. Older people stayed out of his way. And so, with few friends, 'Daft' Peter, as he became known on the estate where he lived, roamed the streets, plotting the eleventh of his attacks that would lead to the deaths of three more victims and his eventual arrest.

The partial paralysis of one of his hands made even striking a match an awkward affair, but Lee was a practised and accomplished fire-starter who often described feeling a tingling sensation in his fingers and an urge to kill before each blaze. The fire he started in December 1979, at a house in Selby Street, claimed the lives of three young brothers. Charles, Peter and Paul Hastie all survived the initial blaze but eventually succumbed to their horrendous burns. Their mother, Edith, and her four other children survived the attack. Tommy Hastie, the boys' father, was away from the house at the time of the atrocity, serving a short prison sentence for burglary. After the flames had been extinguished, suspicious firefighters soon realised that the ashes were tainted by paraffin, but their enquiries revealed that no such fuel had ever been used on the premises. Forensic investigators confirmed the initial fears, and concluded that, in all probability, paraffin had been poured through the letterbox and set alight. And two spent matches were found close by. It was now a job for the police.

By lunchtime on the day of the tragedy, the headline in the early edition of the *Hull Daily Mail* read: 'FIRE HORROR CHILDREN BADLY HURT'. Within hours of the news breaking that Charles Hastie had died from his burns, a member of the public reported overhearing a chilling pronouncement by a man seen drumming his fingers on the railings of the railway walkway overlooking Selby Street: 'One down four to go'.

At first, the motive for the attack seemed reasonably clear. The Hastie family were very unpopular with neighbours. House-to-house enquiries uncovered a history of animosity, petty jealousies and feuds. Much of the bad feeling arose because of the disruptive and anti-social behaviour of the children who had been accused of dropping bricks down chimneys, urinating through letter boxes, leaving faeces on doorsteps, throwing stones at pensioners, petty vandalism and shoplifting. A poison pen letter written to the family a year earlier seemed to corroborate these early assumptions. Scrawled on the back of a cornflakes packet were the following words:

> A family of fucking rubbish. We all hate you, you should all live on an island. (Devils Island) but I'm not kidding but I promised you a bomb and by hell I'm not kidding. Why don't you flit while you've got the chance. We can't get you out normally then we'll bastard well bomb you and that's too good for you.

Although this threat was taken seriously, a new lead opened up the possibility that the attack might have been intended for the house of a known drug-dealer who lived next door to the Hasties. Then, the police received an anonymous telephone call. Lee, apparently remorseful, rang to admit his guilt. By this time, Tommy Hastie's sentence had been waived on compassionate grounds and he, and his family, were asked to listen to a police tape-recording of the confession. Would they recognise the voice? They might have done had Charles Hastie been alive. The police also pursued another line of inquiry by comparing the handwriting of residents in the Selby Street area with the scrawl of the poison-pen letter. There were no similarities.

Just a week after making the call, Lee, as bold as brass, walked into a police station and said he wanted to make a statement about the fire. He said that he had overheard a man in a pub claiming responsibility for the blaze. 'Daft' Peter's ramblings were, of course, treated with some disdain and incredulity by the police and he was dismissed as a time-waster.

Meanwhile, the irate and pain-wracked Hasties knocked on every door in Selby Street hoping to confront the killer of their sons. Windows were broken and there was much shouting and exchanging of obscenities before the police were called to restore order. And then on a bleak January day came the funerals. The cortege, in a deliberate act of tribute and defiance by Tommy and Edith Hastie, wound its solemn way down Selby Street as the curtains fluttered nervously. All Hull knew about the sad deaths but only around sixty people attended the service.

All through the winter, the police doggedly searched for clues to the deaths but met with little success. As time passed, the investigation inevitably began to wind down. Months of painstaking work had revealed little information about the fire, although the file on the murders remained decidedly open. In the spring of 1980, the man who had led the enquiries, Superintendent Ronald Sagar of Humberside CID, thoroughly reviewed the case and decided to take one last look at the gutted house on Selby Street. As he stood examining the boarded-up building, he had a flash of intuition. His conjecture was that Charles Hastie, a vulnerable 15-year-old, might have been exploring his sexuality like other boys of his age and that he could have been drawn into the 'rent boy' culture that afflicted the Selby Street area. Following up his hunch, he mounted a six week stake-out of a local public toilet known to be frequented by touting homosexuals. At the same time, his officers painstakingly compiled a list of youngsters who might have known Charles Hastie. The name of Bruce George Peter Lee was on that list.

A number of youngsters were interrogated to discover if they had known Hastie. Under examination, Lee admitted having a passing acquaintance with the lad but he divulged nothing else and was released. Sagar was not satisfied with the first round of interviews and, a month later, the young men faced further questioning. This time, the Superintendent adopted a more aggressive and confrontational approach, by putting a provocative question. 'You set fire to the Hastie house, didn't you?' Each youngster in turn vehemently denied any involvement with the crime. And then, nearing the end of what seemed to be yet another fruitless session of interviews, Lee was brought in. Sagar repeated the same words. He was astonished at the immediate reply, as Lee admitted his guilt with a single phrase: 'I didn't mean to kill them.' But was this the worthless admission of a simple-minded and intimidated youth browbeaten into making a confession? It could have been perceived as such, had not the police matched the interview tapes with the recording of the anonymous telephone call. Any further doubt about his guilt vanished when, after a night of interrogation, he revealed a catalogue of intimate details about the crime that had not been made public. Finally, Lee explained the motives surrounding his fatal attack, explaining that Charles Hastie had annoyed him by repeatedly clamouring for payment after allowing him sexual favours. Sagar had his killer, but he was in for yet another surprise.

There was something in Lee's lack of remorse and unusually co-operative manner that left Sagar perplexed. Two weeks later, with Lee behind bars in Armley Gaol in Leeds, he got the opportunity to pursue his suspicions in yet another interview. Lee yet again astounded his interrogator with a startling admission of responsibility for two more arson attacks, one of which had resulted in a fatality. There were yet more revelations arising from twenty further interviews, and Lee recorded in damning detail every aspect of his crimes. The harrowing catalogue of destruction included a description of a man showered in paraffin and left to die in a ball of flames – up to that time the official cause of the blaze had been attributed to sparks from an unguarded fire, which ignited his clothing as he slept. There were also details of conflagrations that killed a 6-year-old boy and an 82-year-old woman. The boy's death had previously been blamed on a gas leak, while smoking in bed was regarded as the culprit for the pensioner's demise.

During his soul-bearing Lee, ironically for the first time in his life, learned to trust another human being. He confided in Sagar and revealed all the intimate details of his crimes. And the biggest revelation of all was kept until last. Lee admitted that he had started a fire that led to the deaths of eleven elderly residents of the Wensley Lodge retirement home in Hessle in January 1977. All Hull was shocked by these grisly revelations and the authorities were somewhat abashed and perplexed. The Wensley Lodge fire was the most serious in the area for three decades and had been thoroughly investigated by forensic and fire experts. A committee of inquiry concluded that the fire had been started after a plumber's torch had accidentally scorched floorboards and left them smouldering. The jury at the inquest reached a similar conclusion and returned misadventure verdicts on all eleven victims. Now there was egg on many people's faces.

Lee boasted how he had normally used paraffin to start his blazes. His usual technique, it has to be said, was hardly the work of a professional arsonist. In most cases he used two separate pools of the fuel linked by a fuse of dribbling paraffin, and the delayed action gave him time to escape. But this *modus operandi* was never detected, even by forensic experts. One of these experts, Home Office specialist Graham Daveport, changed his mind about the Wensley Lodge tragedy, and concluded that it had indeed been caused by arson.

While on remand, Lee asked for a Bible. Chillingly, he turned to Matthew chapter six, verse twenty-four, and quoted the following as a key to his awful obsession and motivation: 'No man can serve two masters: for either he will hate the one, and love the other; or else he will hold to the one, and despise the other. Ye cannot serve God and mammon.' What are we to make of this extraordinary reference to Scripture? Well, it would seem that Lee juxtaposed fire for God and ending up hating all of mankind. And he made another statement at the time that was equally macabre, allegedly bragging to the police: 'Those twenty-six are going to put me in the *Guinness Book of Records.'*

Lee was sent for trial at Leeds Crown Court in January 1981. Against a background of repeated confessions, the verdict was a foregone conclusion. Lee pleaded guilty to eleven charges of arson and twenty-six counts of manslaughter, the prosecution accepting the latter on the grounds of diminished responsibility. The trial judge ordered that the defendant should be detained indefinitely at a secure mental institution and the case file was closed. The world might never have heard of Bruce George Peter Lee again but, ever unpredictable, he had a trick up his sleeve, and set the judicial world alight just a month after his conviction when he contacted solicitors and decided to lodge an appeal.

His case was heard nearly three years later, in November 1983. The Court of Appeal heard evidence from Lee that he had given false statements under duress, lied to avoid questioning and co-operated with the police, preferring detention in a hospital to the grimmer alternative of prison. His chief interrogator was also called to the stand. Superintendent Sagar strenuously denied breaches of interviewing procedures and of bullying Lee. After re-examining the evidence, the judges refused leave to appeal in all but three of the cases. A month later, they quashed Lee's conviction for arson and manslaughter at Wensley Lodge after concluding that the forensic evidence supporting the verdict was 'unsatisfactory'. In reaching their decision, they exonerated Sagar of any wrongdoing but castigated forensic scientist Daveport and described his investigation as 'inadequate'. With this in mind, and accepting that Lee could have fantasised about the fire because of the notoriety attached to becoming the biggest-ever mass killer, they had no alternative but to accept the appeal. Lee went back to hospital with a few less deaths to his name and the files were yet again closed. But the media still had doubts about Lee's crimes and the *Sunday Times* published a series of investigative articles about Sagar's methods. He responded in a 1985 newspaper interview, saying, 'No-one feels more sorry for Lee than me and why anyone should think we would want to pin on him deaths that were already recorded as accidental is beyond me.' Incensed at what he regarded as libellous criticism of his handling of the investigation, Sagar instigated action against the *Sunday Times* and, two years later, secured a five-figure sum in damages following an out out-of-court settlement.

Two decades on it is thought that Lee remains in custody although, some years ago, to the great anger of the relatives of his victims, I understand that he was moved to a less secure institution. Perhaps he still keeps a poster of his kung-fu idol in his room. He never did quite fashion a reputation to match that of his kick-boxing friend, but his name is still up there in the blackest of lights . . . just below that of Harold Shipman.

Detective Superintendent Sagar's detailed, honest, compassionate and often painful account of the extraordinary story of Lee, *Hull, Hell and Fire* published in 1999, ends with a telling sentence. If Lee is ever deemed to have served his time and be ready for release into the community, one can only hope that what he told his inquisitor on Wednesday 15 October 1980 is true: 'I'll never ever set fire to another dwelling house as long as I live.'

7

BLONDE, BEAUTIFUL . . . MISSING

Blonde and beautiful, with curves in all the right places, Gloria Bielby was a woman who could stop traffic dead. A 34-year-old former model from a quiet bungalow in Dawnay Road in Bilton on the eastern outskirts of Hull, she was a lady who stood out in a crowd. Her stunning looks and outgoing personality attracted men by the score. Married, but with a hectic social life outside her suburban home, she was a well-known figure in the pubs, restaurants and nightspots of Hull. So how was it that, in 1979, she managed to disappear without a trace? More than twenty years later, after exhaustive enquiries by the police and a mass of speculation, that question is still unanswered.

She was married to a successful butcher, Bernard Bielby, and the couple had an 11-year-old son, Nigel, who was a pupil at a preparatory school in Bridlington. The pair had grown apart over the years, and migrated to different bedrooms. Bernard preferred domesticity, while his wife opted for a more exciting lifestyle and the company of other men, particularly that of handsome 39-year-old Mike Blackburn, a suave vending-machine salesman and rugby player. The phlegmatic Bernard Bielby apparently knew about his wife's infidelity, but was prepared to tolerate it for the sake of his son. But, finally, the couple decided to separate in January 1979.

Gloria was employed as a secretary at the Reckitt and Coleman offices in Hull but, on 1 February, a technical problem temporarily closed the premises. Gloria enjoyed an unexpected holiday in the company of Mike Blackburn, and the pair spent the day travelling by car to Driffield and Bridlington. Blackburn dropped his girlfriend off at her twin sister's house around 9.30 p.m. on that bitter cold Thursday evening, and her brother-in-law escorted her home on foot soon afterwards. Gloria felt she needed an escort, as she feared for her safety after receiving a number of malicious telephone calls. Back home in Dawnay Road, Bernard Bielby greeted his wife, and gave her £3,000. This payment had been previously discussed as part of the separation agreement and Gloria intended to use the money for the purchase of a second-hand Ford Capri.

Around 6 a.m. on Friday 2 February, Bernard Bielby's alarm clock sounded and, as usual, he heard Gloria leave the house. She said nothing as she left, and he wondered if the day of separation had finally arrived. He noted that a considerable amount of clothing, her hairdryer and other personal belongings were missing and assumed that she might be gone for some considerable time. After the temporary closure, the Reckitt and Coleman offices had reopened that day but, mysteriously, Gloria never arrived at her desk. Her boyfriend telephoned hoping to confirm arrangements for the collection of her new car. Told of her absence, he rang her home number. There was no response. Bernard Bielby then telephoned her parents, Mr and Mrs Thompson, to explain that she had probably left him for good and would not therefore be able to pick her mother up as planned. The fears of the family grew as time went on, and the police were notified.

Initially, they did not take the view there had been any foul play. Appraised of her marital history and penchant for the high life, they assumed she had taken the £3,000 and done a bunk, perhaps jetting off to some exotic island with yet another lover. But months elapsed and there was still no word from Gloria. The Thompsons became increasingly concerned at the lack of even the briefest contact from their daughter. Mr Thompson, a civilian employee at police headquarters in Hull, shared his growing alarm with work colleagues and an investigative team was formed, headed by Detective Superintendent Bob Carmichael.

The team began at her place of work. More than six hundred questionnaires enquiring about her habits and contacts were circulated amongst Reckitt and Coleman's staff. The information provided was thought-provoking in the extreme. Several employees reported having seen Gloria regularly get into a red

Morris car during her lunch break between July and August 1978. The descriptions of its driver did not match those of either Bernard Bielby or Mike Blackburn.

Detectives also made enquiries in Dawnay Road. The Bielbys' next-door neighbour, an elderly woman called Elsie Pauling, reported that she had observed Gloria loading suitcases into a red Ford Escort car at around 11 a.m. on the morning of her disappearance. Mrs Pauling was adamant about the day and time of the sighting, explaining that she always cleaned her windows at that hour on a Friday. A naturally inquisitive lady, she had put down her leathers to have a really good look, describing the driver of the vehicle as smartly dressed, about 40 years old, around five feet nine inches tall and of slim build with greying hair. And both Elsie Pauling and her husband Robert claimed to have seen the man before. They said he called so frequently to Gloria's home during January 1979 that they had christened him 'Dapper Dan'. With their detailed description – it bore no similarities to that of the man seen outside Reckitt and Coleman's – an artist's impression of this so-called 'third man' was prepared and circulated across the country. It drew a blank.

The police obviously considered that both husband and lover might have some knowledge of Gloria's whereabouts and Bernard Bielby and Mike Blackburn faced repeated and intense questioning over a number of weeks. Both men strenuously denied involvement in her disappearance. Systematic searches of the house and garden in Dawnay Road also led nowhere.

So where on earth was Gloria Bielby? And if she was dead, where was her corpse? There was a torrent of rumour and speculation fuelled by numerous articles in the press. Many anonymous telephone calls and letters were received by the police, who followed up even the most outlandish theories with dogged determination. Bielby had been an enthusiastic follower of rugby league and there was some suggestion that, at the time of her disappearance, she might have accompanied a touring team from York on a visit to Munchengladbach in Germany. All the players were interviewed but, once again, the enquiries came to nothing.

Frogmen made exhaustive but fruitless searches of almost every watercourse in and around Hull. False reports of the burial of bodies in gardens in Hessle Road and Coltman Street proved equally frustrating. During the investigations a corpse found on the North York moors was thought to be that of the missing woman, but subsequent examination proved otherwise. And the reports of alleged sightings became even more bizarre and fanciful. Gloria had been spotted in Venezuela and she appeared, according to several television viewers, in an episode of the hit series *The Professionals*. One of the most promising leads came in October 1980 when a witness came forward recalling two possible sightings of Gloria and a male companion with vaguely Jewish features. He was described as around 35 years old, five feet ten inches tall, with an athletic build and thick, dark-brown hair. The man was first observed picking Gloria up from work in a red Ford Escort. The couple were next seen hugging in Hull's Prospect Centre by the same witness. Although this information gave some credibility to Elsie Pauling's testimony, the man in the red car was never traced.

Nearly all the people who knew Gloria Bielby were of the opinion that, had she been able, she would have at least got in touch with her parents to reassure them about her safety. However, not everyone shared this view. Workmate and close friend Jacqueline Clyne suggested that, occasionally, she was a selfish opportunist who would dump one boyfriend unceremoniously if a rival with a bigger bank balance came along. Clyne went on to tell the police of an intriguing boast made by her colleague shortly before her disappearance. Bielby bragged mysteriously that she had the opportunity of earning £30,000. Although Clyne recalled being intrigued by this information she explained that, despite her curiosity, her stubbornness prevented her from asking the obvious question. Had she asked where the money was coming from, the mystery of the disappearance of Gloria Bielby might have been solved.

Over time, all avenues of enquiry were exhausted and the investigative process was inevitably wound down. By January 1982, Bernard Bielby had successfully petitioned for a divorce from his wife on the grounds of desertion and the case file began to gather dust. Nothing has been heard from that beautiful lady since that fateful Friday morning in February 1979. Is she out there somewhere sunning herself on some tropical beach, or strolling into a casino on the arm of a rich businessman? Or was she cruelly murdered and cleverly disposed of in an unmarked and untended grave? Over two decades on, it seems unlikely that we shall ever know.

8

FISH!

This book could, with some justification, be called *Fish and Ships*. The sea and its denizens – finny and man-made – fill these pages with a certain pungency. And, as an author uniquely blessed to wax poetical about Hull's most defining product, I can readily identify that smell. Fish! Why do I make such a bold claim? Well, let me explain. My grandfather was a hawker of fish in Leeds during the 1920s and 30s, and I married a girl whose own grandfather and father were fish merchants on Hull Docks. Thus connected, I can write with some conviction on all matters piscatorial. But that's not all. Guess what my mother was called before she married Leonard Markham senior? That's right, her maiden name was Haddock!

Having identified the qualifying chromosomes I can state, quite naturally, that I love fish. The opportunity of further mixing the genes with one evolved from a family so eminently connected to the order *Gadiformes*, is always eagerly taken. I took to my new father-in-law – a well-known character on Hull docks – like, if you will pardon the expression, a 'fish to water', and eagerly accepted his early invitation to see his business from the bony end. At some obscene early hour only inhabited by insomniacs and ladies in childbirth, I was taken to a freezing quayside where an initiation ceremony was performed to blood me, I suppose, in the ways of the dock. Somewhat confused, I was presented with a samovar of steaming grit-flecked liquid that appeared to be the rinsings from a trawler's steam-boiler and a bacon butty the size of a cod-end. Having accidentally overturned what I later learned was a pitcher full of tea and, when nobody was looking, tossed out enough ballast to keep a flock of seagulls grounded for a month, I was taken to a large shed. Indisputably, I liked fish until that moment.

There, contained in large dustbin-sized metal barrels known as kits, were thousands of limp, glass-eyed fish. These shoals of haddock and cod gave off the most penetrating odour imaginable. A sort of finny tear-gas, it crept into every orifice, assailing the nose, clouding the eyes and impregnating every fibre of clothing that henceforth, even after innumerable washes, could not be worn without instant reminders of Captain Ahab's jock-strap. Exposure to the gas, though, was all part of the bonding process – 'you don't smell it after a while' – and the next treat came as a phalanx of keen-eyed merchants arrived for the auction.

The ability of these men to remain upright on a floor surface that was as slippery as eel in a massage parlour amazed me. Fish are naturally lubricated for the business of gliding through the sea with a protective mucus. This substance, which had coated the floor to a depth of several inches, enabled non-skaters like me to perform a passable imitation of a Torville and Dean triple salchow. But I might have been part of a circus spectacular, as several bidders followed my clownish antics with their equivalent of a high-wire act . . . without a safety net.

Soberly dressed in suits and waistcoats, these daredevils, who had an obvious disdain of danger, leapt onto the rims of the kits and proceeded, in a delightful unison that could have been set to the music of *Swan Lake*, to give us repeats of Blondin's famous walk across Niagara Falls. Unerringly, they balanced and skipped from rim to metal rim inspecting the fish with knowing eyes, all the time assessing quality and weight. My mentor, meanwhile, led me to another part of the shed where dozens of monster halibut were laid out for inspection. Close up, what an impressive beast the halibut is! One of the largest of all flatfishes, weighing in at up to 600 pounds, it laid there, they laid there, in ascending order of size awaiting scrutiny.

By this time, the troupes of fish-monkeys had returned to earth and were manhandling the goods. 'What are they doing?' I ventured, observing closely as each fishy tail was lifted in turn. 'They know by sight to within a few ounces what each fish weighs,' he explained. 'A little lift of the tail helps them to decide how much to bid.' The bidding came next but it was unlike any other auction

I have ever attended. The fish hawks gathered round a man in a white coat who was attended by a clipboard-clasping woman who had the physiognomy of a large pollock, although I have to say, in redemption, that she did find rather more use for her appendage than Denis Norden. It was her job to record the bids that came in quick succession.

The apparition in the coat moved from kit to kit, mouthing something as unintelligible as cetacean sonar and the products were somehow sold. I knew not how. All I know is that my taciturn guide – I'd swear he never spoke but I did notice that he was the owner of a pair of rather manoeuvrable eyebrows – was the proud purchaser of several hundred fish. The sale was noted by the pollock with a scribble, the ownership of her close relations being confirmed with a scattering on their scales of small purple labels. I'd mysteriously seen shredded parts of their printed surfaces before, and a subsequent rummage through my honeymoon bag confirmed that my father-in-law, who was the truest of Yorkshireman, would never waste money on shop-bought confetti, God rest his soul.

Within a few minutes, the entire stock of fish had been sold and I was none the wiser as to the method of sale. 'How was it all done?' I asked nonplussed as the first of the bobbers came to collect the kits for trundling to the filleting sheds. He smiled as if to say I had a lot to learn and said: 'The auctioneer starts from a price per kit and works down until a merchant buys. It's as simple as that. Blink and you'd miss it. Now, we'll follow our purchases and show you what happens next.'

The filleting shed would have made the perfect set for a film about the Arctic convoys. Liberal quantities of ice and swilling water gave the place an authenticity only slightly devalued by the fact that the floor kept still. The kits were barrowed in and the filleting began. Two teams of twin slashers, dressed in stout waterproof-aprons and rubber boots, took their places across a table. The last time I saw hands as quick as those was in a Bruce Lee film, but no martial-arts expert ever handled blades like that. Every cod and haddock was deprived of its working parts in a flash of steel, and each man washed the filleted fish in a sluice of running water conveniently situated between the teams. And the pace was electrifying. It was off with their heads in double-quick time, fillet after luscious fillet going, with the precision and tenderness of a florist packing prize blooms, into boxes of fresh ice. Within a few hours these boxes would arrive in the West Riding, and by nightfall their contents would be anointed in batter, the metamorphosis into a dish fit for the gods coming in sizzling and glorious symphonies of hot dripping.

Marriage certainly has its compensations. Oh, and I forgot to mention my role in the business. The in-laws were also the proud owners of several fish-and-chip emporia within the town. I was recruited as the chief taster and head of quality control.

9

WHEN THE BOAT COMES IN

I don't wonder, with all the men lost around the Dogger, we sometimes got human skulls, and that, in the trawl, an more 'an once I've seen a man in oily jumpers, and boots on, shot out on deck with the fish when we've opened the cod end. It made your flesh crawl, shovin' of 'em over again with a capstan bar or your shovels. Lor, the Dogger's a regular ocean cemetery.

Smacksman, 1909

Man was catching fish in the river Humber and the North Sea when Hull was an unnamed creek. The discovery, in the silt, of hewn-out boats in places like Ferriby and Hasholme Carr attests to a quest for fish and wildfowl that has gone on for millennia. Examine coprolite unearthed from the Yorvik Viking-age dig in York and you will discover the microscopic bones of eels and other delicacies. The trade in fresh fish reached out along the Humber and its feeding streams for many miles.

Wyke-upon-Hull, as it was originally known, was a busy trading port long before it was bought by Edward I from the monks of Meaux Abbey in 1293. Fish formed an important element in the prosperity of the town, although imports through the busy ports of Whitby, Scarborough and the long since vanished Ravenser at the mouth of the Humber exceeded those of their inland neighbour. Great quantities of fish were imported in the thirteenth and fourteenth centuries – huge landings of herrings and cod supplemented by lesser quantities of plaice, mudfish, skate and eels coming from France, Flanders and Holland in foreign vessels.

By the early fifteenth century, pioneering Hull merchants organised fishing trips to Icelandic waters. They needed the permission of the Danish king, who then ruled Norway and its dependencies. This practice of English fishermen requiring licences from a foreign power presaged the Cod War by several centuries! In the middle of the century, Hull regularly despatched three or four fishing vessels every year to Iceland, and they returned with holds full of wind-dried herring and cod. Hull ships also fished home waters but, because their catches were not liable to tax, unlike the foreign imports, no records of the landings or fleet sizes were made. For these reasons, this period in Hull's fishing industry remains largely conjectural.

In the absence of organisation, expertise and dedicated docking and processing facilities, the fishing trade of the town continued to be a relatively small-scale operation for hundreds of years. Then, in 1843, a fisherman from the Devon port of Brixham came to Hull with ambitious plans. Using his tried and tested smack, he set sail in rough weather and headed intuitively for the Dogger Bank about sixty miles from the Humber mouth. Almost miraculously, his ship harvested a biblical haul of fish, and the vessel returned to port smothered in fish scales. News of the bumper catch, and the newly located fishing ground, which was thereafter referred to as the Silver Pit, quickly spread, and many more ships joined the fledgling Yorkshire fleet. In 1863, just twenty years after the discovery of the Silver Pit, Hull had a 270-strong fleet of smacks, each of about fifty tons. The railway, which first linked Hull to an expanding national network in 1840, helped to stimulate an unprecedented demand for fresh fish.

Initially the smacks used the pier, which was less than suitable, to land their catches. But, after repeatedly pressing the largely unsympathetic Hull Dock Company to allocate berthing space, they were grudgingly allowed a corner in the Humber Dock, the ships relocating to the newly built Albert Dock in 1869. By 1880, the number of smacks had increased to 420, and that year also saw the introduction of important innovations. For practical reasons, smack fishing had been largely confined to the accessible waters of the North Sea. The realities of time and distance, and the need to deliver fish in fresh condition, restricted the scope for fishing in more productive grounds further from port. Three factors were to change all that: the availability of ice to preserve the fish; the offloading of catches into fast cutters whose sole purpose was to rush the fish back to port; the development of the fleet system, which ensured continuity of supply and longer periods at sea. The industry expanded rapidly to serve the growing need for cheap and nutritious protein demanded by the newly industrialised towns in the Yorkshire hinterland and elsewhere. With a further growth in the fleet came a demand for crews, and the majority of new recruits came from city workhouses, especially those in Leeds and London.

Two further developments spurred a rapid expansion in the industry. Firstly, new technology saw the advent of steam-powered winches and ironclad, steam-powered ships. In addition, Hull built its first dock – St Andrew's – for the sole use of fishing vessels, in 1883. In the ten years between 1885 and 1895, most of the antiquated smacks, which had served the industry so well during its fledgling years, were replaced by steam-powered ships. This all resulted in the port of Hull becoming one of the prime centres for fishing and fish processing in the country.

The twin revolution of 1883 saw social change on a vast scale. The fishermen credited with founding the industry had done so owning and operating their own wind-powered vessels. The introduction of new and vastly more efficient vessels, however, transformed what until then was essentially a cottage industry on a par with handloom weaving in the West Riding. High capital costs attracted major investment and concentrated the ownership of the fleet in fewer, more professional hands. As a result, the fishermen themselves relinquished the ownership of vessels and became employees. Large fishing companies now controlled every aspect of the business.

The concentration of fishing families in huddled terraced houses in the Hessle Road area mirrored those of industrialised populations in the textile and mining areas of inland Yorkshire. Like their urban counterparts, these families developed a fierce interdependency and near tribal loyalties, with generations of young men following their fathers into an occupation that was poorly paid and hazardous in the extreme.

Ironically, it was in that monumental year of 1883 that Hull suffered one of its worst ever calamities. In just one stormy day in May, twenty-six smacks were lost at sea, and 129 men and boys (about 6 per cent of the entire workforce) drowned in the process. In December 1894, 106 men were lost in a single day. Statistically, one fisherman in a hundred would die at work in the period between 1878 and 1882. And those that were injured, maimed and deliberately abused by evil skippers would, perhaps, suffer an even worse fate.

In a factual overview of Hull's fishing past, it is easy to forget the personal cost involved in bringing, what is now becoming a luxury food, to the nation's table. Today, fishing – what's left of it – is a dangerous occupation, but the privations involved in the daily routines of your average smacksman in the late nineteenth century make your hair stand on end. Recruited from the perceived dregs of society, the apprentice boys, who did a great deal of the arduous work on board were, in reality, a form of forced labour. It was the task of the most junior of these raw recruits – some of them only 10 or 11 years old – to cook the ship's food. All five crewmen shared a small cabin and, in an atmosphere impregnated with the stench of sweat, steaming fish-slimed clothing and the nauseating smell of tobacco and putrefying cod livers, they would sleep and eat. The meals were hardly appetising; the monotonous menu consisted of little more than beef that had been towed astern to remove most of the encrusted salt before cooking. Other delicacies included hard biscuits and doughy puddings.

Except in the vilest weather, or in periods of dead calm, smacks were required to fish day and night, seven days a week, for up to twelve weeks at a stretch. Under the fleet system, each ship would be under the instructions of an 'admiral' who would synchronise the hauling up of the trawls every eight hours. Before the introduction of steam-operated winches, this was backbreaking work. The winding in, over a three-hour period, of fishing gear bulging with up to half a ton of fish led inevitably to raw hands and aching backs.

Once the catch was tipped on board the vessel, the messy business of gutting and packing the fish started. After the crew had sluiced away the heaps of blood and offal and recast the gear they might, if they were lucky, snatch a few minutes sleep in their saturated clothing before the next haul began. As hard as it was, this routine was not the most hated aspect of life at sea. For those crewmen who drew the short straw, the most loathed and feared of all the duties of a smacksman was that of ferrying boxes of fish to the awaiting cutters for transhipment ashore. Apart from the loss of a vessel, this process was the major cause of death. The man-handling of slippery boxes of fish, and their transfer by rowing boat to the cutters in often-violent seas, was an extremely dangerous operation. Tragically, many young fishermen – not many of them could swim – were swept overboard and drowned. Others were crushed between the rowing boats and the cutters. The treatment of excruciatingly painful fractures and wounds had to await a return to port.

Even these hardships, though, were as naught compared with the experience of a boy who was actually murdered on board his vessel in 1881. The maltreatment of raw recruits to the fishing industry was a fact of life for decades; exploitation, humiliation and torture went on miles away from scrutiny with only frightened crewmates as witnesses. All this changed after the appalling treatment of apprentice William Papper. Osmond Otto Brand, the 27-year-old skipper of the *Rising Sun* was a psychopath long before the word was coined. His brutality to Papper, a boy of only 14, began shortly after his vessel left Hull on 14 December 1881. Papper is alleged to have made a derogatory comment about a liaison between his sister and Brand. A ship's crewman later reported on oath the following outburst from the skipper: 'Now you bastard, I'll pay you for telling lies about me! I've had something to do with your sister have I?'

Shaking with anger, Brand then took up a knotted rope and repeatedly thrashed the boy, leaving him badly hurt with a deeply gashed wound across his face. An orgy of wickedness was to follow in the next few days. The *Rising Sun* sustained damage to her fishing nets off Spurn. Brand immediately blamed the boy for the problem and punched him to the deck. Dousing Papper with buckets of sea water, he next ordered that the terrified bundle be bound with rope and hoisted aloft on the cross trees which promptly broke with the weight, and spilled the lad to the deck.

All through the Christmas period, Papper was denied food and taunted with bones. By the turn of the year, after spending days on deck with little protection from the cold and the incessant spray, he was reduced to a shivering, vermin-infested shadow. Seeing his predicament, the skipper ordered him to strip naked, and directed a messmate to douse him with icy sea water. With the promise of dry clothes, the boy was pushed below but he was so feeble that he fumbled with his socks, Brand rewarding him for his difficulty with the end of a knotted rope. Further barbarities followed. Papper was immersed in water, jumped on and repeatedly flogged by Brand with a wooden club. The beating coincided with a blast on the ship's foghorn. 'There you bastard, the bell's tolling for your death,' screamed Brand, bringing his weapon down for the last time.

The lad was indeed dead but the skipper insisted he was faking. Frantically, he tried to revive the corpse by forcing hot tea and tobacco into its mouth. When this had no effect, he hung the body over the side of the ship hoping that a buffeting by the waves would restore life. But William Papper was irretrievably dead. Recognising the consequences of his brutality, the murderer cast the body into the deep. He subsequently reported the death at a police station, with an explanation that the boy had been knocked overboard by a wayward sail. Osmond Otto Brand would have escaped justice but for the gnawing consciences of the crew of the *Rising Sun*. Although they bore some passive responsibility for the death of the boy, they reported the crime to the authorities and subsequently gave evidence at Brand's trial. Faced with such shocking testimony, the jury found the accused guilty of murder and he was hanged on 22 May 1882 in Leeds Prison.

A similar act of gross cruelty and murder was perpetrated on another Hull apprentice in February 1882, when the mate on a smack savagely attacked Peter Hughes. Edward Wheatfield starved the boy and forced him to walk naked on the deck with a pail of sea water on his head. Later, the mate repeatedly kicked the lad's hands until the bones were exposed. The torment finally ended when Hughes was smeared in excrement and flung over the vessel's side. Within a few short weeks, Leeds Prison witnessed another hanging.

These two well-publicised cases revealed the darker side of the fishing industry to the wider public for the first time and, shortly after the executions, a Board of Trade inquiry led the way in introducing better conditions. As a consequence of increased awareness and new investment, brought about by the Fisheries Exhibition of 1883, the injection of capital helped to pay for steam-powered ships. By 1895, Hull had 410 new ships and a workforce of around 5,000 men.

In 1895, the North Eastern Railway (they had bought out the Hull Dock Company in 1893, consolidating the management and operation of the docks and railway) built an extension dock doubling the berthing areas and the lengths of fish quays. With every modern facility at its disposal, the fleet extended its range of operation to include the productive grounds off Iceland and in the Barents Sea. The next few years, until the outbreak of the Great War in 1914, marked a period of unprecedented prosperity stained only by one day of infamy on 22 October 1904.

At sunrise on that autumn day, Hull's forty strong Gamecock fleet was fishing peacefully in the Dogger Bank grounds, some two hundred miles from home. It is hard to credit what happened next. Out of the mist appeared the Russian Baltic fleet; seven battleships, six cruisers and several torpedo boats all bearing down on the little trawlers. Illuminated in the glare of Russian searchlights, the craft were mistakenly identified as Japanese torpedo-boats. At that time, Russia was at war with Japan and its Baltic fleet had been despatched to Port Arthur to rendezvous with the Pacific fleet. Thinking they were under attack, the panicked Russian officers ordered their big guns into action and, for twenty minutes, 300 salvoes ripped into the Hull ships. On board the trawler *Crane*, the skipper and the third hand were killed instantly. The two bodies and seven injured seamen were transferred to the *Gull*. She was also hit along with her sister ships the *Mino* and the *Moulmein*. With the *Crane* sinking, the attackers ceased firing and steamed away.

Back in Hull there was outrage. Angry relatives lined the docks as the ravaged trawlers returned to port. Protests were made to the Russian government, which agreed to recall its Baltic fleet, court martial the offending naval officers and pay compensation amounting to £65,000. More money was promised locally, and King Edward VII led the way by donating 200 guineas to a relief fund for the dependants of fishermen killed and injured. For valour, Henry Smith of the *Gull* and William Smith of the *Crane*, were awarded the Albert Medal. Later, in August 1906, a memorial to the victims of what fittingly became known as the Russian Outrage, was unveiled outside the church of St Barnabas on the corner of Hessle Road and the Boulevard. Ironically, the Russian fleet steamed on regardless to its destruction. Under the command of Admiral Rozhestvensky, it was sunk on 28 May 1905 in the Tshushima Strait by the Imperial Navy of Japan, commanded by Admiral Togo.

During the conflict with Germany between 1914 and 1918, much of Hull's fishing fleet was dismembered. The more modern trawlers were requisitioned by the Admiralty for use as minesweepers and the fishing grounds were left to regenerate. All boded well for a resumption of fishing after 1918, but the worldwide economic recession of the 1920s bit deep and the industry recovered only slowly. Hull ships ventured further from port in search of heavier catches. The depletion of fish stocks had been recognised as an obvious consequence of over-fishing since the days of sail, and the progressively less productive North Sea diminished in importance as Hull vessels made pioneering voyages to the Barents Sea. In 1928, large numbers of ships began exploiting the even more remote waters in the Arctic Sea, making spectacular catches of cod off Bear Island. Much of this fish provided a staple food for the working classes. The growth of fish-and-chip shops in almost every urban and rural community providing vital calories and nutrition at a time of continuing depression.

By 1931, the entire industry was suffering from over-production and some vessels were laid up. Adverse economic conditions five years later led to a vast reduction in the 'box fleet', and large numbers of inefficient, coal-hungry smaller ships went to the scrap yard. Recession brought further problems. In Hull, trawler owners attempted to reduce the historic premiums paid to crews in relation to the amount of cod liver oil delivered for processing. The disgruntled men organised a strike, and an industrial court largely settled on the side of the fishermen. The recommendations of the inquiry's chairman, Sir James Baillie, helped to redress a number of other long-standing issues about pay and working conditions. And then came the second of the world wars. Hull trawlers again found themselves at the explosive edge of the conflict.

After the end of hostilities in 1945, Hull built up a modern distant-waters fleet. Over half of the nation's ships – some 137 vessels – were registered in the port by the end of 1959. In 1961, an innovative new ship, the *Lord Nelson*, joined the fleet. Hitherto, trawling had been exclusively carried out by the so-called side-winders, with catches hauled over the ship's side. This technique adversely affected the design of vessels by restricting the possibility of constructing weatherproof processing areas for the crew amidships. The *Lord Nelson* introduced the new method of trawling from the stern position, allowing built-in protection for the gutting and washing of fish. The ship also part-froze its catch. A second all-freezer vessel – the *Junella* – joined the fleet in 1962.

The advance of technology facilitated the introduction of sturdier and more commodious ships, wireless telegraphy, VHF transmitters, ship-to-shore radios, radar, echo-sounding equipment and, in more recent years, satellite navigation. While these all contributed to comfort and safety, the life of a trawlerman continued to be dangerous. Massive outlays on the introduction of new craft and high running costs demanded intensive and sustained periods of fishing. Vessels undertook ever longer and ever more arduous voyages to locate dwindling stocks of fish that were increasingly over-exploited by fleets from a host of European nations.

With massive diesel engines, the constantly throbbing trawlers were cauldrons of sound. The background creaks forever accompanied the ship's grinding routine; eighteen hours of grab and slash, followed by a thirty minute meal-break capped by five or so fleeting hours of sleep. With every man allotted a task, the drudgery went on day after day. Only the shipboard humour and camaraderie, thoughts of the next meal, the possibility of a catch bonus at the voyage's end and the rare prospect of making skipper one day kept up the spirits. But there was no shortage of apprentices, who signed on at 17 as 'deckie learners'. For all the danger, here was an occupation that had a manly image like no other. Despite the backbreaking work there was something else about the job that appealed to seamen. Oddly enough, and this is a conclusion reached by a renowned sociologist who examined the industry in detail during the 1950s, 'some men find, despite the extremely long hours, a curious sense of relaxation on a trawler. There is never an unexpected psychological challenge.'

However, there were physical challenges aplenty and a constant fear of death. One of the most tragic losses of life at sea occurred in January 1955. Two trawlers, the *Lorella* and the *Roderigo*, were fishing off the North Cape in deteriorating weather. They hauled in their gear to ride out the storm but conditions got much worse. *Lorella* radioed this message: 'Boat deck solid with frozen snow. Lads digging it out since breakfast. Terrible lot on bridge top and they are going up there at daylight if possible.' *Roderigo* responded: 'Same here George, and the whaleback is a solid mass.'

Both ships were encased in ice and, buffeted by hurricane-force winds, they were becoming increasingly unstable. *Lorella's* last transmission came as the light faded: '*Lorella* going down, heeling over. *Lorella* going down, heeling over.' Some two-and-a-half hours later, the sea claimed its second victim. The *Roderigo's* final message, which was repeated in Morse code until the transmission ceased, was, '*Roderigo* going over'. Hull lost two ships that day . . . and forty men.

There were many other tragedies. The most discussed loss of all was the sinking of the *Gaul*. In February 1974, this vessel was lost with all thirty-six hands while fishing off Norway's North Cape. She disappeared from the radar screen with not a word from her skipper, and not a piece of wreckage was ever found. A Wreck Commissioner's enquiry was formally held in Hull that October. At the end of a searching investigation, it was concluded that the ship had foundered in heavy seas. But controversy raged. The bereaved relatives claimed that the vessel had been engaged in clandestine surveillance work for the Royal Navy. Their reasoning was that the northern fishing grounds offered the ideal location for snooping on Soviet Navy submarines sailing from their base in Murmansk. The Ministry of Defence denied this allegation with some vehemence, but the allegations rumbled on. Eventually, in 1998, Deputy Prime Minister John Prescott reopened the investigation into the tragedy after a government survey of the wreck revealed important new evidence. Since then investigators, assisted by a small army of submarine robots, have compiled a dossier of new evidence that is designed to allay the suspicions of family members that the *Gaul* was engaged in spying. This evidence, much of it on video, is due to be put before hearings scheduled for 2003.

And still the rumours fly. One vital piece of evidence has, to my mind, escaped close scrutiny to this day. Three months after the *Gaul* sank, one of her lifebelts was found floating eighteen miles off the Norwegian coast. This was insignificant in itself, but what was most telling was the presence on the surface of the lifebelt of microscopic plant life. This, declared a forensic scientist, could only live in freshwater. Where had the lifebelt been? In the freshwater pens of the Russian fleet in Murmansk?

Trawling, then, was always an extreme occupation that brought multiple deaths, and pushed men and their ships to the very limits. And, increasing competition from foreign vessels during the twentieth century only served to exacerbate the very many natural hazards that were the fisherman's lot. In the first year of that century, a British-Danish convention established a three-mile fisheries limit around Iceland, the Faroes and Greenland. However, by degrees the limit was extended, culminating in the imposition of a twelve-mile exclusion zone in 1958. So in went the frigates!

For the next eighteen years, until 1976, the aptly named Cod Wars raged between Britain and a progressively more belligerent Iceland. Relations between the two countries went from bad to worse with the extension of the fishing limit to 50 miles and then 200. This was followed by litigation in the international courts, small-catch quotas and a confrontation between the trawlers, their warship escorts and the patrol vessels of the Icelandic Navy. This all culminated in the breaking-off of diplomatic relations between Britain and Iceland in 1976. The closing-off of the Icelandic fishing grounds affected Hull like no other port. Its ships and infrastructure were geared to the exploitation of these grounds. Without them, the industry collapsed. Ships were withdrawn from service, scrapped and sold abroad. The whole character and physical appearance of Hull changed markedly within two decades. The old docks were closed and filled in, and the reclaimed sites were put to more fashionable use.

Today, very little fish is landed in Hull and one must visit its Town Docks Museum and the restored *Arctic Corsair*, anchored behind High Street on the river Hull, to gain some insight into the trawling trade. Or you can talk to retired fishermen, many of whom are still resident in Hessle Road. In 2001, a video was produced by local historian Alec Gill recording the lives of the fisherman of Hessle Road. In introducing his tribute to these indomitable men of the sea, the author said: 'George Orwell talks about society standing on the shoulders of the miners and I believe the port of Hull prospered on the backs of the trawlermen.'

But not just the trawlermen. The story of Hull's fishing industry is about much more than the stalwarts at the cod-end of the business. Read the excellent *Fish Dock – The Story of St. Andrew's Dock, Hull* by Michael Thompson, published in 1989. A former trawlerman himself, Thompson gives a revealing insight into the trades that depended on Hull's rich harvest from the sea. With precious photographs of a time long gone, he shows the work of the 'swingers', the 'winchmen', the 'bobbers', the filleters, the offal men and the wives who mended the nets. Other scenes depict an ice-making factory, the fish market, fish lorries and steam trains. In his evocative text, even the telegram boy, dock policemen and local taxi-drivers get an affectionate mention. One particular highlight of the book comes in two final pages devoted to 'Fish Dock Characters'. Reference is made to Cloggy Walsh, the Liverpool Street maker of the indispensable fish-dock clogs. Jim 'If It Swims We Have It' Kelsey, who had a famous fish-and-chip shop on Brighton Street, also has an entry. And then there is an account of arguably the best-remembered character of all: a resident of Harrow Street, Walton Denton, better known by his nickname of 'Dillinger'. A practical joker, he was a regular customer in the fisherman's Star and Garter pub (it was commonly known as Rayners) having once ridden into its bar on a pony! One of his party pieces was to lurk outside a Hull store and rearrange babies into different prams while their mothers shopped inside. A whole chapter is devoted to the exploits of Walter Denton in another superb memorial to Hull's fishing folk, *Good Old Hessle Road* by Alec Gill, published in 1991.

In his final pages, Thompson lists the bald statistics year-on-year: the numbers of vessels involved in the trade, and the tons of fish landed. Thereby hangs an incredible tale.

10

THE CHIMNEY'S GONE AFIRE!

A geyser of hot blood pluming into the sky. A fire-hosing haemorrhage and a brief, all-staining deluge – aquamarine, white and crimson mingling and swirling. Convulsions, sonar screams and a final crash of the great fluke. Amid a frenzy of lance throwing, the whale is dead.

Such were the awful scenes that marked the end of one of nature's most persecuted animals. An animal that formed the basis of a global industry that, over several centuries, exploited many species almost to extinction. Whale fishing – despite the fact that the great beast is a mammal, the pursuit of whales is commonly referred to as fishing – has been carried on ever since man first went to sea. Initially a small-scale enterprise using kayaks, wooden spears and sealskin floats, whaling satisfied local needs particularly among communities in the polar regions. The industry was developed as early as the ninth century by the Norwegians. Norman settlers in the Bay of Biscay further refined the techniques of whaling from the twelfth to the fourteenth centuries. It is known that the Basques were hunting whales off the coasts of Greenland and Labrador before 1450 and had established a processing factory overlooking the Strait of Belle Isle between Newfoundland and Labrador by the early 1500s.

Over time, whaling accounted for almost all the species of the animal. They included: the seventy-five-feet long common, or Greenland whale; the more diminutive white, or beluga whale at up to eighteen feet in length; the famous cachalot, or sperm whale of the southern oceans which measured up to eighty-four feet from head to fluke; the tusked narwhale at around sixteen feet. Whalers also captured vast quantities of seals especially when hunting for their bigger cousins proved difficult.

Technical advances by the Dutch in the seventeenth century led to the deployment of a large Arctic fleet and the building of a dedicated processing factory at Spitzbergen. The Dutch were then able to supply half the population of Europe with oil, and this trade reached its zenith in 1680 when the industry could muster 260 ships and 14,000 men.

Yorkshire entrepreneurs were uncharacteristically slow in recognising the commercial opportunities. It was only in the 1750s and 1760s that pioneers like captain, later Sir, Samuel Standidge, set up substantial whaling ventures. A few small but reasonably successful ships such as the *Berry*, the *Britannia* and the *British Queen* operated from Hull in pursuit of both whales and seals. The virtual Dutch monopoly, however, was gradually eroded as problems associated with the French Revolution almost ended the trade by 1789. Until 1785 Hull whaling accounted for only a small proportion of the national industry but, following the third great collapse of American whaling in 1784, the town's share of the business increased markedly. Encouraged by a bounty from the government for every ship of 200 tons engaged in whaling, the British fishery increased. Ships from Hull, many strengthened and adapted to cope with the rigours of sailing through ice, regularly ventured to the waters off Iceland and Greenland and to the grounds between Jan Mayen and Spitzbergen. Lacking experienced crews, captains often recruited displaced Dutch harpooners and boat-handlers, and ships' complements were also augmented by the signing-on of labourers who traditionally made up about a third of a whaler's crew. By 1790, Hull supplied a tenth of the national demand for whalebone, and the proportions rose to a third by the turn of the century and a half by 1805. In that year, Hull ships landed 5,200 tons of oil and vied with London as England's premier whaling centre. Catch returns for the port were the best ever in 1820 when 60 ships brought home 360 tons of whalebone and 7,978 tons of oil. Despite the bounty, only 164 British ships were engaged in whaling by 1815 and, by 1824, the bounty was finally withdrawn.

In 1824, most of the Hull fleet, after a series of poor catches, abandoned the traditional hunting grounds off Greenland and began to penetrate the seas beyond Cape Farewell, patrolling the migration routes in the Davis Strait and off the coast of Labrador. Those productive fishing areas, located in a narrow 300 mile box, were known as the South West Grounds.

The Hull fleet was made up of prize ships captured during conflicts with the French and Americans, some converted Baltic trading vessels and a number of purpose-built whalers. With a general displacement of around 300 to 350 tons, all these craft were reinforced by strong stanchions, cross-bars, stout planking and half-inch ice plates, enabling them to withstand the rigours of sailing in Arctic seas. Sailing with an initial crew of around thirty men and boys including a captain, a ship's surgeon, harpooners, boat-steerers, lancers, line managers, carpenters and coopers, they usually left Hull in early March on a deployment of between four and five months. Crews had the traditional ambition of returning with 'full ships' by the date of the famous Hull fair in October. Twenty or so extra hands were usually taken on board at either Stromness in Orkney or Lerwick in Shetland, and the entire voyage to the fishing grounds took a tedious three weeks. During this period, the men were occupied in the mundane routines of the watches and in the maintenance of the fishing gear. They also regularly participated in the daily religious services that were a constant feature of whaling life.

Boredom was instantly forgotten with a cry from the crow's-nest. The triumphant shout, 'There she blows!' caused a fever of activity and the launching of the ship's boats as the mother ship was berthed in a specially cut, makeshift dock in the ice. Typically equipped with two harpoons, eight lances and eight hundredweight of stout rope, each of the seven boats had a crew of six or seven hand-picked men. Some of these boats had a harpoon gun mounted in the prow. Invented in 1731 this vicious weapon was dangerous and unreliable, although later versions were more effective. Launched at the beginning of the whaling season, these craft were up to twenty-eight feet in length and five feet nine inches in breadth. They had to contend with dark days and poor weather, the persistent swell and the unpredictability of the quarry. The constant hazards of using razor-sharp equipment and racing ropes led to many accidents and fatalities.

The skill and experience of the boat-steerer in getting close enough to a breaching whale was everything. The success of the enterprise and the lives of the men depended on it. Once harpooned at very close range – the head had to be avoided as it was impenetrable – whales invariably sounded (dived very quickly). Only the heavy ropes, up to a mile long, kept the animal tethered to the surface boat. As soon as the harpoon struck, a signal flag would be hoisted on a staff to alert the mother ship and prepare the crew for action. The sailors on watch responded with a vigorous stamping on the deck with attendant shouts of 'A fall! A fall! A fall!' This insistent call for other boats to be launched was derived from a Dutch term, meaning to jump or leap. Meanwhile, the injured beast would dive with great rapidity, and the friction caused by the scorching rope on the gunwales of the boat raised clouds of smoke and threatened fire. Only by constant dousing with pails of seawater was a blaze averted. On occasions, the whale would disappear under the ice and the rope would have to be cut instantly to avoid a fatal collision. An axe was kept handy for such an eventuality but the harpooners were always reluctant to lose their catch. And besides, rope of the exacting quality used in whaling was extremely expensive.

The whale would remain submerged for half an hour or more but, needing air to breath, the exhausted beast would inevitably surface. Sometimes its eventual capture would be preceded by a struggle marked by a violent rearing and shaking of its tail, with the noise of the thrashing being carried up to a distance of three miles. At the breaching, the deadly lances would be put to work. Plunged with great accuracy between the wounded animal's ribs, these lances were 'churned' from side to side to inflict the maximum trauma until, in a death flurry, the whale spewed its last and the 'chimney went afire' in a dramatic blow of blood. Despatched, the huge carcass was towed to the parent ship – one mile per hour was a good rate of knots – and tied securely onto the larboard side to await the process called flensing. Then the gruesome business of slicing up the animal began.

Over time, detailed techniques evolved to enable even the largest carcass to be stripped within four hours. Primitive winches only allowed the enormous weight of the animal to be raised about one fourth out of the water, so most of the flensing had to be done at great personal risk in the sea. The brave and nimble flensers, who were shod with spurs to assist their movements on the body of the whale, first removed the tail before taking their blubber spades and knives to the belly and the under jaw. The flensers were assisted in their work by young boys, who skilfully kept their boats alongside the carcass and handed out the specialist tools.

Striped lengths of blubber weighing up to a ton in weight were next hauled aboard the vessel where they were cut into smaller pieces and stored in casks. The whale was then turned with ropes and the process was repeated on the other flank. The whalebone was also removed. Sometimes, when sea conditions permitted, a boat would be manoeuvred directly into the jaws of the whale to enable this valuable commodity to be removed with comparative ease. Also known as baleen, this horny, fibrous, laminated structure consisted of two extensive rows of plates. In a good animal, the jaws could measure fifteen feet long by fifteen inches thick and provide one hundred large and four hundred smaller pieces. They served as the whale's food-filtration system, straining out plankton from tons of seawater. When the flensing was completed the carcass, or kreng as it was known, was cast adrift.

In so-called primitive Arctic cultures, almost every part of the whale was utilised. Its flesh was a food staple and the oil was used for fuel. The baleen and the bones made tents, sledges and boats and the sinews were fashioned into twine. A use was even found for the diaphanous membranes; in the absence of glass, they served as makeshift window panes.

The industrial world, on the other hand, discarded most of the animal. The stripped bodies attracted sharks, bears and flocks of sea birds as 'along the floe edge lay the dead bodies of hundreds of flensed whales, and the air for miles around was tainted with the foetor which arose from such masses of putridity.' Only the oil-rich blubber and the baleen, together with small amounts of ambergris (a secretion found in the intestines of the sperm whale used in perfumery and cookery) had a commercial value. The blubber yielded tons of pale honey-coloured-oil. The oil was a valuable domestic commodity used extensively in street and domestic lighting, in soap, leather and paint manufacture and as a lubricant. It was either extracted by boiling in large copper vessels at processing plants on shore (the processing plants in Hull known as the Greenland Yards were on the banks of the river Hull in the Cleveland Street area) or rendered down (especially on the American ships) in large vile-smelling vats aboard ship. Each large whale produced nearly two tons of baleen. This was simply dried to await manufacturing at specialised factories back in port. Fibrous along its length, baleen was made into a wide array of products. It was cut into lengths to form the stems of parasols and umbrellas and was used to provide the stiffening in ladies corsets. It was an ideal substance for the manufacture of brushes and brooms, particularly for road and chimney sweeping, and was in great demand for covering such items as whip handles, walking sticks and telescopes. Immensely strong and flexible, whalebone was also made into fishing rods, springs and shafts. But first catch your whale.

Guided only by instinct and experience, whaling was a precarious occupation, a boom-and-bust endeavour that could make fortunes or lose them. While some ships could return to port 'clean' without a single whale, others were stuffed to the gunwales with bounty. One vessel from Peterhead – Hull's most successful rival in the trade – captured forty-four whales during the 1814 season. That year also marked the start of a golden era for Hull captains that lasted until 1830. During that period the Hull fleet averaged fifty-eight ships, a figure that rose to sixty-five in 1819, with the best-ever returns being realised in 1820. For a few short years, whaling profits soared, and the trade received a boost following the end of the French wars. The price of oil reached £19 10s per ton, while baleen made an equally attractive £200 per ton. Those at the sharp end, however, saw only modest rewards. Unlike the men of the American whaling fleet operating out of the port of New Bedford in Massachusetts, Hull crews were not paid on the number of whales caught. Although wages were above the seaman's average, they received only a basic wage topped up with bonuses known as 'oil money' and 'bone money' and a small additional payment to take account of government bounties. As an incentive to the all-important harpooners, ten shillings and sixpence was offered for each captured whale. In theory, whaling normally exempted men from impressed naval service. But try telling that to the press gangs!

Fishing of any description has always been regarded as the hardest and most dangerous occupation in the world. Even today, it is at the top of the league in terms of deaths per-thousand-operatives. The pursuit of humble sprats and mackerel is hazardous enough but minnows like these do not crush their would-be captors to pulp with a flick of the tail. Whale fishing rightly has the reputation as the supreme challenge in the eternal harvest of the sea. So what type of men volunteered for the Hull fleet? The harshness of the industry drove out all but the toughest of men. But were they callous butchers and flint-hard, heartless old salts from the Captain Ahab school of mariners? The answer for the most part is surprising indeed.

The real history of Hull whaling is to be found in the logbooks, catch returns and ships' journals kept by men like William Eden Cass, who was a surgeon on board the *Brunswick* in 1824. Cass records many fascinating features of life on board the vessel, including details of the Christian services held by Captain Blyth every Sunday. Christianity, it would seem, imbued many voyages with a sense of divine purpose, and many ships left port flying Methodist bethel flags as a sign of faith. Such actions reflect the gentler attributes of the outwardly cruel and pitiless crews, who saw the capture of whales as a noble opportunity to test their mettle by harvesting one of God's mightiest creatures. Cass puts it thus: 'let us not relax our exertions but rather plough on with increased energy, until the abundance of the sea shall be converted to God.' Cass goes on to describe the preparations for the slaughter ahead. He refers to the appalling weather and the ominous 'streams of heavy ice named cape ice' encountered as his vessel rounded Cape Farewell. His log also records the peculiar sailor's traditions associated with this barren place. These included men who had never been to the polar regions being required to hand over a pound of tobacco or sugar, and to dress up in a variety of silly costumes – as Neptune for example – for the amusement of their shipmates.

This induction ceremony, which mimicked the 'crossing the line' tradition at the Equator, was one of the few moments in any voyage when whaling crews could relax and forget about the privations ahead. Most men though enjoyed the experience of seeing new lands and creatures. In their brief leisure hours they collected native carvings of seals, sleds and polar bears, made models and unwittingly produced a new art form. This is known today as scrimshaw, and involved carving images of whaling life on bones, teeth and tusks. The other regular diversion was the ritual dispensing of the 'mess pots' or grog ration every Saturday evening and there are also reports of the more adventurous seamen sliding down crevasses and icebergs!

It is interesting to note that Cass's ship, the *Brunswick*, arrived back in Hull in September 1824 having caught just ten whales. The vessel's catch-returns for the twenty-one years between 1814 and 1834 – the figures are preserved on the flyleaf of Captain Blyth's copy of *The Life of Christ* – show a whale tally of 271 'fish' and an oil return of 3,430 tons. The most successful voyage was that of 1823 when thirty-six whales were landed. The least successful years were those of 1832 and 1833 when the ship returned to Hull 'clean'.

Crews came to Hull from all over Yorkshire. The excitement of 'running away to sea' led many a young lad to the Humber yards. But with press gangs on the prowl, it was never plain sailing. The Royal Navy was constantly in need of men, particularly experienced salts who had honed their skills in the most difficult trade afloat. Naturally, the Admiralty coveted the sailors of Hull. Press gangs converged on its docks and impressed any fine fellow with concussion and a king's commission. Any unsuspecting cabin boy was fair game for these ruthless bands, and whaling captains had to resort to ingenious methods to retain their precious crews.

Even whaling ships in the process of embarkation were not immune from raids by the press gangs and a number of reports survive recounting pitched battles on deck. Serious injuries were commonplace and several deaths occurred. The court actions that followed were generally dismissed by Hull juries, which had an overriding sympathy for their whaling neighbours. Ships' captains even smuggled crews aboard in boxes and barrels. Some crewmen wore female disguises in an attempt to fool the press gangs, while others adopted the tactic of boarding and disembarking at remote beaches and coves miles north of the port. The most celebrated ruse involved the installation in one ship of a brass tap fitted inside the vessel below the waterline. The deliberate flooding of the ship, and the sight of all hands pumping furiously to keep her afloat, had the desired effect of keeping the press gangs at bay. After they departed, the tap was closed and the vessel was pumped dry and made ready for sea.

Catch returns show that whaling was full of uncertainty. Adverse weather and dwindling stocks brought about a disastrous season during the fateful year of 1830. Out of a total of thirty-three Hull ships, eight limped home without having caught a single whale between them, and eight vessels were left in the grip of the sea ice.

Ice entrapment was a constant peril. The journal of William Elder, a crewman aboard the whaler *Viewforth* graphically recalls the fate of his ship:

> There remains very little prospect of us getting out indeed my mind is made up for a winter in the Arctic regions the worst of it is that we are very short of Provisions & so are the other two ships we are now on a Biscuit and a half a day and $^1/_2$ pound beef and about $^1/_2$ tea cupful of meal the cold too is very intense the ice at the top of my bed is about $^1/_4$ of an inch thick.

Tragically, the *Viewforth*, and her sister ships the *Duncombe* and the *Jane*, were on the eve of quitting the fishing grounds in October 1835 and returning home when the weather closed in. The plunging temperatures encased all three vessels in ice. Two hundred miles from the nearest Danish settlement, the men were marooned, and the cold became so intense that they could only remain on deck for a very short time. They lay below in their hammocks, their breath forming minute particles of frost overhead. With food running out and the encroaching ice threatening to crush the ships, the crews endured the long weeks with great solace and much prayer. The mate of the *Jane*, who also kept a journal, recorded that even his oil lamp and the ink in his pen froze solid. Ravenously hungry, the men ate seals, bears and foxes to stay alive although many unfortunates died through a combination of malnutrition, frostbite and scurvy. Eventually, after four terrifying months in the ice, the weather relented and the whalers limped home. All the church bells in Hull town peeled out a welcome as the ships moved into the Humber Dock in February 1836.

The disasters at sea, combined with over-fishing, and a declining demand for whale products – oil was gradually replaced as a lighting fuel by coal gas – signalled the death knell for the industry. By 1852, the Hull whaling fleet was reduced to just a handful of ships. The duration of the industry spanned just 105 years.

The last of Hull's sailing whalers was the *Truelove*. She made nearly eighty voyages capturing around five hundred whales and thousands of seals, including a haul of 13,000 in 1849. For a time she competed with the steam-powered vessels that attempted to revive the trade during the 1850s and 1860s. Ironically, the economic pressures brought about by the Crimean War in 1854 helped to inflate oil and baleen prices, causing some owners to speculate in the fitting out of new ships. One of these was the ill-fated *Diana*. In 1886 this thoroughly modern vessel became fast in the pack ice. Entombed, she was carried south all winter long. Finally breaking free, this floating mortuary managed to lumber into Hull after fourteen months. Her captain's body had been consigned to a tarpaulin on the bridge. Another logbook kept by a cooper, Joseph Allen, records the dreadful ordeal, which claimed a total of twenty-five lives: 'We cannot sleep, we cannot even eat what little food we have, we cannot rest below deck, in the cabin, upon deck, anywhere. Restless, uneasy, anxious, we will not have a moment's peace of mind or body so long as we are in this awful ice.'

A contemporary newspaper account of the tormented ship from the April 1867 edition of *The Scotsman*, is even more chilling:

> Coleridge's ancient mariner might have sailed in such a ghastly ship – battered and ice-crushed, sails and cordage blown away, boats and spars cut up for fuel in the awful Arctic winter, the main deck a charnel house not to be described. The miserable scurvy stricken, dysentery-worn men who looked over the bulwarks were a spectacle, once seen, never to be forgotten . . . most pitiable of all were the ship's boys, their young faces wearing a strange aged look not easily described.

Refitted, the *Diana* made two more voyages to the cold north. Returning to Hull at the conclusion of her last adventure, she ran aground on Donna Nook, where pounding waves effectively signalled the end of Hull's whaling tradition. There is a poignant reminder of the *Diana* in Hull's Spring Bank Cemetery. A fast-fading image of the ship is engraved into a tombstone – the tombstone of her 64-year-old captain, John Gravill.

Hull's whaling fleet is now long gone, but much of the paraphernalia of the industry remains. The Hull Town Docks Museum has logbooks and other records of the slaughter, paintings of ships, models, specimen lances, harpoons, blubber spades, flensing knives, marlin spikes and numerous items made from whale products. You can even view the interior of a fully equipped whaling-boat and hear, in the background, haunting sound-recordings of the great creature's sonar. For me, however, there is only one way to understand the awesome but brutal majesty of this bloody trade. Like Rudyard Kipling, you must read the *Cruise of the Cachelot* by veteran whaler Frank T. Bullen.

When this book was published in 1898, Kipling wrote to its author saying: 'It is immense – there is no other word. I've never read anything that equals it in deep-sea wonder and mystery; nor do I think any book has so completely covered the whole business of whale-fishing and at the same time given such real and new sea pictures'. With a harpoon in his fist, Bullen saw the whole spectacle at close quarters:

> Up, up it went, while my heart stood still, until the whole of that immense creature hung on high, apparently motionless, and then fell – a hundred tons of solid flesh – back into the sea. On either side of that mountainous mass the waters rose in shining towers of snowy foam, which fell in their turn, whirling and eddying around us as we tossed and fell like a chip in a whirlpool. Blinded by the flying spray, bailing for very life to free the boat from the water with which she was nearly full, it was some minutes before I was able to decide whether we were still injured or not. Then I saw at a little distance, the whale lying quietly. As I looked he spouted and the vapour was red with blood.

Sadly, the chimney continues to burn.

11

TRAWLERS WITH TEETH

It is doubtful if we could have defeated the Germans, at any rate as quickly as we did defeat them, if it had not been for the assistance which the Royal Navy received from the fishing community.

Admiral Sir Reginald Bacon.

In both world wars, fishing vessels and their conscripted crews were vital in achieving victory. Every ounce of national muscle had to be harnessed in taking the fight to Germany. The converted trawlers and some newly commissioned vessels offered platforms for both offensive and defensive operations. In addition, their skippers and crews provided invaluable maritime knowledge and expertise. And, as one might expect, the fishermen of Hull played a leading role in both conflicts.

Trawlers were built for fishing and had to be converted for military use. Conversion, especially in the Second World War, usually led to the raising of the bridge onto a higher deck, the removal of the ship's lifeboat from the stern to a position amidships and, sometimes, the construction of an additional deckhouse forward of the bridge. Armaments consisted of one large gun with a four-inch calibre – this was sited on a platform at the break of the forecastle – and several heavy machine-guns placed both port and starboard. Trawlers were frequently called upon to counter the scourge of the U-boats and they were equipped with stern-fitted depth-charge chutes and throwers.

The military potential of the trawling fleet was recognised well before the outbreak of hostilities in 1914. In 1907, Admiral Charles Beresford conducted a tour of the east-coast fishing ports concluding that, in the event of war, trawlers should be requisitioned for minesweeping operations to free up warships for engagements with enemy vessels. In 1914, the Admiralty duly acted and over 800 vessels from the Hull and Grimsby fleets – some newly built in the Cook, Welton & Gemmell yard at Beverley – entered service. The Admiralty naturally acquired the most modern trawlers. The older vessels were left to operate in their traditional role as fish catchers.

Fiercely independent, many trawler skippers, although eager to answer the call of king and country, were ambivalent about the notion of naval discipline. To acknowledge the maverick tendencies of these men, and properly to elevate their status, the Admiralty introduced the new rank of Skipper Royal Naval Reserve. Many of the skippers and their crews went on to serve with great distinction.

The tasks allotted to the trawlermen were hazardous and included the clearing of minefields. With their cutting gear, they would sever the anchorage cables allowing the devices to float harmlessly to the surface. Once visible, they would be dealt with by rifle fire, which was directed at the sensitive horns causing them to explode. The trawlers would also lay mines within the German shipping lanes and, more dangerously, attack U-boats.

The U-boat menace was not confined to World War Two. The German Navy also had a deadly submarine capability throughout the Great War between 1914 and 1918. With few detection aids, the puny trawlers were charged with seeking out these submarines and sinking them. Indeed, one ferocious battle between the converted drifter *Dawn* and a U-boat is regarded as one of the most illustrious in Hull's long history. The commander of the *Dawn* was none other than the irrepressible Edward Spencer Rilatt, from the Hessle Road area. He was known as 'Mad' Rilatt, especially to the sailors of the Kreigsmarine.

Commenting on this fearless war hero, one observer noted that 'his head literally used to steam' when his ire was up. He was the proud owner of an incandescent temper and would answer a stranger's enquiry with the riposte: 'Rilatt's the name and, if you must know, it's Mad Rilatt!' To emphasis his claim to insanity he would snatch off his cap when roused, fling it to the floor and jump on it until it had apologised. One can only imagine the reaction when a U-boat attacked his vessel. One day, as part of a three-ship minesweeping operation, the *Dawn* engaged a U-boat. Rilatt's outstanding seamanship and the accurate fire of his gunner, who lost two fingers in the action, sent the submarine to the bottom of the sea. After the engagement, the entire crew was commended for bravery. Such encounters though, were meat and drink to Rilatt.

Earlier in the war he devised a novel strategy for dealing with the U-boats, and his success in beating the German captains at their own game led to him being mentioned in despatches. As one minefield was cleared, the persistent Germans were in the habit of returning the next day to lay another, and this routine of laying and clearing mines persisted for months. The wily Rilatt suggested that one minefield should be left intact. The tactic of allowing the Germans to 'get tangled in their own muck' received favourable consideration by the Admiralty. Sure enough, the ruse worked and a submarine sailed into its own trap. Some hours later, the damaged vessel was found washed up on a beach. Rilatt went on to serve with even greater distinction in the Second World War. He became an honorary Lieutenant Commander and was awarded the MBE and the Croix de Guerre.

During the First World War, Hull lost 135 trawlers to enemy action, of which 73 were unarmed vessels engaged only in fishing when they were attacked. One of the worst atrocities occurred on 3 May 1915. On that one black day, seven trawlers – the *Bob White*, *Coquet*, *Hector*, *Hero*, *Iolanthe*, *Northward Ho* and *Progress* – were sunk in the Dogger Bank. The German tactics can only be described as dastardly. U-boats would surface once their captains had determined through periscope sightings that their targets were unarmed. Trawler skippers would then be given the ultimatum of either surrendering their vessels or having them blown to smithereens. Most skippers chose the latter option. Along with their crews, some were taken prisoner but, more often than not, they were set adrift in their own lifeboats, forced to watch in torment as their ships were sunk along with the precious catches. Is it any wonder that returning crews enlisted on armed ships in a bid to exact revenge? Before the German captains gave the orders to sink the trawlers with showers of bullets or with time-bombs strategically placed below the water lines – expensive torpedoes were reserved for more important targets – they would sometimes confiscate the registration documents as grisly souvenirs. Afterwards, they would disappear beneath the waves, leaving the trawlermen to an uncertain fate.

By 1915 only about a quarter of Hull's trawlers were left to continue fishing. Prices rose as a consequence of shortages. The port's share of the overall national catch increased as the remaining crews, courageously dodging the U-boat threat, exploited those fishing grounds in the Icelandic and Barents Sea that remained open. With the end of hostilities in 1918, the armed trawlers were decommissioned, and the lucky vessels that had survived the war underwent conversion prior to rejoining the fishing fleet. Within a generation, though, the filleting knives were once again swapped for bayonets. Some men, like the redoubtable Rilatt, got their second set of call-up papers.

Euphemisms are widely used in war. Anodyne words mask the true horror of death and destruction. Naval losses have always been collectively referred to in terms of tonnage sunk, as though the losses of ships were mere statistical entries in an accountant's balance sheet. But those were real ships crewed by flesh-and-blood men. The roll-call of trawler names scratched from the Hull inventories during World War Two makes grim reading. Between 1939 and 1945, the port lost nearly its entire fleet to the war effort. The names *Adonis*, *Argyllshire* and *Avanturine* head a list of some one hundred craft sunk in those years.

The fishing industry had expanded in Hull during the inter-war years, with some 277 modern trawlers entering service. Most of these vessels were requisitioned by the Admiralty in 1939, and became part of the Royal Navy Patrol Service. There were never enough ships to satisfy the national demand for minesweeping, anti-submarine patrol and convoy duties. Local shipyards in Beverley, Selby and Goole certainly did their best, providing an impressive 60 per cent of Admiralty orders. The Beverley firm of Cook, Welton & Gemmell again significantly bolstered the war effort, building eighty-three such ships. Some of the new ships went into service with Britain's allies, and the United States Navy received twenty-four armed trawlers in 1942.

During the 1920s and 30s, one of the big stars of the day was the comedian, Harry Tate. It is from the comedian that the trawlers, drifters and whale catchers requisitioned by the Admiralty took their nickname: 'Harry Tate's Navy'. I believe there was a similarly inspired description for the Home Guard: 'Fred Karno's Army'. Self-deprecating they may have been, but the crews of the 'rust stained and weather beaten arse-end Charlies' that made up the improvised fleet based in Lowestoft, had teeth. And they were determined to use them in every theatre of war from the Atlantic to the Indian Ocean, and from the coasts of Africa to the Arctic Sea. Armed trawlers were never more than featherweights in a deadly contest that invariably saw them outrun and out-gunned. Fast German E-boats, destroyers and dive-bombers all took a heavy toll. Four episodes in the proud history of Hull's armed trawlers serve to illustrate what odds they faced.

One of the first opportunities for real action came in April 1940. Eight trawlers of the Anti-Submarine Striking Force were despatched from Scotland to Namsos in Norway to assist in what turned out to be a hasty evacuation of the British Expeditionary Force. Penned in by the cliffs of the narrow fjords, the ships were vulnerable to attack from the air, and three vessels were sunk. The surviving ships took refuge under the steep, thickly wooded sea-cliffs. During lulls in the bombing, the crews would briefly go ashore to chop down greenery to use as camouflage. Eye-witness accounts suggest that the remaining five trawlers looked like mobile Christmas trees. In the thick of the action was the Hull trawler *Arab*. She had already rescued the survivors from a bombed-out sloop when her courageous skipper headed straight into an inferno, bringing his ship alongside the blazing pier at Namsos. The flames threatened to ignite an adjacent ammunition dump and send it sky high, and only the quick intervention of the skipper and crew averted a catastrophe. For his bravery, the skipper of the *Arab* won the Victoria Cross and four of his crew were also decorated.

Another Hull trawler, the *Warwick Deeping*, joined the fray in October 1940. She and a sister trawler – the *L'istrac* – were deployed to the English Channel as part of an invasion defence force. They were immediately set upon by a flotilla of German destroyers, and the *L'istrac* soon fell victim to shellfire and a torpedo. Torpedoes were then fired at the almost defenceless *Warwick Deeping*. Fortunately, in haste to take up her action stations, the vessel had left port only partially loaded with stores and coal. This caused her to ride high in the water, causing the torpedoes to pass beneath the *Deeping* without impact. The German crews were mystified at their failure to sink the trawler but they pursued her doggedly, and concentrated shellfire finally brought her to a stop. Thankfully they broke off the action, and turned away, allowing the crew of the sinking *Warwick Deeping* to abandon ship. Amazingly not one of her complement of twenty-two was killed. The ship went down five miles south of the Isle of Wight. In recent times, her wreck has been located, and salvaged items such as her range-finder and compass binnacle have found their way to the Maritime Museum in Bembridge.

In June 1941, a third Hull vessel made a name for herself. The little *Moonstone* took part in combined anti-submarine operations in the Red Sea. Using her sonar equipment, the ship detected a submarine and immediately launched an abortive depth-charge attack, resuming the action an hour later when renewed contact was made. Suddenly, a mile astern, the Italian submarine *Galileo Galilei* surfaced. *Moonstone* wheeled hard round and went full-steam ahead with all guns blazing. The Hull ship was only a third of the size of the enemy vessel but, undaunted, she ploughed on sending a four-inch shell slamming into the submarine's conning tower and killing those inside. The humiliated Italians immediately surrendered and lowered their flag, offering themselves as prisoners. Such a large number of men could not, however, be safely taken into custody on the *Moonstone*. The skipper reloaded his guns and bellowed out a warning to the Italian commander that he must not scuttle his boat. Soon afterwards, all the captives were taken aboard a destroyer and the enemy submarine was towed to Aden for a refit and re-commissioning in the Royal Navy. The skipper of the *Moonstone* won the Distinguished Service Cross.

Some months later it was the turn of the *Lady Shirley* to fly the Yorkshire flag and take her proud place in naval history. Built in the 1930s, this venerable girl of 470 tons was affectionately described by one crewman thus: 'We always knew when we were at our full speed of ten knots because the bridge windows began to rattle. Nine knots was when the bridge flag-locker shook; eight knots down to five produced minor shakes in the bridge ladder. An extra burst of speed needed in emergency shook the whole bridge works in harmony.' In September 1941, the *Lady Shirley* sailed into Madeira for repairs, and received a rapturous reception. But garlands and fresh fruit were not the only diversions. The ship's signalman noted a bizarre occurrence in his log: 'On our second day in harbour, a funeral procession slowly passed the ship . . . little did we know that we were being thoroughly scrutinised, for we learned afterwards that it was a fake ceremony organised by the Nazi *gauleiter.'*

Suitably shipshape, the vessel was ordered, along with the *Erin*, to escort the *Maron* to the Canary Islands. Shortly afterwards, she was given new orders and was soon on the trail of a marauding U-boat. A tell-tale 'ping' on her ASDIC precipitated a depth-charge attack. Damaged, the German submarine was forced to surface. For twenty-three minutes a fierce firefight ensued, with *Lady Shirley* scoring nine direct hits with her four-inch gun. The big gun of the U111 remained strangely silent. Intelligence reports later revealed that, in their haste to engage the enemy, the German gunners had forgotten to remove the tompion (a watertight plug) causing the breech to explode. Forty-five of the German crew were taken prisoner aboard the British ship as their own boat sank, their presence in the hold averting a certain tragedy. Unbeknown to the skipper of the *Lady Shirley,* the entire action had been witnessed through the periscope of a second U-boat, and its commander sent frantic signals back to his base in Lorient. Naturally, the German commanders were loath to endanger any more lives and the torpedo doors of the second submarine were kept firmly shut. *Lady Shirley* meanwhile steamed triumphantly back to her home base in Gibraltar where she got a rousing welcome. Winston Churchill himself cabled his personal congratulations. The skipper of the gallant ship was awarded the Distinguished Service Order and a number of ordinary crewmen were also decorated. There is a sour end to this tale. Only a week later, *Lady Shirley* was mysteriously lost at sea. Although a secretly planted limpet-mine has been suggested as a possible cause of the loss, no conclusive evidence has ever been produced to explain her disappearance.

The service rendered by the converted Hull trawlers during both world wars was a brave and an illustrious one. The dedication and outstanding professionalism of Edward Spencer Rilatt epitomised the important contribution that the plucky citizens of this Yorkshire port made to the defeat of Nazi Germany. On a happy note, Rilatt, who had 'nattered the life out of the Admiralty to let him serve his country again', ended up with a chest full of medals and as Commanding Officer of the Boom-Defence Vessel *Barbican* at Swithergate, Scapa Flow. He died peacefully in 1957, with his boots off, and his funeral was held in the Fisherman's Bethel on Hessle Road.

12

THE BIGGEST FLEET AFLOAT

Some ships are the mechanical equivalent of Greta Garbo; beautiful and alluring with just a hint of mystery. Who could fail to fall in love with the sleek lines of an old-time steamer with her funnels puffing and her skirts awash? And who could remain impassive at thoughts of travelling steerage to strange new lands aboard such wonderfully named vessels as *Calypso, Argo* and *Romeo*? But these ships, once part of the biggest privately owned merchant fleet in the world, are all gone; scrapped, melted down and flung at the Germans. And gone too is the company that at its height employed 10,000 men – the famous Wilson Line. Its flag flew from more than sixty vessels, but is now remembered only in the history books and in a few precious models.

It is fascinating to review the development of a muddy creek that, within a few hundred years, became known as 'King's Town-upon-Hull'. This Yorkshire town eventually challenged the dominance of London and Liverpool as it became England's third busiest port. For the greater part of the last millennium, Hull was an unimportant backwater, subservient in commercial terms to both Hedon and Beverley. Hedon had the advantage of its thriving Haven, with direct access to the Humber, while the busy wharves of the important market town of Beverley could easily be reached via the river Hull. But size was everything. The introduction of bigger, ocean-going ships sparked the need for deeper anchorages with ready access to the North Sea. For over four hundred years, the inhabitants of Hull had lived within the walls of their fortified town, whose only moorings were along the banks of the river Hull. Then, international trade beckoned, and naval architects responded with the creation of larger ships whose dimensions demanded deeper water.

Recognising the potential of their town, the visionaries of Hull acted with typical business acumen. They promoted an Act of Parliament to authorise the construction of a dock extending from the Beverley Gate along the line of the old town-moat. The Act was sanctioned in 1774. Four years later Hull had the honour of possessing the first enclosed trading dock in Great Britain. Known quite simply as the Dock, this nine acre facility was a commercial triumph, and its success prompted the creation of the New Dock in 1809. In 1829, a third dock, the Junction Dock, was dug between the two previous docks, all three docks entirely replacing the line of the old town moat. The creation of Junction Dock was a important event in Hull's rise to international importance as a trading centre. The opening coincided with the establishment of what became Hull's most famous shipping company, when Thomas Wilson went into partnership to create the firm of Beckinton, Wilson and Company.

Steam power transformed the world. Hull waved off its first steam-powered trading vessel – the *Caledonian* – in 1815. Its modest destination was Thorne but, by 1820, there were several ships sailing to Hamburg, the first foreign port accessed by any Hull steamer. Wilson and his partners, Beckinton and Hudson, initially had four sailing ships in their modest fleet – the *Patriot*, the *Ivanhoe*, the *Wave* and the *Susan* – all engaged in the lucrative business of transporting iron to Gothenburg. They also operated several vessels between Hull and Dunkirk. However, the partners soon recognised the ascendancy of the new steam-driven vessels and they quickly introduced three paddle steamers to their fleet. The *Superb*, the *Innisfail* and the *St George* returned such good profits that more ships were built. When the energetic Wilson took the helm, with the retirement of both Beckinton and Hudson, the enterprise was known as Thomas Wilson, Sons and Company.

Hull was connected with the railway network in 1840, and this boost to its trading fortunes encouraged the construction of yet more ships and the opening of new routes linking Hull with Stettin, St Petersburg and Riga. In 1867 the senior partner, David Wilson, retired, handing over responsibility to Charles and Arthur Wilson. The drive and business aptitude of these two men created a shipping empire that came to be known across the globe.

The opening of the Suez Canal in 1869 brought further

opportunities. Routes were established connecting Hull with Bombay, Colombo, Madras and Calcutta. The pioneering *Orlando*, built in Hull in 1870, was the first steamship to open up a direct link between the port and India. Success bred success, and the ever-expanding firm inaugurated trading links with Boston and New York. It also acquired the rival shipping company of Brownlow, Marsdin and Company, whose seven zoologically named craft – *Tiger, Panther, Zebra* and the rest – joined a massive fleet of nearly sixty ships. These ships had tonnages that varied from 450 to 4,000, and they generally had names ending in the letter 'o': *Borodino, Rinaldo, Fido, Yeddo, Kelso* and so forth.

Booming trade facilitated further investment in bigger and better ships most of which, interestingly, were locally built by Earle's Shipbuilding and Engineering Company. This firm 'also earned a great reputation among English ship builders, having launched many notable vessels at one time and another, including ships of war for the British and other Governments, steam yachts for the late Czar, and large passenger-ships for the Atlantic lines'. The expansion in trade also funded a lavish expansion of port facilities in Hull. A contemporary account of a visit to Wilson's offices revealed that the company now enjoyed palatial accommodation. Indeed they were thought to be the largest such offices in Britain. The same witness described the commissioning of a new Wilson ship. Straight off the slip, the *Romeo* was heralded as the fastest steamer sailing from Hull. Prosaically, she had a length 275 feet, a beam width of 34 feet 6 inches and a depth of hold of 20 feet. But no expense had been spared in fitting the vessel out, with mahogany, satinwood and maple being used for the salon and cabins.

Rich profits paid for the very best offices and ships. The burgeoning Wilson fortune also brought civic responsibilities and opulent lifestyles for the Wilson partners. The senior partner, Charles Henry Wilson, served in the office of Sheriff of Hull in 1870 and he became the port's MP in 1874, representing Hull for thirty-two years. He was a local magistrate for the East Riding of Yorkshire and chairman of the Hull Orphan Asylum and a generous supporter, with his brother, of other local charities and institutions. His business interests included a shareholding in the

Central Dry Dock Company and directorships in the Hull Dock, North Eastern Railway and Hull and Barnsley Railway companies. He was also chairman of the Hull Steam Fishing and Ice Company, and a partner in the engineering firm of Amos and Smith. A prodigious worker and a champion of his native Hull, Charles Henry Wilson was made a freeman of the city. Then, in 1906, he was rewarded with a peerage, becoming Baron Nunburnholme of Kingston-upon-Hull.

Outside of his interests in shipping and philanthropy, Charles Wilson is probably best remembered for his self-elevation to the squirearchy. The purchase of Warter Priory near Pocklington from Lord Muncaster in 1878 gave him ownership of a noble mansion and 8,400 acres of 'some of the loveliest scenery in Yorkshire.' Arthur Wilson, the younger partner, was equally determined to enjoy his wealth and status. He purchased another expensive mansion, Tranby Croft, on the western outskirts of Anlaby within sight of the Humber. Here, he entertained lavishly, devoting his leisure time to card playing and fox hunting.

The mansion at Warter was built near the site of an Augustinian monastery that was founded in 1132 and finally dissolved in 1516. The country seat of a gentleman who could afford the very best in life, Warter Hall, as it was originally known in the eighteenth century, was extensively extended and furnished. The major French and Italian Renaissance-inspired additions were commissioned by Wilson. They included a great hall fitted out with carved oak-panelling, executed by the distinguished Beverley firm of J. E. Elwell and Sons, a clock tower, a porte-cochere and an exquisite marble staircase. Set in stunning grounds, complete with a lake and kitchen gardens, Warter Priory had nearly 100 rooms. Over thirty of these were bedrooms. The running of such an extravagant pile was labour intensive, and over sixty staff attended to the family's every need. Stuffed with treasures from all corners of the globe, the mansion was a showcase, and its owner took every opportunity of entertaining guests in the most opulent style. A report in the *Hull News* of January 1899 gave a breathless account of a party for 300 guests, who included Prince Henry and Princess Daisy of Press.

Arthur Wilson had imperial aspirations of his own. Tranby Croft was an eighty-room mansion, set in thirty-four acres, accommodating a cricket pitch, boating lake, lily pond, three vineries and peach and nectarine houses. It glittered with electric lighting, crystal chandeliers and huge gilded-mirrors. Like his brother, Arthur Wilson moved in royal circles. At a charitable bazaar, organised by his wife Mary in 1888, he entertained the Duke of Edinburgh and his consort the Grande Duchess Marie of Russia. The event raised £5,000 for the establishment of an orphanage. His real passions, however, lay in field sports.

Unlike Charles, Arthur Wilson had no political ambitions but he was a passionate sponsor of horse racing and a keen huntsman. For twenty-seven years, from 1878 until 1905, he was Master of the Holderness Hunt, and his fondness for field sports was often remarked upon in the press. The most famous fox-hunt under his direction was held in January 1882, when more than 4,000 spectators watched him share a stirrup cup with the Prince of Wales at Brantingham Thorpe, then the residence of Mr Christopher Sykes.

Towards the end of his exceptional career, the indefatigable Charles Henry Wilson embarked upon a rescue plan that would have daunted a man half his age. The business that had been an integral part of the Wilson's rise to riches collapsed, and 2,000 workmen in the proud Earle's Shipbuilding and Engineering Company faced ruin. With typical boldness Wilson stepped in to save the enterprise and invested some £250,000 in a modernisation programme. And even as late as 1903 – just four years before his death – he was keen to expand his empire still further. His business already operated one of the world's biggest fleets, but he was keen to establish more routes and, in conjunction with the North Eastern Railway Company, he added steamship services linking Hull with German, Dutch and Belgian ports.

Arthur Wilson died just two years after his brother, on 21 October 1909. The family firm was sold to Sir John Ellerman and became the Ellerman-Wilson Line. Tranby Croft was eventually converted for use as a girl's school and the building survives to this day. Warter Priory, however, suffered a worse fate. For twenty years, Charles Wilson's widow continued to live in the rambling and increasingly crumbling mansion. In 1929, it was sold to the Honourable George

Ellis Vestry who did little to arrest its structural decline. That decline, ironically, can be partly blamed on poor design and the use of inferior building materials. Following Vestry's death and a further sale, Warter Priory became a gaunt and leaking shell fit only for demolition. So its contents were sold; an auction in 1969 disposed of Gobelin tapestries, three grand-pianos, Chinese porcelain, pictures, prints, assorted silver wares and over a hundred big-game trophies including the heads of Indian elephants, rhinoceroses, warthogs and leopards. By 1972, the building had been expunged from the map. Its site is now occupied by a group of anonymous farm buildings. Fittingly, the huge Warter estate is currently owned by another successful Hull businessman.

The Wilson legacy lives on in Hull. The city's continuing success as a major port is testament to the achievements of a remarkable dynasty. But what personal memories of the family remain? After his death, Arthur Wilson was conveyed on a farm rulley to his final resting place in Kirkella Church. But where is the grave of the Baron? He breathed his last in his beloved Warter Priory and is remembered on a plaque in the local church of St James, although I can find no tombstone. Is it possible he was cremated and his ashes scattered at sea?

In his life, Baron Nunburnholme spent large sums of money supporting the church of St James. There is ample evidence, in the extravagance of the monuments to other members of the Wilson family, that no expense was spared in providing eternal tributes to their past lives. Here lies a sad reality. Even the most expensive and durable marble-moulds will crumble without regular maintenance. On inspection in the graveyard, you will find that not a flower has been laid on the family tombstones in decades. Invaded now by rank grasses and weeds, the finest handcrafted materials weep and decay.

The pride of St. James was once the Nunburnholme family-chapel, an exquisite domed mausoleum built in 1905 to the memory of Isabel, daughter of the seventh Duke of Roxburgh and the wife of Guy Greville Wilson. The chapel, which once accommodated an elegant recumbent effigy of the lady in marble, has been described as one of the finest churches in the Wolds. It suffered the same fate as Warter Priory, although thankfully its intricately worked wrought-iron gates and its stirring effigy are preserved in a church aisle. Nearby is the simple plaque showing Baron Nunburnholme and his wife. For a while the entire church, redundant through lack of a congregation, looked doomed to follow the priory and chapel into oblivion, but in recent years it has been saved for use an educational centre by a charitable trust.

On a lighter note, a benign statue of Charles Henry Wilson, first Baron Nunburnholme, surveys the busy urban scene from a perch on the corner of Alfred Gelder Street. Wherever his bones or ashes lie, his soul can be content in the knowledge that the Humber is today one of the busiest shipping lanes in the world.

13

WHAT'S IN A NAME?

Some Yorkshire place-names send the conjectural cogs racing, as images of topographical features, historical events and people crowd the imagination. I have in my personal lexicon the following treasured entries: Booze, Kettlesing, Fill Belly Slack, Boggarts Roaring Hole, The Whams, Jump, Great Cockup, Clint, Boot of the Wold, Shivering Moss, Soldiers Lump, Wine Haven, Hawkswick Chowder, Greedy Gut, Black Beck Swang, The Tongue, Hades, Elysium, Lost John's Cave. And then there are two of my all-time favourites; the Land of Nod near Holme-on-Spalding Moor and the Land of Green Ginger in Hull. The most interesting town in Yorkshire has a host of such names.

The gazetteer of Hull street names is an index of the city's origins, distinguished citizens and achievements. A walk, particularly around the city centre and the environs of the old town, prompts a historic roll-call. In fact, even a short stroll puts clothes on the bones of many of the subjects referred to in other chapters of this book. Just an upward glance at the names rolls out a pantheon of the great and the good. Take a walk along the ancient thoroughfare where the city's 700 years of development first took root. This pilgrimage down High Street – it was originally called Hull Street – follows the banks of a river that gave the city its very name. Then wander into Blackfriargate and Whitefriargate following in the steps of the friars who once trod the monastic estates hereabouts. Trinity House Lane takes one past the grand façade of the mansion that has for so long held the rudder on the town's maritime affairs. Then, of course, there is Tower Street, a name that evokes the terrible Hull Castle where scores of religious zealots were imprisoned. And, further afield, you will find David Whitfield Close.

Also honoured with street names are the famous aviatrix Amy Johnson in Amy Johnson Court, the emancipator of the slaves William Wilberforce in Wilberforce Street and local architect and MP Alfred Gelder in Alfred Gelder Street. Other local worthies also get their names on high. Pearson Avenue recalls the generosity of ship owner Zacchariah Charles Pearson, whose park was given to the people of Hull in 1860. Coltman Street brings to mind a prominent local family and most notably the larger-than-life Joseph Coltman, a clergyman who was so fat that he had to be wheeled into his pulpit in a contraption known as a dandy horse. There is also Thomas Ferens, who made his way in life from the humble status of a clerk to become a Liberal MP and the joint chairman of prominent Hull company Reckitts; he has his sign in Ferens Avenue.

Most modern citizens, of course, stare up at the names of their illustrious forebears with gratitude and some pride. But I wonder what Hull commuters make of the plate that names a congested modern highway after the rugby league hero whose premature death was mourned by the entire city in October 1985? Clive Sullivan Way is a name to be cursed on a busy Monday morning at a quarter to nine.

The naming of some Hull streets was also inspired by people and places in other parts of the world. Havelock Street alludes to Sir Henry Havelock, the distinguished soldier who played a leading role in the Indian Mutiny. Sibelius Road strikes a note for the great Finnish composer, while Freetown Way commemorates the twinning of Hull with the port in Sierra Leone. There is also a plate that reminds us of the horrors of the First World War; Mons Street is a testimonial to the infamous battle of August 1914. And there are two most unusual references to fighting ships; the plates Ark Royal and Endymion Street fly the colours for these important naval vessels.

For me though, the most interesting street names are those that speak eloquently of Hull's origins. Salthouse Lane refers to the valuable salt deposits that were once found there, Dagger Lane was the place where knives and daggers were made and Silver Street was named after the bullion trade that was carried on in the vicinity. Other names take us back centuries to the very origins of the town.

The tongue-twisting Wincolmlee is probably named after an island meadow surrounded by marshland at Wyke – the lonely creek where Hull had its birth. However, a more popular explanation for the origins of the word was provided by a lady who kept a local alehouse. A spinner of yarns, she was said to have beguiled her gullible customers with tall stories while at the same time winking at her in-the-know regulars. From this practice was derived the compounded words 'wink' and 'lie' (lee). Moving on, Stoneferry was the place where the river was crossed by a stone-paved ford and Drypool Way began as a hamlet adjacent to the 'dried-up' pool.

One of the most captivating names in the entire town is Strawberry Street, which lies on the site of former strawberry fields and tea gardens. The area had a somewhat mixed reputation. In its early days, it was home to a respectable community but between 1820 and 1850 it was 'chiefly the resort of the poorer inhabitants whose drunken quarrels often caused the landlord of the public house to appear before the magistrates.' At the time of the Drypool Feast in August, the gardens were inhabited at night by 'the lowest and vilest blackguards in Hull'.

The most evocative street name of all though, and our perambulation leads us neatly back to the core of the old town, is the Land of Green Ginger. No other name in the entire county has generated so much intrigue and curiosity. The Land of Green Ginger. Surely this is a fictional creation inhabited by some wonderful creatures from Middle Earth rather than a nondescript street in the middle of Hull? Go there now and there are no spicy nasal greetings, only the enigmatic and much photographed street sign that hints at a colourful past.

Read a dozen old guidebooks on Hull and you will discover twelve different explanations of the origins of the name, The Land of Green Ginger. One tome suggests that the roots of the name grew from the Norman word 'Ginge' meaning a spring or a stream issuing from a 'Green'. Another argues that the land in question merely belonged to a local boat-builder by the unlikely name of Moses Greenhinger. His name was corrupted and hey presto! One fanciful version explains that a druggist dropped a piece of imported ginger onto fertile ground and it grew like Jack's beanstalk. But the suggestion I like best, and I think it is the most plausible, is that the area where the street now runs was used for the cultivation of ginger. The story goes like this. Ginger was first imported into England in 1530. Like all essences and spices, it was a valuable commodity and highly prized. Henry VIII is reputed to have enjoyed a delicacy called 'green ginger'. This was a sweetmeat prepared, according to an ancient recipe, by steeping ginger roots in a concoction of wine, honey, lemon juice and cloves. The mixture was left to infuse for several months. During Henry's reign, an up-and-coming Hull merchant by the name of John Monson – he was a member of the Guild of St George – was given a small consignment of West Indian ginger which he planted near to his home on Old Beverley Street in Hull. His family had first experimented with the spice on their estates at South Kelsey in Lincolnshire and had successfully raised a crop on an area of land that was thereafter called the 'Field of Green Ginger'. In a manuscript dated 11 March 1592, Monson recorded in his own handwriting that he had 'sett' his exotic roots in the 'Land of Green Ginger', a name that supplanted the original Old Beverley Street for evermore. Interestingly enough, Monson was included in the royal entourage when the King visited Hull and it is fascinating to suppose that 'green ginger' might have found its way onto the sovereign's table. Modern botanists reject the ludicrous idea that a tropical plant such as ginger could be grown successfully in the cold climate of the East Riding. But so-called experts have consistently underestimated the resolve and ingenuity of past generations. Given the novelty of the spice, and its appeal to the King's palate, surely an enterprising gardener such as Monson could have devised a method of cultivation involving the careful application of heat? John Monson died in 1599 and was buried on 10 June in the south transept of Holy Trinity Church. His pungent legend lingers on. To my mind, the next time councillors choose a name for a new road, they could do no better than calling it Monson Street.

14

DRESSMAKER TO THE QUEEN

No offence, but on life's catwalk, one would imagine the ladies of Hull having as much rapprochement with the garment houses of London and Paris as Nora Batty. Lacking a Mayfair, or a Rue De Faubourg St Honore, Hull has rarely aspired to the heights of haute couture. However, one incredible lady, for a brief period between 1890 and the outbreak of the First World War, took a town more familiar with shawls and thigh waders to the very pinnacle of fashion.

Born Emily MacVitie in Cheltenham in 1856, she left school at an early age and began a dressmaking apprenticeship at Marshall and Snelgrove's famous emporium in Scarborough. Despite the long hours and the drudgery of her job, which involved mundane tasks such as cleaning and picking up pins, she was quick to learn and developed a keen eye for the finer elements of dress design. At the end of her apprenticeship, she emerged as a thoroughly competent seamstress, skilled in every aspect of the trade. Bursting with confidence she married Haigh Clapham, and persuaded her new husband that they could run a successful business. Pooling their skills and savings, the pair bought a yellow-brick house in Hull in 1887 and, to a somewhat incredulous reaction, announced themselves to the world. The signboard fixed to the elegant entrance of 1 Kingston Square gave a promise of glamour and Gallic panache. The name Madame Clapham shone out onto the dull streets of Hull.

As we have discovered elsewhere in these pages, the Hull of the period was rapidly expanding. Fishing, shipbuilding and a wide range of commercial developments created a nouveau riche whose ladies aspired to the elegant fashions that were becoming increasingly popular in London and Paris. Shrewdly recognising the possibilities of supplying exclusive clothes to the well-to-do families of Hull and the East Riding, Madame Clapham studied the emerging trends and began adapting the designs of the best London and Paris fashion houses to produce her own unique styles.

She used only the finest materials and embellishments. Quality and attention to detail were of paramount importance, and clients soon appreciated the beauty and exclusivity of a Madame Clapham dress. Within four years, her business had begun to flourish to such an extent that the adjacent accommodation at 2 Kingston Square was purchased to provide more space. By the outbreak of the First World War, the property at number 3 had also been added to the business that, at its height, employed 150 people. The social life of Hull had been transformed due to the rapid growth of the local economy, and the perennial round of balls, musical evenings, race meetings and weddings gave rise to a demand for fashionable attire. Having forged a reputation by producing exquisite garments for a long list of wealthy patrons, Madame Clapham increasingly attracted clients from further afield. Each season, she would travel to meet these customers in York, Harrogate, Grimsby and London. And she would make frequent visits to Paris to keep abreast of fashion trends.

Many of the local glitterati would attend personally at the fashionable Kingston Square, which had been laid out by the Revd Robert Jarratt around 1801 to improve the area. The grandeur of the new showrooms with their thick carpets, comfortable sofas and colourful curtains created an ambience that pampered the most discerning of clients. Ladies were made to feel utterly at home, and models or mannequins elegantly displayed examples of lingerie, evening gowns and day wear as tea was served in china cups. Sumptuous fabrics were everywhere. One young visitor referred to 'folds of silk and net, of pale cloth and velvet, embroideries of pearl and silver and dull gold and lace, petticoats with pleated frills and lacy blouses.' Once they had commissioned a particular creation, ladies would return for the all-important final adjustments, and three fitting rooms equipped with wall-to-wall mirrors allowed the intensive scrutiny of every stitch. A stickler for detail, Madame Clapham would often recommend that clients return for a final fitting wearing their chosen jewellery and accessories so that any last-minute adjustments to the overall ensemble could be made.

In the Ferens Art Gallery in Hull there is a beautiful oil painting of Muriel Wilson. Sumptuously attired in a flouncy ivory-silk gown, this leader of the Hull avant-garde was one of Madame Clapham's most prestigious clients. Indeed Sir Osbert Sitwell, in his autobiography, referred to the enormous boost given to her career by the patronage of the Wilson ladies. Such national exposure gave the name of Madame Clapham a cachet far beyond the provincial bounds of Hull, and her gowns were soon in demand from the aristocracy. Lady Duff Cooper, the Duchess of Norfolk and Baroness Beaumont all became customers.

Madame Clapham was immensely proud of her creations. A comment in the *Hull Lady* magazine of 1901 reflected her growing list of prestige clients: 'To give you some idea as to the large connection I have,' she said 'I may tell you I make dresses for most of the county and leading society ladies, also a great many for royalty, and I send dresses out to ladies living abroad whom I have never seen.' In that year of 1901, she received so much royal patronage that she felt confident to add the words 'Court Dressmaker' to her letterhead.

An article in the *Hull Lady* for 1902 paints a vivid picture of the opulent scene in 1 and 2 Kingston Square: 'I particularly noticed a French model gown in black velvet, handsomely embroidered with ecru lace appliqué, and a princess robe in blue Orient satin, charmingly trimmed with blue mousseline de soie. There were also several lovely evening cloaks about, one, which specially took my attention, being in banana-coloured cloth, with beautiful old muslin-collar and necklet of ermine.'

The same article refers to commissions for other distinguished society ladies such as the Countess of Londesborough and Lady Mildred Denison, although Madame Clapham was keen to point out that she took a great interest in her female customers from Hull. In 1911, she was asked to give an estimate for a robe and mantle that Viscount Chetwynd intended to wear at the Coronation of George V. She undercut the more fashionable suppliers in London and won the order, adding further to her reputation for quality garments. By far her most important client was Queen Maud of Norway, the daughter of King Edward VII. Summoned to London, Madame Clapham displayed a range of wares to her royal customer and secured a valuable commission. And, although her new client never visited Hull, Madame Clapham and her entourage of assistants and mannequins often visited the Queen's apartments in Sandringham.

Royal endorsements created a glowing reputation for Madame Clapham's couture, with every young girl aspiring to wear one of her garments. The comments of one excited 17-year-old customer demonstrate just how popular the Kingston Square emporium had become: 'Today I went with mamma to Hull for the day to get a coming out frock!! Oh joy, oh joy!! Girls brought in soft piles of silk and satin to exhibit to me. The satin frock has a very simple body draped with gold embroidery. It ought to be perfectly lovely we think.'

Within a few short years of launching her business, Madame Clapham was the talk of the town. Her reputation helped to attract orders from fashionable ladies everywhere. But a growing number of orders required an army of seamstresses and embroiderers. Hull and its environs supplied a more than enthusiastic workforce. A job in Madame Clapham's workrooms was something of a status symbol, and young girls eagerly signed up to seven-year apprenticeships. In the early days, recruits regarded a job there as a privilege and were generally unpaid for the first year. The positions were invariably offered to the daughters of better-off families who were in a position to support them. Apprentices began by performing mundane tasks such as tidying rolls of fabric, picking up pins, replenishing pincushions or making strap-holders for the shoulder bands in evening dresses. Gradually, they would be tutored in a range of specialist skills. Fully trained apprentices, who met the exacting standards imposed by Madame Clapham, went on to work in the various departments devoted to skirts, bodices, sleeves and embroidery. One former employee, Mabel Nutbrown, who worked in the establishment between 1929 and 1940, recalls her relief at not being dismissed after her probationary period: 'After you had done seven years it was really traumatic because they usually used to sack people and you would sit in fear and trembling for the whistle to blow and you would have to go upstairs. But I was one of the lucky ones.'

Working hours were half-past eight in the morning until six o'clock in the evening, with only a break for lunch. There were no other stoppages for refreshments and the girls were expected to work on Saturdays until one o'clock. For a week's work, 'Our full wage after seven years was one pound and ten shillings three ha'penths', recalled Mabel Nutbrown. Workrooms were cold, draughty and uncarpeted, and the girls worked in austere conditions using long wooden tables and hard stools. Most of the stitching was done by hand and there were few mechanical aids except for flat irons called 'gooses'. A code of silence was imposed on the workrooms, and strict discipline and exacting standards produced garments of an incredibly high quality. Despite the dourness of the environment, the girls took immense pride in their work especially when they were involved in creating scintillating gowns for prestige clients. 'To me it was a wonderful experience,' remembered Mabel Nutbrown, 'because the materials you used were absolutely out of this world and when the dresses were presented at Court it was wonderful.'

Although work at Madame Clapham's was hard, her staff developed a fine work ethic and strong teamwork, readily cooperating to assemble complicated garments. And, if any operative accidentally pricked a finger, her colleagues would immediately spring into action with a well-practised routine, chewing on cotton swabs to dab away the offending stain. And when the supervisors were not looking, there was always time for a snigger and a recitation of a favourite rhyme about tacking:

> Tack with blue, sure to rue!
> Tack with green, not fit to be seen!
> Leave in a tack, sure to come back!

The girls would also enjoy a titter when assembling gowns for the more amply proportioned clients, quipping 'Once round the waist, twice round Hyde Park!' Madame Clapham, who rarely fraternised with the workshop girls, did not appreciate such levity. A large imposing lady with striking blue eyes, rosy cheeks and rash of blonde hair, she was a sober Christian Scientist who rustled through the salon in her trademark floor-length dress complete with train. With an eagle eye and an acerbic tongue, she was most definitely not a lady to be trifled with.

Inevitably, the fashion-bubble burst. The outbreak of the First World War ushered in a period of austerity. Its aftermath and the social values of the 'Roaring Twenties' brought new attitudes to female attire inspired by the movie industry and dances like the charleston. Out went the elaborate gowns with their petticoats, trains and bustles, and in came shorter, straighter and sexier dresses that reflected the mood of emancipation and greater personal freedom. Young people everywhere adopted the new styles, and orders for traditional Clapham clothes dropped, although the older generation steadfastly refused to move with the times. Greater competition caused the Kingston Square business to contract, and some staff were put on short time. To bolster her business, Madame Clapham decided to offer a corset-making service and she also began to sell some ready-to-wear outfits manufactured in London fashion houses. But the steady decline accelerated and, with the advent of the Second World War in 1939, the salon almost closed. There was a brief upsurge in demand for quality clothes after 1945 despite the rigours of rationing. However, by this time, the era of the court dress was over, and Hull's sixty-five year romance with the world of high fashion came to an end with the death of Madame Clapham in 1952. She was 96.

The business was continued by Madame Clapham's niece from the premises at 3 Kingston Square until her own death in 1967. Finally, a Hull legend was no more. Today, Kingston Square is still a fashionable address, and Madame Clapham's former premises are occupied by the Kingston Theatre Hotel near the Hull New Theatre. Over the hotel's entrance portal is an original cast-iron nameplate, and the ornately figured word 'Clapham' reminds visitors of its distinguished history. Inside the hotel is the Clapham Restaurant. Many Clapham creations have been preserved for posterity. Hull Museum Service owns a collection of sumptuous gowns and, some years ago, a Clapham exhibition was staged in Wilberforce House. The dresses are currently conserved in storage pending further displays.

I have my own personal memento of Hull's fashionable past. Twenty or so years ago, I was wandering past a semi-derelict Georgian property abutting Prince Street when curiosity led me inside an old shop. There I discovered a discarded, but beautifully made, wooden coat-hanger with a brass hook. I have it still. It is painted black and embossed in gold letters are the words, 'THOS BACH COSTUMIERS – HULL' I wonder if he knew Madame Clapham?

15

THE RESTAURANT OF YORKSHIRE

The bomb had Powolny's name on it. It was dropped from a German aircraft on 7 May 1941, one weapon in a lethal consignment of eighty tons of explosives that ripped out the commercial heart of Hull. When the smoke cleared after a frantic and prolonged battle with fires that raged throughout the night, Hull counted the cost. There were 203 people dead and many more injured. The city lost something else that night. It lost a certain style and sophistication which, in over six decades, has never been satisfactorily replaced. It lost the much-loved 'Restaurant of Yorkshire'. It lost Powolny's.

Powolny's. An awkward sort of name redolent of cheap Polish sausage. A name that would have modern image-consultants in a flat spin. But the name was of no consequence. Its elegance and glittering persona, backed by sumptuous food and service, created a catering icon and one of the best restaurants in Europe. How did it come about and who was this Powolny fellow, the remarkable foreigner who brought such sophistication to the old streets of Hull?

The 17-year-old Ernst Adolf Powolny, a native of Zittau in Saxony, came to Yorkshire in 1858 and settled in Leeds. An adventurous and hard-working young man, he found a job in a local catering firm. His natural aptitude as a chef soon became apparent to his friends who, after four years, persuaded him to open an establishment of his own. With little money, he took the plunge and opened a small but successful restaurant. By this time, the émigré was a naturalised Yorkshireman, and the penchant for 'eating all and paying nowt' soon rubbed off on a go-getting young man. Within a short time, he had saved up enough funds to move his kitchen to an upmarket address in Bond Street. Cultivating a clientele that included the aristocracy, civic dignitaries and the nouveau riche of the Leeds factories and mills, he built up a profitable business and a reputation for exquisite cuisine and fine wines served in an ambience of unparalleled style. For thirty years, attention to detail and superb culinary skills marked out Maison Powolny as one of the best restaurants in the county. The use of fresh ingredients and exciting new recipes captivated the dull palates of our sober Northern race. 'It's absolutely amazing what you can eat there,' said one delighted customer. 'Do you know something? They offer three types of turtle soup freshly made on the premises. They actually keep the live turtles in the cellar.'

After a lifetime's work, the great Powolny retired from his business in 1897, bequeathing his chef's hat to his family. But his influence did not end there. By the turn of the century, a limited company had been formed to look at opportunities in other cities for the family business. Its owners looked fondly east to Hull.

At the beginning of the twentieth century, Hull embarked on a programme of urban renewal befitting its standing as an international port and manufacturing centre. The prominent architect and town councillor, Albert Gelder, spearheaded a campaign for the redevelopment of the land beyond the confines of the Old Town and the circle of docks. Gelder's daring scheme was to create a piazza – an open public space to grace buildings designed to mirror the town's sense of confidence and pride. The creation of City Square swept away a conglomeration of nondescript buildings north of Princes Dock. A wide boulevard was named King Edward Street as a tribute to Queen Victoria's son, and radiated out to link with Prospect Street and the countryside beyond. The exciting new street would be filled with shops, theatres and restaurants. The potential of marketing the Powolny legend to the newly affluent residents of Pearson Park, the Avenues, Spring Bank and Beverley Road encouraged the limited company to buy into the scheme. Redevelopment proceeded as planned and, by the autumn of 1903, the last gravy-boat had been buffed up and Powolny's was ready for business.

The first things to note about the imposing restaurant were its central position on King Edward Street and the imposing façade, which was no less than sixty-feet wide and crowned by a clock tower. Clad in dazzling light-coloured stone, the building was somewhat over-embellished with pilasters, balustrades and aesthetically superfluous mouldings. But it captured the confidence of the age, signalling an end to austerity and the beginning of a less class-conscious future. These themes were also reflected inside. The interior offered a grand café, continental restaurant, luncheon bar and smoke room. No expense was spared in fitting out these facilities. The finest marble flooring, mahogany doors, oak panelling, thick carpets, polished mirrors, marble-topped tables, crystal chandeliers, silver-plated wares and crisp linens created a sumptuous atmosphere that vied with any restaurant in the country.

Powolny's was formally opened on Saturday 3 October 1903 after a mouth-watering advertisement had been published some days before in the *Hull Daily Mail*. The town's hottest attraction was reported as specialising 'in soups of every description, particularly turtle, hot and cold ornamental entrees, fancy ices, aspics, patisserie, pate foie, bonbons, chocolates, savoury and sweet jellies, creams, truffled viands, all made on the premises by competent chefs and able to be packed securely to travel any distance.' Oh how the readers must have salivated! And how the fishermen of Hessle Road must have wondered at the restaurant's funny name and how a German upstart came to be selling pâté foie. 'What's that?' they might have asked between mouthfuls of brawn or black pudding. 'Bugger me, chicken livers . . . is that what it is? Does it come with fried onions?'

The new manager of Powolny's was also of foreign extraction. The suave and personable Monsieur Charles Colomb hailed from Neuchatel in Switzerland. With vast experience of running prestige establishments in Monte Carlo, London and Bexhill-on-Sea, Columb was persuaded to relocate to the far from avant-garde environs of Hull. This was an ambitious move by the directors and an indication of the faith they had in Hull.

Monsieur Columb had an opportunity to show his true colours just three months after the restaurant opened. The flag was hoisted on the clock tower on 13 January 1904 when 170 members of the Holderness Hunt and their guests attended an evening dinner in honour of the retiring hunt-master, Mr Arthur Wilson, the distinguished director of the famous shipping line. Wilson had held the post for some twenty-five years and was well respected by the county elite. The choice of Powolny's as the venue for this glittering occasion says much about its standing in the county, and Monsieur Columb and his army of liveried staff made sure that the event was the social highlight of the year. The *Hull Daily Mail* wrote in glowing terms about the town's newest attraction and praised the food, organisation and ambience to the hilt.

Expensive banquets were fine for the rich and famous, but what did Powolny's offer to ordinary people who could only just scrape together enough money for the occasional treat? Well, it could provide a five-course table d'hôte lunch for two shillings and sixpence or the full seven-course beanfeast for just one shilling more. This sounds reasonable looking back a hundred years or so, but it must be remembered that, in 1901, even chief engineers in the trawling fleet were only earning forty-six shillings per week, with deck hands taking home just over a pound. Monsieur Columb moved on in 1905, handing over the reins of management to Monsieur H. Constantine who helped make the restaurant a fixture in the social life of Hull. He, in turn, was succeeded by Monsieur Petro Louis Dermond in 1910.

Such was its popularity that, by 1913, it had been enlarged. A single-storey extension was built at the rear to cater for private luncheons and dinners. Then came the dreadful events of 1914. Although Powolny's managed to remain open during the First World War, the impact of the new world order brought about a change in its character. Henceforth it would be more populist in outlook. Its name was shortened to Polly's and simpler, less expensive menus were introduced – a 'special four-course luncheon was on offer at 1s 9d' in 1931, for example – along with tea dances. This meant the ever-present Bijou Orchestra had to learn the all new tunes inspired by jazz and the charleston. The band played on, and the restaurant went from strength to strength. Powolny's was a multi-faceted business. The promotional literature advertised its availability for ball suppers, whist drives, regimental and masonic suppers, garden parties and weddings. All Hull brides of the period aspired to cutting their cakes within its expensive walls, and many a hard-pressed father spent his life savings to do his daughter proud. The business was also extremely active in outside catering. Powolny's kitchens provided the food for the luncheon party held at the Guildhall in October 1926 in honour of Edward VIII. On one occasion the restaurant even catered for a function south of the Humber. Making use of the regular ferry, it ingeniously carried a cargo of fresh-fruit salad in milk churns. Other incredible feats of mass catering included the provision of a banquet to celebrate the centenary of the London and North Eastern Railway in Darlington and a massive bun-fight at the British Empire Exhibition in Wembley.

The mantra of perfection was constantly recited by the ubiquitous Monsieur Dermond, who was a true perfectionist. Every day he could be observed tweaking here, and cajoling there, in his immaculately pressed double-breasted suit, wing collar and bright bow-tie. He had animated relationships with the temperamental chef, Georges Cottin, and his volatile assistant Groppo. A strict code of conduct was imposed on waitresses. The finer points of silver service had to be practised to perfection and they had to keep their aprons and table linens perfectly clean. One poor dear, who really took Dermond's warnings to heart, is reported to have said to a diner: 'Now, here's your fish and mind you don't get a mark on the tablecloth.'

Powolny's was the in-place for the young and debonair and a rendezvous for the rich and famous. They were never far from the gaze of the local press who seemed to have a permanent reservation at a table next to the front door. The reporter's pencil must have been white hot on the night an Indian maharajah tried to whisk the restaurant's young cashier away to his palace. And there must have been great excitement when the great aviatrix Amy Johnson – a native of the city – stopped by for a celebratory lunch. Other famous diners included Joachim von Ribbentropp, who went on to become Nazi Germany's Foreign Minister, Owen Nares the film actor and Wally Whiting, the son of a diamond-mine owner in South Africa. Less well known was the crew of the airship R38, which also played a significant part in Hull's history. Prior to the airship dropping into the Humber in 1921, a number of its American aircrew had enjoyed Polowny's legendary hospitality. Indeed, several of the dashing young men made friends with the restaurant's female staff. In fact, on that tragic August day, it had been agreed that the girls would wave to the crew as their vessel passed majestically overheard. The party assembled outside, but excitement turned to helpless horror as R38 spilt asunder in flames and dropped into the river.

There was another setback for the restaurant in the early morning of 6 April 1934. This time, the flames were closer to home. A fire – it was thought that a discarded cigarette in a telephone kiosk might have been the cause of the blaze – reduced much of the restaurant to ashes. Amazingly, by July of that year, it had been repaired and the restaurant reopened for business to banner headlines in the local press.

Shortly thereafter, the charismatic and tireless Monsieur Dermond died. He left the business to his son Paul who immediately took on a new partner, Freddie Gamble. Together this pair embarked on a marketing campaign to restore its former glories. One of the adverts is a reminder of rather outdated social attitudes: 'The Smoke Room Bar is being modernised and will continue to function for "Gentlemen Only". Even in these enlightened days, we find that there are times when we must escape from the too vigorous attentions of our wives and sweethearts.' How things change. Gentlemen smokers were kicked out into the street, and the world has become a gynarchy!

All that remains of Powolny's is its site, which is now occupied by an uninspiring chain store. Some souvenirs, secretly purloined when the waiter's back was turned or kept by former staff, occasionally turn up. But apart from the odd inscribed ashtray or plate nothing much remains except for the memories of the ageing few. Hull lost something else that fateful day in May 1941. It lost part of its character and a deserved reputation for unashamed glamour that, even in the new millennium, has never been equalled.

Whatever happened to old Ernst Adolf Powolny? Well, he spent eighteen years in retirement in Harrogate and died at the age of 76 in 1915. He is buried in Woodhouse Cemetery in Leeds.

16

WHEN HULL WAS CINEMA CITY

The development of cinema can be traced to the pioneering work of a Frenchman – Augustine Le Prince – who shot the first-ever moving pictures on Leeds Bridge in 1888. Le Prince began a cinematic revolution that first came to Hull in October 1896, when Randall Williams amazed audiences at Hull Fair with moving pictures from his bioscope. Magic-lantern shows were soon consigned to the toy cupboard and, by the end of the century, fairground operators were regularly entertaining thousands of cinema-goers. And the price of admission? It was 2d for adults and 1d for children. Many people were open-mouthed at the visions before them. At one opening performance, they are said to have 'gazed in astonishment at the sight of an orange being sliced up'.

Noting the popularity of this new form of entertainment and its obvious economic potential, several Hull businessmen began showing films in the town. One of the first to be shown was the astounding 1896 film of the fight of the century between boxers Corbett and Fitzsimmons for the heavyweight championship of the world, which drew large crowds to the Theatre Royal. Suddenly, everybody wanted to invest in the phenomenon that was moving pictures. Indeed, the mushrooming of converted and purpose-built premises across the country caused the government to pass the Cinematograph Act in 1909. The national craze spawned a rash of investment in Hull and, in the year the Act came into force, the Palace Theatre, the Assembly Rooms, the Alexandre Theatre and the Bijou Empire were all showing moving pictures. Some entrepreneurs also converted shops in the city centre to show films, and the conversion of 44 Whitefriargate into the Electric Theatre was typical of the period. The scramble to get in on the act did, however, lead to some rash investments. The farcical creation of the aptly named Garden in Anlaby Road led inevitably to disaster. It opened for business in 1912 and was located in an open field alongside Anlaby Road. Patrons had to contend with the vagaries of old deckchairs, traffic noise and the worst excesses of an English summer. Not surprisingly, the Garden closed after only three months.

Over time, all manner of suitable premises were adapted to serve the new purpose. The Criterion on George Street began life as a waxworks and the Picture Playhouse on Porter Street was originally a Methodist chapel. However, by far the easiest and most common conversions were of existing music halls and theatres. Two particularly fine examples of the work of the eminent theatre-architect Frank Matcham were remodelled to show films. Regrettably, both of these – the opulent Dorchester on George Street and the Palace on Anlaby Road – have since been demolished.

Hull's first purpose-built cinema was built in 1910 and was known as the Princes Hall. Scores of other picture palaces followed in its wake. The Regal in Ferensway took just seventeen weeks to build. Some of the early cinemas were nothing more than sheds with a ragbag collection of seats. But many of the new attractions were architecturally imposing and ornate: soaring columns, triumphal arches and sweeping entrance steps in the image of ancient Rome created the grandest ambience for that special night out. The Majestic (formerly the Criterion) on George Street even had a pair of imperial lions at its entrance. Inside, the cinemas were lavishly equipped and appointed. Extravagant use was made of tropical timbers, rich plasterwork, marble and plush seating for hundreds of people. One cinema had a coal fire in its foyer – the Central on Prospect Street – and affectionately became known in the neighbourhood as 'The Cosy'. Every supplementary facility was provided for customers. The attractions included shops, male and female toilets, fashionable floor-coverings in linoleum, cafes where smart waitresses in black-and-white uniforms served elegant teas, full-scale orchestras, commissioners in braided caps, bell-boys in brass-buttoned jackets and pork-pie hats and torch-wielding usherettes.

Cinemas were denounced by some as a social evil, especially in view of the amorous antics reserved for the double back-seats where incognito snogging could go on uninterrupted. These daring novelty seats, very popular amongst courting couples, were first introduced at the Central in Prospect Street in 1915 during the First World War. Interestingly, during that conflict, film managers were charged by the government not to show 'anything depressing – people need their spirits keeping up.'

It has to be remembered, of course, that the early films had no soundtracks. Pianos, organs and orchestras provided the appropriate accompaniment to events on the screen and during intervals. Sophisticated apparatus – drums, sheets of sandpaper, coconut shells, tins, sheets and buckets of glass – simulated the sounds of gunfire, rushing water, galloping horses, thunder and lightning and crashes. Experimental talking-pictures were, though, already being shown at the Princes Hall from as early as 1914 but audiences would have to wait until 1929 for sound and vision to be successfully combined. This ushered in a golden age of cinema that would last until the advent of mass-ownership television in the 1960s. In that pre-television age, regular screenings of *Pathe News* brought animation to the stories people were aware of from newspapers and radio. Posters would be displayed on busy street corners advertising the coming of new films, and property owners who allowed their gables to be used as hoardings received complimentary tickets. Trailers also blazed a cavalcade for new films.

At the peak of their popularity in Hull, there were thirty-eight cinemas in the city. It is estimated that there was one cinema seat for every nine inhabitants. At one time Hull had more picture houses per head of population than any comparable city in the north of England. In 1935, 200,000 people a week visited Hull's twenty-six cinemas, which had a total of forty thousand seats. The city had twenty-eight cinemas in 1953. With no sign of audience numbers dwindling to any great extent, that year saw the planning of a new cinema to replace the much-loved Cecil. Together with the Ritz on Holderness Road and the National on Beverley Road, among others, the old Cecil was destroyed by enemy bombing during the Second World War. Much of the precious archive of Hull's cinematic history also went up in smoke on that fateful night of 7–8 May 1941, as the Cecil was the administrative centre for eleven cinemas. But the phoenix rose – it was the first cinema in England to be constructed on a new site since the end of hostilities – in 1955, providing a 2,052 seat auditorium and a restaurant with 100 covers.

Cinemas offered cheap and stimulating entertainment for the masses. For millions of people, a visit to the cinema was the highlight of the working week. In often drab, routine lives, films offered escapism, and the weekly outing was often combined, after the show, with a drink in a local pub and the purchase of 'one of each' from the nearby fish-and-chip shop. And musical entertainment was an integral part of the cinema experience for decades. In the interval between films, orchestras and magnificent organs provided dazzling repertoires of sound. The celebrated Compton Organ Company, the largest theatre-organ makers in the world, installed a new instrument in the newly built Astoria at the corner of Holderness Road and Lake Drive in 1934. It had an immense melodic range, encompassing 'the thrilling peal of the cathedral organ, the brilliance of a full symphony orchestra and the rhythm of a modern dance band'. Its console was fitted with an interior coloured-lighting-system that could be synchronised with the music or images on the screen. The Fitton and Haley organ in the Carlton Theatre on Anlaby Road was hailed as another wonder, and its manager boasted that it could produce every nuance of sound, 'anything from the noble noises of a church organ to the call of a cuckoo or the crying of a child'. This organ was later removed to the old Cecil just down the road where, during the 1930s, it proved a star attraction alongside the swing-along music of Betting de Boer and his Orchestra. Yes, cinema-goers got all this . . . and change from a shilling!

In that golden era of the 1930s, prominent Hull businessman J. Arthur Rank, the son of the founder of Rank's Flour Mills, became interested in the evangelical possibilities of film. An ardent Methodist and a Sunday-school teacher, he was inspired to make several religious films, and his developing expertise allowed him successfully to enter the commercial market towards the end of the decade. His movies, introduced by the image of a strongman striking a huge gong with a hammer, became immensely popular and he went on to control more than five hundred cinemas and a business empire that became known as the Rank Organisation.

A visit to the cinema was *the* hot date. The first tentative holding of hands during some particularly tense scene led on to many a romance. The typical adult-ticket-price at the time was 6d or less for the standard seats. Children had a novel way of paying for their seats, which persisted from the early days right up to the advent of the Second World War. They were allowed to pay in kind, by presenting clay jam-jars at the box offices. In return they got free admission and an orange, and cinema managers recouped the deposits from jam manufacturers. And the little angels came in their droves on Saturdays.

Who can fail to forget those famous matinees? Never have so many unwashed urchins with pockets full of 'spice' and ammunition for their 'spud' guns been so tightly packed under one roof. By-laws and fire regulations strictly controlled the numbers allowed into auditoria, of course, but on occasions, cinema managers scratched their heads in disbelief at seeing so many youngsters without seats. These matinees were such riotous events – at least until the lights dimmed – that most establishments needed to employ a ringmaster and 'chucker out'. One such gentleman, who is still remembered with affection and not a little terror, was Naggy Boynton. A severe-looking man with a military bearing, ginger beard and walking stick, he patrolled the aisles and kept order at the Magnet on the corner of West Dock Avenue and Hessle Road. And he had other duties. His particular cinema – there were dozens like it – was classified as a 'flea-pit' and he was charged with patrolling the lines during the screening of such matinee treats as the *Three Stooges* and the *Bowery Boys* with a brass aerosol-dispenser filled with disinfectant. It has to be said that such delousing was necessary. Boynton's other task – he had an equally mangy mule to assist him – was to wander the streets of Hull, hauling around a mobile advertising hoarding with details of the following week's films. Amazingly, he survived a month of Saturdays in the front line, trying to keep order and the bugs at bay. But it was a hopeless task. Many adolescents, having rifled the pockets of their fathers, took the opportunity of lighting their contraband fags under cover of darkness. And some had no qualms about using their 'spud guns' and pea-shooters on the girls and dropping assorted litter that included orange peel, sweet wrappers, fish-and-chip papers and lighted cigarettes. Some particularly vile creatures created a tidal wave on the sloping floor by urinating when Boynton's back was turned. But when the projector rolled there would be a hushed silence, as serials such as *Batman* left the children on a knife-edge. They just had to come back the following week!

Cinema was the mass entertainment for decades. And then along came Logie Baird and his new-fangled television and, over the years, ticket sales slowed. Efforts were made, of course, to entice customers away from their armchairs, and blockbuster films, particularly the biblical epics, increased audience numbers. Gimmicks like three-dimensional films and new technology in the shape of curved screens and stereo sound-systems helped staunch the flow but, by the end of the 1950s, the golden days were at an end. In addition to television the advent of pop music and the availability of record players provided alternative entertainment, especially for young people. In 1959 many Hull cinemas were closed. The list of casualties in that year included the Rex on Endike Lane, the Eureka on Hessle Road and the Regis at Gipsyville on Hessle Road. In the period between 1959 and 1961, Hull lost sixteen cinemas. Many were demolished for building sites or road widening. Others were converted into shops or bingo halls and for a time it looked as though the cinema, like the old-time music hall, might become extinct. Happily, Le Prince's vision flickers on.

17

HEROES OF THE HUMBER

Read any book about great Hull characters and you will find few references to two men who, by their selfless acts, deserve a prominent place in the annals of the city. In common with many of the great and good of the nineteenth century, both were inspired by their sincere Christian beliefs. They are Thomas Thompson and John Ellerthorpe.

'Friend, this Tower, with its wide view, was built in 1825 at Thomas Thompson's expense, for you to see the Humber and the lovely land on every side.' These words are a translation of a Latin inscription composed by Thomas Thompson for his Prospect Tower, a belvedere that still stands in the now incongruous setting of Castle Hill Hospital in Cottingham. Built at great expense as a vantage point, the tower was to be furnished with a table, a map identifying local landmarks and 'suitable extracts from our best poets as subjects of profitable conversation.' But why should any man lay out the not inconsiderable sum of £200 so that his friends could enjoy the view? Why? Because that man was Thomas Thompson, one of the most generous benefactors in the history of a city that still hardly knows his name.

Thomas Thompson was born in Swine in 1754. After obtaining a basic education under the Revd William Stead, he left the village school at the age of 16 and entered the Hull counting house of Russian and Baltic merchant William Wilberforce (whose grandson was to become world famous as the emancipator of slaves). Thompson worked diligently as a clerk, broadening his education in his spare time by studying Greek, Latin and French. But it was his religious experiences that really began to shape his life. His conversion to Methodism and the preaching of the Revd Joseph Milner at Holy Trinity Church gave him moral parameters that were to produce a career that would grace any age. For over fifty years, with hardly a blemish on his character, Thompson, who was described by his employer as 'a man of the first character in Hull', attained the rarest heights. He successfully combined careers in banking, business and politics with integrity and an overriding commitment to his fellow man.

By the force of his intellect, Thompson quickly made an impression on his employer. His steady advancement enabled him to marry Philothea Perronet Briggs, a fellow Methodist of some piety, in 1781. The couple lived at 17 Lowgate in Hull, moving into 25 High Street (now Wilberforce House) in 1798. This imposing property was used by Wilberforce and his partner as a business base and it was shared by Abel and Smith, a fraternity of bankers. In the offer of more commodious accommodation and partnerships with both firms, Thompson had clearly made his mark.

At the end of the eighteenth century, banking was becoming more sophisticated. The safe keeping of specie and the advancement of short-term business loans were still the core businesses for most banks but, gradually, financial institutions like Abel and Smith began to issue their own handwritten notes and to cater for a wider clientele. Under the direction of Thompson, the bank from High Street in Hull widened its sphere of operations and developed trading links with London, Yarmouth, Nottingham, Manchester and Thirsk, as well as in Archangel, St. Petersburg, Riga, Konisberg and Pilau.

Under the guidance of the new partner, both firms returned handsome profits and Thompson, had he chosen the obvious option, could have led a life of some ease. But he was fired by religious convictions and became concerned with the needs of those less fortunate than himself. He looked no further than the fields that surrounded his Hull home. Thompson had his roots in farming stock and he was painfully aware of the injustice of the ancient system of tithes. This was in effect a 10 per cent tax levied by the clergy on produce. Thompson lucidly condemned the levy and urged immediate reform. His repeated protestations on behalf of farmers had a special resonance in the years 1799 and 1800 when Yorkshire harvests were badly affected by rain. Thompson was chairman of the Hull Guardians of the Poor at that time and he lobbied hard to help not only agricultural workers but also the urban poor, a process that proved highly successful. At his insistence, soup kitchens were set up in Hull in January 1780. They served 4,000 destitute persons in that month alone. In May, another 6,000 people were fed, and an estimated one person in five of the city's population took advantage of the free food. All the while, Thompson continued writing his pamphlets and preaching in Hull and in outlying hamlets. During his orations, he was often pelted with stones.

Thompson, of course, had ample funds to spend on his growing family and shortly after attending to the urban poor he turned his mind to building a new family home away from Hull and its unhealthy atmosphere. He chose a suitable plot north of the town on a hill in Cottingham and immediately began planting trees as a way of landscaping a modest mansion, which he dubbed Cottingham Castle. Business and his moral commitments did not allow him to commission building works until 1808 when boundary walls and stables were erected. The main construction was delayed 'in the hopes that materials would be cheaper' until 1814. Two years later, the project began in earnest at an estimated cost of £1,800, although 'if I finish it for £2,100' confided Thompson, 'I shall be satisfied.' Built of white brick on two storeys, embellished with towers and mock castellation, the property was used by the Thompson family during the summer months. The cold drove them back to their cosier quarters in High Street as the nights drew in. Cottingham Castle did not survive as long as some Thompson creations, and suffered the ignominy of demolition in 1861.

Agricultural reform always figured large on the Thompson agenda and in 1803 he published a treatise promulgating the economic and social value of endowing cottagers with what was termed 'three acres and a cow'. Some years later a pilot scheme was launched in Cottingham to test the efficacy of the proposals. In the same year, the author also produced a philosophical study on religion and civil laws, and his appetite for affecting change inspired him to run for Parliament, which he entered in 1807. His candidacy was endorsed by Lord Carrington, a sponsor who was highly impressed by his financial abilities.

As the Honourable Member for Midhurst in Sussex he entered the chamber as its first ever Methodist lay-preacher in the momentous year when legislation for the abolition of slavery was passed. The Hull MP, William Wilberforce, who was a close confidant of Thompson, saw his life's work accomplished to great acclaim. Throughout Thompson's twelve-year stint as an MP – he said that the experience had 'spoiled a very good banker and made a very bad MP' – he remained in the shadow of his famous friend. The pursuit of more pedestrian causes failed to register with the Hull electorate. Interestingly enough, it was Wilberforce who opened the way for Thompson's son to become the governor of Sierra Leone, the newly established colony for freed slaves.

If a man's work is a portrait of himself, Thomas Thompson left us the most appealing picture in the entire gallery. In addition to his duties in Westminster – his maiden speech urged the introduction of a minimum wage for cotton weavers – he continued his thriving business. He also embarked on an exhausting round of preaching engagements, produced articles for the *Methodist Magazine*, wrote a succession of books, became chairman of the Hull Dock Company in 1810 and occasionally found time among his marital and parental responsibilities to plant a few trees!

In 1812 he addressed the House, proposing a bill that would require MPs who had been declared bankrupt within the previous six months to give up their seats. He spoke again in 1813, when he addressed the important issue of renewing the East India Company's charter. He opposed the monopoly saying: 'the people of the North Country could build ships to sail round the world, as well as the East India Company' and he also encouraged the promotion of Christianity in China. As a consequence of his oratory, several clauses were introduced to further the evangelical crusade. Back home in 1814, he instituted a scheme to give land to the poor of Cottingham. A selected parcel of land was divided into twenty strips and let for two shillings per annum. The new landowners built cottages on these strips, growing crops on the remaining areas of land for sale. Dubbed the 'Paupers Gardens' the venture was eventually named New Village.

In 1815, Thompson entered the fray, alongside many firebrand

MPs, on the vexed question of the importation of foreign corn. The Corn Laws were designed to keep British agriculture in business and Thompson, as always, rallied vigorously behind the farmers. There was, however, an angry faction within the electorate that saw only the possibility of cheap bread and, in consequence, violence loomed. An alarmed Thompson said that he 'did not expect to escape without some mark of popular vengeance'. And, alluding to sentiments in his home town, he remarked: 'my name is written on the walls accompanied with strong expressions of disapproval (he was being polite!) but my Friends there do not expect that my House or Bank will be attacked.'

During the following year, the ever more confident Thompson continued to ruffle Parliamentary feathers, speaking on a wide range of issues in eleven debates. He emerged as a leading advocate for poorly paid agricultural workers, rousing the Commons with a speech that suggested, 'like sheep, farmers have been shorn down to the skin.' Then, with even greater passion, he attacked the corrupting influences of the state lottery. This lottery had been introduced during the war with France to raise much needed revenue. Its prizes though were not paid in money but in government stock and that, in turn, could only be used to buy more shares in a subsequent lottery! Lotteries, fumed Thompson 'were nothing but cheats and frauds upon the public and the injury that the country suffered by their destroying the moral bounds and ties of society was only known to those who were acquainted with the state of the poor.' Now in full flight, Thompson rounded off a busy year by speaking up for the Greenland whale fishery, the plight of Holderness wool producers and the treatment of children in the cotton factories.

His heavy workload and the frequent nightmarish journeys to London – it took two days over appalling roads – had a deleterious affect on his health. As was the custom, every ailment was addressed by frequent bleeding, called 'tapping the claret', by the many patients who swore by its efficacy. An eminent Hull physician also prescribed such potions as Elixir Paragoric, James's Powder and leeches. Despite his deteriorating condition, he conducted an exhausting round of preaching.

Thomas Thompson made the last of his orations in the House of

Commons in 1818. He supported moves to introduce a national chain of savings banks and spoke twice on the forgery of banknotes. Shortly afterwards, he left Parliament to concentrate on his business and religious interests. He also found time to write, publishing in 1821 *Ocellum Promontorium; or short Observations of the Ancient State of Holderness, with Historic Facts relative to the Sea Port and Market Town of Ravenspurne in Holderness.* His *History of the Church and Priory of Swine* was to follow in 1824, but a double tragedy intervened. In 1823, his beloved wife died and a month later, he lost his daughter.

Thompson kept on working at his bank, and the loss of his loved ones only served to strengthen his moral resolve. In the autumn of 1826 he noticed from the vantage point of Cottingham Castle that three corn mills continued to grind on the Sabbath. He was upset by the outrage and 'called one of the Millers out of his Mill, and reasoned with him on his conduct, as being contrary to the laws of God and man, and mentioned his liability to be fined on complaint being made to a Magistrate.' Following his intervention, all three millers discontinued their Sunday work.

Thompson finally gave up his own work in 1828 at the age of 74. He went abroad for the first time in his life and was taken ill in Rouen, finally dying in a Paris hotel. He was buried in the French capital. A tribute in the *Hull Advertiser* of September 1828 recorded his passing: 'It has seldom fallen to our lot to record the death of an individual more highly respected for his talents and various excellencies than this lamented gentleman.' With the death of Thompson, Hull and the whole of Holderness lost one of its greatest and most generous champions. And his enormous generosity continued even after his death. In his will, he made plain his desire that his servants should be paid for the remaining period of the year in which he died. In addition, they were to receive an extra year's wages.

The next time you pass Wilberforce House in High Street, remember its lesser-known occupant. And do call in to the Hull Docks Museum to see the portrait of a remarkable but barely remembered man.

*

John Ellerthorpe was a simple, largely uneducated man who never deliberately involved himself in any activity likely to alert the public gaze. And yet, for all who know his incredible story, he makes an indelible impression. So, what did he accomplish to deserve, in my mind, the raising of a civic statue alongside those of Wilberforce, Nunburnholme, Johnson and the rest? Well, he was a one-man lifeboat service. By his own unassuming account he saved over fifty people from drowning . . . without a boat.

Like thousands of his contemporaries, he was the son of a seaman and destined to follow his father in the coastal trade. Born in Rawcliffe on the banks of the Aire in 1806, he spent his early days mostly in the care of his grandmother who ran the town's Anchor public house. The coarseness of the clientele, and the unhealthy influence of his constantly inebriated father, who owned a Humber keel, were hardly good examples for a boy. 'He was brought into daily contact with the worst of men,' records his biographer, the Revd Henry Woodcock, 'listening to their ungodly conversation and seeing their drunken habits; his father was an habitual drunkard and took no interest in the intellectual and moral improvement of his children.' The lad often accompanied his father on sailing trips and seems to have acquired many of his faults. Years later, looking back with great regret on this early period of his life, he admitted to being a 'drunken blackguard'.

When Ellerthorpe was 10, the family moved to Hessle where his mother became interested in Wesleyan teaching. Disgusted by the dissolute behaviour of her husband, she began regularly to attend services, taking her son along on one occasion to listen to the famous oratory of preacher John Oxtoby. The young Ellerthorpe was moved by what he heard and later said, 'I was truly converted under his sermon and for some time I enjoyed a clear sense of forgiveness.' It would seem, though, that the redeeming effect was only transitory for, within a short time, John had joined the ranks of the hundreds of rough-and-ready seamen whose conduct attracted opprobrium from the wider community.

Beginning work at the age of 14, he spent three years on the brig *Jubilee* plying the route between Hull and London. Clever, adaptable and quick to learn the ropes, he quickly progressed to the *Ellen* and then to the *Westmorland,* sailing for four years between Hull and Quebec. After a spell in the Baltic trade, he was ready for the command of his own vessel, and he became the proud captain of the *Magna Carta* on the Hull to New Holland circuit. During this period of steady advancement, by his own admission, he was as dissolute as his father, particularly in the consumption of strong liquor.

There was a problem early in his career when an incident aboard the *Ellen* almost ended in him being sent to prison. The *Ellen* worked the Sheffield to London route. After one voyage, she was tied up in the capital awaiting vital repairs, her captain lamenting the cost of mending her torn flying-jib. Ellerthorpe, who was on this occasion the ship's mate, eagerly volunteered for the task on the understanding that if there was any surplus canvas he would be allowed to make himself a pair of trousers for free. The deal was struck, the repair was completed to the captain's satisfaction and John got his trousers. All was well as the vessel sailed back to Yorkshire. Then the scheming captain told him he would not be paid. And then he did something far worse by accusing his shipmate of stealing the trouser cloth. The *Ellen's* owner reported the matter to the police and Ellerthorpe was arrested and locked up. But he pleaded his innocence, and justice ultimately prevailed when a not-guilty verdict was returned.

In 1846, something profound happened to John Ellerthorpe. In a repeat of the visit he paid to the chapel with his mother all those years before, he again went to listen to a sermon, and the oratory he heard in the Nile Street Chapel in Hull changed his entire life. From that moment on, this retired seaman – he had abandoned the sailor's life and entered the service of the Hull Dock Company in 1845 – became a devout Christian.

Although he suffered from an acknowledged 'hastiness of temper, and ruggedness of disposition which cost him a vast deal of watching and praying', he did his best to lead the life of a Christian from then on. By 1856 he had become the foreman of the Victoria Dock. This allowed him to attend chapel on a regular basis and, given the opportunity, he frequently prayed and visited the sick. On some days he comforted as many as twenty afflicted families, and he did this for weeks on end. When Hull was blighted with a cholera epidemic in 1849 – it claimed the lives of 1,860 people; one in forty of the population – he spent hours comforting 'those from whom others shrank lest they should catch the contagion'. And, with others, he preached in the vile garrets, obscure yards and wretched alleys such as those off Leadenhall Square.

All this would, of course, have marked him out as an exceptional man but he had an additional natural talent, and 'betook himself to it as natively and instinctively as the swan to water, or the lark to sky.' Quite simply, he was an amazing swimmer.

Ellerthorpe was always around water. The casual observer might assume that all seafarers have a natural inclination to swim. This is most definitely not the case. Many Hull fishermen eschew this essential skill on the rather tenuous basis that, if they could swim and fell overboard, they would be left to fend for themselves. On the other hand, they argued, vessels were always turned about to rescue non-swimmers. Swimming, it must be remembered, was not taught in schools or indeed by many parents at this time. Youngsters like John Ellerthorpe had to learn for themselves.

He discovered his astounding aquatic ability shortly after his move from Rawcliffe, when an older boy threw him into the harbour. Far from floundering, Ellerthorpe crossed the harbour no less than thirty-two times. The next day he went back for more and swam the length of the harbour twice. Soon he was swimming several miles up the Humber. On another occasion he swam out to a ship that had overturned in the Humber and brought her safely to shore. For this act of heroism, the master of the vessel gave him five shillings.

In the early years, John swam mainly for pleasure, and his prowess in the water attracted the envy of all his friends. He was particularly adept at what he termed 'the porpoise race', which involved deep diving and reappearing at the surface at some unlikely spot. He took many risks in those early days, and later recalled his foolhardiness with some wonder: 'I look upon those perilous adventures as so many foolish and wicked temptings of Providence.'

Over time, the playfulness and impetuosity of youth gave way to a more serious appreciation of his talents, and John began to use his skill for the benefit of others. The great rescuer excelled at his art, and practised it at all times of the year and in every season. He never hesitated and often risked his life to save people in danger. Frequently this meant diving into freezing water in the depths of winter to rescue people trapped under vessels. To add to the hazards he faced, more often than not his rescues were carried out in pitch darkness and in very muddy water.

Ellerthorpe became proficient at his art with no training, and learned how to cope with the thrashings of drowning men by trial and error. He later related that, on many occasions, when he assumed someone he was taking back to shore was dead, the 'corpse' suddenly came alive and grabbed him by the head. This was very dangerous for both parties and Ellerthorpe came close to being drowned many times. Although he became proficient in rescue techniques, those he was attempting to save invariably panicked and made his job much more difficult.

Incredibly, John Ellerthorpe saved not only his father from drowning but also his son. In all, he rescued more than fifty people between 1820 and 1861. Woodcock records some thirty-nine such incidents in great detail. In total, twenty-two people were saved from drowning in Hull, five in Hessle, three in New Holland, two in London, and one in each of the following places: Bridlington, Castleford, Barton, Quebec, Toronto and off the Humber Bank. Three girls, six women, fifteen youths, one elderly man and fourteen other men 'in the strength and vigour of their days' all had cause to thank the Lord for the help of John Ellerthorpe. It is amazing to think that some fifth and sixth generations of families alive today owe their very existence to the crucial intervention of this unselfish man. In his own way, he really did change the course of history.

It is satisfying to record that, in his own lifetime, Ellerthorpe became a local celebrity and was widely recognised and rewarded for his achievements. Local newspapers followed his exploits closely and wrote breathless accounts of his bravery. He was also praised by the Prime Minister, Lord Palmerston, and by civic leaders in Hull. In 1836, he was awarded an inscribed medallion by the Royal Humane Society. Finally, on 6 November 1861, this 'Hero of the Humber' was presented with a gold watch and an inscribed purse containing twenty-three and a half guineas in recognition of his steadfast commitment to his dock work and his achievements in saving lives.

John Ellerthorpe died at the age of 62 in July 1868. His passing was marked by a large public funeral at which many of the mourners spoke eloquently about the life of a remarkable man. In the years since his death Hull has rather forgotten about its inspirational hero, but there is still a chance to make amends. On the bicentenary of his birth in 2006, might I suggest that Hull City Council organises a commemorative, competitive swim across the Humber, inviting the very best swimmers to attend? And, in diving pose, can we have that long-awaited statue to the man? But where would he go? Where better? With his jaw fixed firmly towards the Humber, put him outside The Deep.

18

NONE SUFFERED MORE: HULL IN THE BLITZ

Many people in Hull and elsewhere expected to see bombs raining from the skies as soon as the Second World War started in September 1939. There was a good reason for this: the 1930s was a decade in which many became almost hysterical about the prospect of a German bombing campaign. And it was widely believed in official circles that such a campaign would trigger defeat by demoralising the civilian population and devastating our cities. But the raids by the Luftwaffe simply did not materialise in the six months or so after war was declared. Instead what has become known as the 'phoney war' lulled many into a false sense of security. The first sustained phase of war in the air was the Battle of Britain, which took place between June and September 1940. This was an attempt by the Luftwaffe to gain air superiority over southern England, a necessary pre-requisite to an invasion. But as things started to go wrong the Germans adopted a new tactic – sustained night-attacks by bombers on British cities. Their intention was twofold: firstly, to destroy Britain's armament factories and, secondly, to ruin the morale of the British people. The blitz had arrived.

Starting in August 1940 the blitz would go on until May 1941. As time passed it became less about attacking strategic targets and more about shattering the confidence of civilians. All the big industrial centres were attacked: London, Glasgow, Manchester, Liverpool, Birmingham. Then, in February 1941, the Germans switched the focus to the major ports. Hull, facing on to the North Sea and easily recognisable from the air, would be a sitting duck for German bombers based in Holland and Belgium.

The Luftwaffe planners examined their reconnaissance photographs of Hull and prepared lists of major targets: St Andrew's

Dock; Albert and William Wright Docks; City Docks; Victoria Dock and Timber Yards; Alexander Dock; King George Dock; Electricity Power Station, Skulcoates; Gasworks, Stoneferry; Waterworks, Clough Road; Oil Refinery, Salt End. In the city, preparations were made to repel the expected onslaught. A high concentration of searchlights – a 'dazzle-barrage' – was deployed to disorientate inexperienced flight-crews and anti-aircraft batteries were installed along the Humber approaches at places like Spurn, Stone Creek and Little Humber. By 1940, Hull was defended along its river corridor by thirty-eight heavy guns (twelve were eventually relocated to augment the defences of London), massed city-based batteries, which eventually included two rocket firing 'Z' batteries manned by the Home Guard, and seventy-four air balloons. These presented a formidable shield. Night after night, the defenders of Hull took up their stations and waited.

In the first, anxious months of conflict many people who had lived through the traumas of the previous war experienced the same strange feelings of unreality. Far removed from the carnage of battle, they saw the mounting destruction in mainland Europe as something distant and abstract. And comforted by the age-old adage about fortress Britannia and assured by promises that the war 'would be all over by Christmas', in typical Yorkshire fashion they got on with life. Indeed some optimists even ran out after air raids to pick up hot splinters of bomb casings to keep as souvenirs. The young were especially excited by the audacity and daring of the German pilots. After one largely innocuous raid, hundreds of sightseers walked to see their first bomb crater near the Lambwath stream on the road to Warne.

But the relatively benign phase was about to end. The first major raid took place on the night of 12 December 1940. Two Yorkshire cities – Sheffield and Hull – were the targets. Now the gloves were off and the real war had begun. On a clear and frosty night that was ideal for bomb aiming, the Luftwaffe came en masse, bringing terror to inner Hull. Soldier Bill Davenport from Halifax had just left a Hull pub and he can remember lingering on the corner of Alfred Gelder Street, listening to the approaching drone of aircraft. Criss-crossing shafts of light stabbed the night sky as sporadic gunfire at some distance caught his attention. Then he heard the scream of a German bomber and ran.

Instinctively, he dived behind a low wall to escape from a shower of incendiaries, as the devices sputtered in devastating fountains of white fire. Soon every other street in Hull seemed to be filled with roaring flames, and the silhouettes of factory premises, church steeples, chimneys, wharf-side gantries and ships stood out against the deepening orange glow. Heeding the shouts of a frantic warden, Bill sprinted for an air-raid shelter. But he never made it to the door. He recalls the moment when a bomb struck:

> At that moment there was a sound like a mighty hosepipe swishing and an explosion which lifted me right off my feet. I remember hearing a tinkling showering of glass and a heavy rumble of falling bricks and wood and before that had even finished I heard a wail, a cry of a child. There was a house across the street with the front wall completely off, rooms open to the sky like a doll's house and in the blackness of what must once have been the front room a child was screaming loudly. I ran across, stumbled over the piles of rubble, window frames, joists and into the blackness towards the skin-crawling sound. I found the child, her thin arms, felt for her body, her legs . . . and stopped as my hand leapt upwards from a warm stickiness. I forced my hand down again and felt the frayed pulp and splintered bone.
>
> I picked her up, she must have been about eight, and ran as fast as I could to the street shelter. There a First Aid woman quickly laid bare the thin little stump below the knee and covered it with a clean dressing and a kind of elastic, rubbery type of bandage. Someone produced a stretcher padded with blankets and within no time at all the child was wrapped up tightly and carried off to an ambulance post.

This was the reality . . . and the worst was yet to come.

The German planes returned in the spring of 1941, with 1 March witnessing the heaviest raid so far. The incendiaries did their deadly work, as fires in a North Bridge warehouse packed with 20,000 wooden crates, guided the Luftwaffe crews in. That terrible night, hundreds more phosphorus bombs were dropped right across the city. Blazing like a torch, the varnish tanks in the Skulcoates factory went up in flames, and scores of high-explosive bombs rained down in a second baptism of fire. Within minutes of the bomb doors opening, the flames from the burning mills soared to prodigious heights, as dozens of firemen fought a valiant but futile battle at their pumps, where three of the heroes died.

On the following morning, millions of people across the country turned on their wireless sets to hear the news from the BBC that an anonymous 'east-coast town' had been blitzed. Evacuees, especially young children, who had already begun to flee the devastation in large numbers, immediately prayed for their relatives in Hull.

Parents were obviously keen to protect their offspring from the deadly consequences of the air raids, and many elected to send their children to the comparative safety of the countryside. The evacuation scheme also covered mothers, expectant mothers and other vulnerable people such as the aged and the infirm. Hull evacuated some 92,000 of its citizens during the war years. The majority of these were unaccompanied children, with many of the youngsters going to villages throughout the East Riding and beyond. Typically, a group of fifty-four children from the Holderness Road area of Hull went to the village of Bishop Wilton near Pocklington some forty miles or so north-west of the city. The *Hull Daily Mail* maintained a keen interest in these evacuees and their welfare. In its 10 October 1941 edition it recorded that, despite many stories of evacuated children being treated badly, many from Hull received a warm welcome from their temporary parents.

The personal memories of these evacuees are no less interesting:

> The day I was evacuated we came on a bus . . . the local children were all stood round looking at us. I remember them looking very pretty, in little bonnets, dressed entirely different from us. I don't know how we were allotted but because I'd sat with these two girls on the back of the bus, I was billeted with them. I went up on the hill to Mrs Stead's. The picture is so vivid; it was the hugest back kitchen you've ever seen with flagstones. Turkeys used to walk in and out while we were eating.

Unaccustomed to rural life, some evacuees in other outlying areas, found the experience confusing: 'We don't get our milk from a mucky cow like that mister,' complained one little lad who was billeted on a farm; 'we gets it from a clean bottle.' Two other children who were staying in far grander accommodation in a country manor, collared the butler with the enquiry, 'When's the bloody breakfast coming?' The shocked servant apologised to the lady of the house, who responded with the words, 'I've been wanting to say that for years!'

Once the raids became more frequent, it is estimated that almost one third of the city's population left the central areas every night. Only the foolhardy, and those who were prepared to take their chances in the far from bomb-proof shelters, stayed at home. If these defiant residents had known the intensity of the firestorm ahead, many more would have chosen to flee the town. Seventy-eight bombers targeted Hull on 13 March 1941. A massive formation of 378 aircraft, carrying a bomb payload of 316 tons, revisited the town on 18 March. Thankfully, a large number of bombs missed their targets.

Then, on the night of 16 April 1941, the truly awful meaning of the word blitzkrieg became agonisingly apparent. The Luftwaffe decided to unleash a new weapon of terror. Conventional bombs, whose nose cones were fitted with acoustic attachments that whistled and screamed on their way to earth, were bad enough but the moaning sounds generated by parachute mines were something else. Floating and swinging eerily to earth beneath parachutes, the mines were packed with explosives that could take out whole streets in one mighty blast. During that April raid, one of these devices landed on the public air-raid shelter in Ellis Terrace killing every one of the sixty people sheltering inside. The exploding hurricane also destroyed hundreds of nearby houses, and five hundred people lost their homes.

And less than a month later, the planes were back. Guided by a bomber's moon, at just after eleven o'clock on the night of 7 May 1941, the Germans unleashed their full armoury of weapons despite the efforts of the anti-aircraft gunners. Incendiaries came first, thousands of them, and the chandelier-type parachute flares quickly started fires in Montrose Street and in the Spring Bank area. Within minutes, it seemed that an inferno had taken hold of the entire city. Seen from above, this vision of hell guided the bombers to their allotted targets, as sticks of bombs rained down on factories, warehouses and homes. A total of 464 fires merged into one massive blaze, and later reports suggested that the burning city could be seen from as far away as the coast of Denmark. Hull was threatened with total annihilation. Firemen, assisted by crews from nearby towns, battled for hours to quench the flames. Such was the intense heat generated by the blaze that window glass melted, and molten flows joined the torrents of pumped water gushing from burning buildings. Water mains were ruptured following repeated explosions, and firemen pumped supplies from the river Hull in a desperate attempt to contain the flames. More reinforcements joined in the battle to save the city, with some firemen dying alongside their machines. With their mission accomplished, the German aircraft turned for home, leaving their target to blaze on.

Burn it did. All night long the fire crews fought valiantly to beat the flames. And they succeeded. By eight o'clock next morning, the exhausted but thoroughly relieved Hull fire chief was able to telephone his counterpart in Leeds with the following brief, but poignant, message: 'All fires now under control'.

The bombers returned, however, on the following night with renewed ferocity. The Riverside Quay was completely burnt out and the timber yards and the industrial buildings in the Stoneferry area and along the line of the river Hull were attacked. When hundreds more fires were finally extinguished, Hull counted the cost. More than 400 people were killed during those two nights of mayhem, and many more were seriously injured. Fatalities were concentrated in the central areas of the town, but many people cruelly died in outlying air-raid shelters in Regent Street in West Hull, St Paul's Street in North Hull and Nornabell Street in East Hull. Many residents lost everything as a result of the bombing and in the eighteen days after the raids some 460,000 communal meals were served to displaced families. The town also lost – either destroyed or seriously damaged – many prominent buildings and businesses. The sad inventory included the Central Fire Station, the Corporation Garage, the Mytongate Telephone Exchange, Holmes Tannery, the Eagle Oil Mill and the retail premises of Thornton-Varley's, Edwin Davis, Hammond's, Powolny's and Reed and Mackman.

After the May raid, apart from two major attacks on 18 July 1941 and 14 July 1943, the bombers returned only intermittently, with little consequence for Hull. Indeed, only the red faces of the hapless German crews in their debriefing rooms caused any heat. On 19 May 1942, a number of aircraft dropped their bomb loads well away from the city. This was because a blazing anti-aircraft battery illuminated by incendiaries drew the attack. The night of 25 July 1943 witnessed another cock-up by the normally efficient Luftwaffe, when every one of the fifty aircraft that carried a combined bomb-load of seventy tons, returned to base with full pods. There was another abortive attack on 20 March 1944, but there were further deaths. Late in the war, Hull had the dubious distinction of being one of very few targets attacked by cannon-firing Junker 88s, when the aircraft descended without warning and raked a crowd of people outside the Savoy cinema on Holderness Road.

It is interesting to examine a German account of the penultimate great raid on Hull. The *Bundesarchiv* in Frieburg provides a view from the cockpit of a Heinkel 111 bomber:

> There in front of us is Hull. In the distance our target area glows fiery red with one large fire and about twelve medium and small fires close by. In unbroken succession other bombs are exploding among them. We are still about three minutes flying time away, and all at once an amazing sight unfolds – surely unique in its way. We are approximately at the edge of the great city so that its vast expanse of houses lies before us, when, immediately alongside the big fire, an enormous explosion occurs. A giant flame shoots into the sky, and like a flash of lightning, lights up the whole city. Every single house, the street patterns, the open squares – right down to the Humber – are dazzlingly illuminated and distinct in every detail. All around us the sky is bright. So bright, in fact, that we can see in front of us three of our attacking planes and, further off, many silver-grey barrage-balloons, poised in the air, plump and still. A unique picture indeed! We on board the He 111 have seen and experienced much action over England, but this stupendous explosion is in a class of its own; indeed we would not have thought it possible. A veritable bullseye!

In November 1944, Hull was visited by the Secretary of State for Air, Sir Archibald Sinclair MP, who described the city as 'this battered but unconquerable stronghold of British sea and air power.' Addressing a packed meeting in the Guildhall, he said: 'I travelled this morning through the blitzed areas, and could see how tragic the sufferings of Hull have been. The Luftwaffe bombed your city eighty-three times, and we think this afternoon of those who were killed or maimed in this protracted struggle. We think too, with pride, of our watchful and heroic defenders.'

Like the stalwart Londoners who endured some of the worst bombing of the war, the citizens of Hull kept up their implacable spirits throughout the ordeal. Acts of selfless courage brightened the dark days of war. On one occasion, a worker in the Rank's Flour Mill rushed into its burning stable to rescue a number of the delivery horses. Calming the terrified animals by pulling sacks over their heads, he led them to safety through an inferno. Another act of heroism saw a policeman knocked unconscious by an exploding bomb as he attempted to extinguish an incendiary. The man was blinded for three weeks. In spite of two broken jaws, a fractured wrist, three broken fingers and facial wounds that required a hundred stitches, he was back on duty within six months.

The determined citizens of Hull are also credited with devising pioneering techniques for rescues from bombed-out buildings. The personnel of the rescue services initiated a method of safely removing slabs from the roofs of collapsed shelters. The efficiency of this procedure was quickly recognised by the Ministry of Home Security, which introduced the so-called 'Hull Lift Method' nationwide. Such resolve in the face of extreme adversity is best summed up in one of Hull's proudest boasts: 'During the bombing, no ship from this port ever missed a tide.'

When the raids finally ceased much of the central heart of the city lay in ruins. In statistical terms, the death and destruction caused by the air raids was minimal compared with that inflicted on German and Japanese cities. In personal terms, however, the devastation was huge and Hull suffered more, in proportionate terms, than any other city in Britain. In total, there were 815 air-raid alerts and more than 1,000 hours under alerts. The official figures, published in 1944, show that 1,200 citizens were killed in the raids and 152,000 rendered homeless. Of the 92,660 occupied houses in the city, only 5,938 escaped damage, while more than 5,000 were completely destroyed. Half the central shopping area was levelled and three million square-feet of factory space was lost. The premises razed included two of the town's three flourmills and several oil and cake mills. Twenty-seven churches, fourteen school and hospital buildings and a theatre were also burnt to the ground. Two hundred and fifty domestic shelters and one hundred and twenty communal shelters were destroyed. It is also worth noting that most of Hull Corporation's buses were written off. Parked overnight in the central bus station, they were an easy target for the bombers. The few vehicles that escaped damage were subsequently dispersed to the city parks.

It is little wonder that Herbert Morrison, a minister in the wartime Cabinet, acknowledged the city's ordeal. He wrote in his autobiography that, due to the fact it was an easy target, 'the town that suffered most was Kingston-Upon-Hull'. One visitor to the city in May 1941 noted that the most spectacular ruins were along the banks of the river Hull, particularly along the east side. Here he saw the smouldering remains of the tall flourmills and stores. And, even worse, to the east and north the many streets of predominantly working-class housing that had been flattened. One of the most impressive bomb holes was in Holderness Road, where there was a crater twenty yards across filled with greenish water. By the side of the crater stood the ruins of the Ritz Cinema.

One odd consequence of the destruction was the proliferation of insects during the warmer months. Thousands of tons of oilseed rape and linseed had been only half burnt in the conflagration. The piles of rancid grain served as a breeding ground for millions of grasshoppers and crickets, whose distinctive calls could be heard from deep within the piles of rubble. In the First World War, poppies blossomed on the scenes of battle. In Hull, a previously rarely seen flower, the rose-bay willow herb, proliferated in much the same way as its botanical cousin, and the swathes of purple spikes covered the bomb sites well into the 1960s.

Of course, there was a grand plan for Hull to arise phoenix-like from the ashes. Hull Corporation recruited the eminent architects,

Sir Edward Lutyens and Sir Patrick Abercrombie, who were charged with drawing up a blueprint for renewal. Vying with the precincts of ancient Rome, this new Hull was never built. Only now, in the new millennium, have the lofty ambitions of that plan – this fascinating document is still available for inspection in the Central Library – been achieved.

19

THE TIGERS ROARED

'Some people think football is a matter of life and death. I can assure them it's much more serious than that.' With no sense of hyperbole, so remarked the great Liverpool manager Bill Shankly. This bluff, no-nonsense Scot also said, 'of course I didn't take my wife to see Rochdale on her anniversary . . . it was her birthday.' It is a long time since any manager of Hull City Association Football Club uttered anything to match the sentiments of Mr Shankly. Only the turbulent recent history of a club that was, for a time, threatened with extinction now seems to make the headlines. Things, however, could have been so much different. And, if events on the pitch had gone better on one fateful day in March 1930, the 'Tigers' could well have been among the elite of English football.

Hull has the unenviable distinction of being the biggest city in Europe never to have been in the top league. Amazingly, the club has never played at Wembley. The city certainly has the population base to sustain large crowds and, once roused, there is no lack of support for the club. So why have the 'Tigers' consistently failed to make the big time? The club has had its fair share of big-name signings over the years and yet its trophy cabinet has remained permanently bare. Is it all down to that agonising 'so near and yet so far' FA Cup run in season 1929/30?

At the beginning of that season, Hull City were in the old Second Division, having just missed out on promotion the previous year. Club manager Bill McCracken had assembled a squad of promising players. The talents of prolific goal-scorer Kenneth Macdonald and team mates Jimmy Howieson, Stan Alexander, Douglas 'Dally' Duncan and Sam Weaver gave the fans hope that promotion to the First Division might just be within their grasp.

The season began well but the team's form had faded by the

start of 1930 when the FA Cup draw saw Hull travel to the ground of Division Three South leaders, Plymouth Argyle. Before a 28,000 crowd, Plymouth were narrowly beaten 4–3, thanks mainly to a hat trick by Stan Alexander. When the black balls came out of the bag for the next round, Hull had some luck. A home draw pitted them against Second Division rivals Blackpool. Although the 'Seasiders' had secured more league points that year than Hull, the Yorkshire side had already beaten them on their own pitch and hopes were high of a repeat performance. Around 23,000 expectant fans crammed into the Anlaby Road ground for the match. Contemporary photographs show that they wore 23,000 assorted flat-caps and trilbies! Many of these were thrown into the air at the final whistle, as the 'Tigers' claimed a famous 3–1 victory with goals from Stan Alexander, Ronnie Starling and Paddy Mills. Bring on the big boys!

In anticipation of the next encounter, the Hull players were pampered with a visit to Hull Corporation's Electric and Vapour Baths. The excited mood of the city rose with the prospect of an away game against either Swindon or First Division championship contenders, Manchester City. Swindon, playing at home, held City to a draw in the first match but, in the replay at Maine Road, they were resoundingly thumped by the astonishing margin of ten goals to one. Game on!

On 15 February 1930 an exodus of around three thousand fans left Hull, some travelling over the narrow Pennine roads by car and others going on specially chartered trains from Paragon Station. Meanwhile, the 'Tigers' left back, Matt Bell, failed a fitness test, and manager Bill McCracken had to make a late and risky tactical change to his team. Jimmy Howieson, a forward, was selected to occupy the vacant position at the back, and his place up front went to Ronnie Starling. After just three minutes, the heads of the visiting supporters dropped. Hull were one down and almost everyone in a crowd of 61,574 expected a rout. But the Yorkshire side rallied and a goal by Paddy Mills after half an hour levelled the score. At half time, the away fans were optimistic. And they had every reason to cheer when, in the second half, Billy Taylor popped in the winner. The 'Tigers' were in uncharted waters, and the draw for the quarter-finals was anticipated with bated breath.

'Number 7, Newcastle United' said the black-ball plucker, 'will play number 2, Hull City.' This time a contingent of 6,000 excited fans left Hull. The *Hull Daily Mail* recorded, 'Never before has there been such a large exodus of people from Hull to one place in the same day.' The place was a bulging St James Park, where 63,486 supporters screamed themselves hoarse in a fiercely competitive cup-tie. Newcastle had most of the possession in the first half, and took the lead with a goal by Tommy Lang. Hughie Gallagher, Newcastle's legendary Scottish centre-forward, had been expected to trouble the Hull defence but close marking by Jimmie Howieson kept him quiet. Eventually the 'Tigers' drew level with a goal from Stan Alexander following a cross by 'Dally' Duncan. And the visitors hung on, as tigerish tackles and desperate saves by keeper Fred Gibson kept the score level. Gibson's efforts were loudly applauded in the national press, and the *Daily Mail* also praised his team mates, Bell, Goldsmith and Childs. That journal's summary of the game seems to point to a crudeness and naivety that compares unfavourably with the skill levels and tactics of the modern game. Nevertheless, at the time, Hull City were buoyed by highly complimentary reports such as, 'Ninety minutes of tearaway football, kick and rush all the time, no clinging to the ball, no nerves and no inferiority complex.'

There was an upbeat mood in the town in anticipation of the replay at Anlaby Road on Thursday 6 March 1930. The whole city was en fete that spring afternoon, and the local council and city traders allowed their employees to leave work early to join a record crowd of 32,930. With rattles whirring and fans cheering wildly the game began, each side probing for an opening. Despite their best efforts, neither team was able to break the deadlock in the first half. But it was a different story after the break when the inspirational Jimmy Howieson broke free and scored a fine goal. Newcastle came back and pushed hard for an equaliser. The Hull fans prayed that their team would hang on. Only the true football supporters will know how excruciating such moments can be. And then came the longed-for final whistle. The crowd went mad and looked forward to the FA Cup semi-final. There was now a very real possibility of walking between the famous twin towers at Wembley.

This time the magic bag delivered a truly daunting tie. City were drawn to play the powerful Arsenal on a neutral ground, Elland Road in Leeds. Under legendary manager Herbert Chapman – who had won three league titles in a row while in charge of Huddersfield Town – the 'Gunners' were pulling out all the stops in their determination to become the leading club in English football. This ambition was epitomised by Arsenal's dealings in the transfer market. David Jack had been signed from Bolton Wanderers for a world-record fee of £11,500. Alex James, described as one of the ten greatest British players of all time, was captured from Preston North End for £8,750. In 1928 James had been part of the 'Wembley Wizards', the renowned Scotland team that thrashed England 5–1 at Wembley. And there was also Cliff 'Boy' Bastin, who Arsenal had bought from Exeter City for a substantial fee. Bastin, who was only 18 in 1930, was one of the most prodigious talents in the country and would go on to win every honour in the game before he had turned 21. The newspapers, noting that Arsenal had the most expensive forward line of all time, gave the Second Division strugglers from Yorkshire little chance.

In the run up to the semi-final the form of both teams could not have been more different. In the league Arsenal beat Manchester United and Birmingham City. The 'Tigers' on the other hand suffered three consecutive defeats, including a 4–0 mauling at the hands of Charlton Athletic. This was hardly the morale boost the club needed ahead of the biggest match in its history.

The big game was scheduled for 22 March. On the day City were accompanied by 11,000 of their fans, who had travelled in special trains from Hull. The 47,549 capacity crowd probably expected the lions of Arsenal to rip the underdogs apart but, encouragingly, City began brightly and after only fifteen minutes they scored. We have all assumed that the lob from distance was a technique first employed by Pele when he audaciously tried to beat Gordon Banks during the famous England–Brazil World Cup game in 1970. Well, according to the report of the Hull City–Arsenal match, Jimmy Howieson got there first! Following a poor clearance by the Arsenal keeper, Lewis, the bold Howieson lobbed the ball straight back on the volley and it flew over the head of the hapless custodian and into the net from a distance of forty-five yards. Full of confidence after such a stunning opener, City pressed forward in numbers and, fifteen minutes later, scored again. 'Dally' Duncan let rip with a powerful drive that sliced off Arsenal defender Hapgood and beat Lewis 'all ends up'. At half time, quite remarkably, the score was 2–0 to the Yorkshire team. Just forty-five minutes away from Wembley!

What magic words did Herbert Chapman impart to his players during the interval? Whatever the secret, the 'Gunners' came out with all guns blazing. They competed for every ball and tried everything to get back into the game. With only twenty minutes to go, the inevitable happened. Jack repaid a considerable portion of his transfer fee when he scored from inside the box. The 'Tigers' fought valiantly to repel an Arsenal attack desperate for an equaliser. Dourly they hung on, until seven minutes from time when 'Boy' Bastin beat the entire Hull defence and smashed the ball into the top right-hand corner of the net. It had taken a wonder goal to keep the aristocrats from London in the cup. A leader in the *Hull Daily Mail* captured the moment: 'Whatever disappointment may linger in the breasts of Hull City players and their thousands of supporters at the team's inability on Saturday to completely spike the guns of the Arsenal, the unfinished semi-final cup tie at Leeds was a game that will remain vivid in the memory.'

Four days cranked by and, all fired-up, the teams met again for the showdown at Villa Park in Birmingham. Ominously, Hull had been weakened by injuries to key men. But the players strode out confidently to meet Arsenal, whose main tactic was to keep the tightest of shackles on danger man Howieson. It turned out to be a controversial match marred by two highly-debatable refereeing decisions that went in favour of Arsenal. The first came in the eleventh minute when the Londoners scored a disputed goal through David Jack, following a centre by Williams. There were many spectators in the crowd who swore that the ball had gone over the dead-ball line before Williams crossed. The referee would later be severely criticised for letting the goal stand. The 'Tigers' stormed back in search of an equaliser but their hopes were dashed after another shocking decision by referee A. H. Kingscott of Long Eaton. After fifty minutes Mr

Kingscott ordered off Hull centre-half Childs for allegedly aiming a kick at Alex James. No one else in the ground believed it was even a foul and the referee was barracked mercilessly for the rest of the game. Childs thus gained the unwanted distinction of being the first player ever to be sent off in a FA Cup semi-final. With Howieson marked out of the match, and Hull reduced to ten men, a comeback was never on the cards. The 'Tigers' battled hard but the vital opening never came. At full time, it was 1–0 to the triumphant 'Gunners', who went on to beat Huddersfield Town 2–0 in the final.

There was widespread disgust in Hull at the performance of the referee. Indeed, the irate Hull City chairman, Dr Durham Pullan, resigned in protest at the match official's poor decision-making. And the local and national press also joined the lively debate about Kingscott's disastrous showing. Commenting on the sending off of Childs, the *Hull Daily Mail* reported: 'On the face of it the dramatic dismissal of the City centre-half suggested drastic punishment for sheer pertinacity, and for the remainder of the game the official in charge got no peace from a crowd that obviously resented his action. I have never heard such continuous booing before on a football ground.' The *Leeds Mercury* noted: 'Hull City's bad luck was in being the losing side in a battle, which neither side deserved to win. An atom of good luck might have turned the game the other way.'

If Hull City had retained eleven men, if they had scored twice against Arsenal and if they had gone on to lift the FA Cup, who knows what football honours might have followed? Success breeds success and the 'Tigers' could have developed a team to emulate the achievements of Manchester United and Liverpool. As it turned out Hull's form deteriorated after the clashes with the Londoners and the team finished twenty-first in the Second Division and suffered the ignominy of relegation. It is instructive to note that Arsenal went from strength to strength after lifting the Cup, which was the first trophy they had ever won. In the 1930s they dominated English football, winning no less than five league titles. According to one historian of the 'Gunners', the last few minutes of the semi-final against Hull were 'among the most important ever played by the club' and proved to the turning point in Arsenal's history.

20

THE GREATEST WEMBLEY FINAL OF THEM ALL

Rugby league suits the northern psyche. It is the most physically demanding contact sport in the world played without the use of body armour. There is a myth, of course, that rugby is an aberration, a contorted offshoot of soccer, and that it was invented by a pupil at Rugby School. A day-boy, one William Webb Ellis, is said to have taken the ball and run with it, 'With a fine disregard for the rules of football as played in his time, thus originating the distinctive feature of the Rugby game. AD 1823.' This is, of course, complete nonsense. The game was invented in the north of England, where teams like Hull Football Club and Kingston Amateurs helped to develop a sport that has slowly shrugged off its whippets and flat-cap image and is now played worldwide.

Hull. One united city, but two diametrically opposed rugby league teams that have existed separately, despite early calls for amalgamation, for nearly 150 years. Over the years, the river Hull has been the dividing line that has separated the fans of these great rivals. Babies from the west of the river are christened in Hull FC kit, infants from the east of the river sport the colours of Rovers. But how can one moderately sized city – which also has a club in league football – sustain two teams? The answer lies in the popularity of this grassroots sport with the wider population and the partisan following it attracts.

Hull Football Club – one of the oldest rugby sides in the world – was the first to take the misshapen ball to its bosom in 1865. The club was formed by a group of former public schoolboys closely connected with St. Mary's Church in Lowgate. The incumbent at the time was the Revd Scott, and old records show that his five sons made up the nucleus of the team. Even in those early days the team had a close rival. A group of men from humbler origins had established the White Star club in East Hull. Before long, the two teams merged and Hull Football Club has been in existence ever since, playing first at a ground at North Ferriby. It was the first in the area to join the Rugby Football Union.

The success of the team must have stirred working-class pride across the city. A number of shipyard apprentices – the eldest was a lad of just 18 – got together to create another new club, Kingston Amateurs, in 1882 and the team was renamed Kingston Rovers in 1885. Rovers' inaugural matches were probably played on rough ground in Albert Street. The first pitch of any importance was on a field at the rear of the Star and Garter pub on Hessle Road, and one of its touchlines was a line of paving stones!

The pioneers of Hull rugby football helped codify the rules and shape the modern game. Their recommendations led to a reduction in the number of players in a team, from an initial twenty to fifteen and, finally, thirteen, following an experimental game between Batley and Halifax. That game abolished the line-out and led to the adoption of a spherical ball. One commentator, who had witnessed the failure of the round ball in a scrum noted, 'the ball as it deserved to, burst.' Hull Football Club also contributed to the formulation of the arcane principles of passing, tackling, scrumming and scoring. Then in 1895, the most successful northern-rugby-clubs took the momentous step of breaking away from the Rugby Union to form the Northern Football Union. Hull Football Club joined the new body immediately, but their rivals delayed affiliating until 1899. It is fascinating to record that the Hull shipping magnate, Arthur Wilson of Tranby Croft, whose name crops up in several chapters of this book, kicked off Hull's opening match against Liversedge on 21 September 1895.

With two ambitious teams playing in the same city, the scene was set for decades of rivalry that would make the skirmishes between Spartacus and the legions of Rome seem like bun fights. The teams met in their first ever Northern Union match at the Rovers ground in Craven Street off Holderness Road on 16 September 1899. Even that initial encounter generated the passionate involvement of the fans, and some men slept overnight in the best stand to guarantee themselves a good view. Playing in their distinctive black shirts Hull, whose nickname is the 'Airlie Birds', were defeated by Rovers (the 'Robins') who secured an 8–2 victory. This was the first of many derby matches that have electrified the entire city and divided family allegiances almost to the point of open war.

There is one wonderful example of fan eccentricity and loyalty that really underlines the utter passion for rugby league in Hull. 'Airlie Birds' supporter Cyril Smith recalled an incident from the fifties. He describes travelling to watch a derby match between the two teams. As he approached St Matthews church at the top of Boulevard, he noticed that a large crowd had gathered, generating much laughter and banter. Two men were in the thick of it, dressed from head to toe in Hull FC colours. Curious to see what happened next, Smith watched as the crowd dispersed and followed the two men who, with feigned gravity, carried a coffin draped in red and white with a dead cock-robin on its lid. The procession moved ceremoniously down to the ground to the strains of 'Old Faithful' – the Hull anthem – and the 'Death of Cock Robin', afterwards making a circuit of the pitch. Finally an 'Airlie Bird' mascot was reverentially placed on the centre spot and the intercession of the gods was invoked for a good victory. Then the match could get under way!

But the most important game between the two clubs took place in May 1980, when the first ever all-Hull Challenge Cup final was contested on the famous turf at Wembley. There was a prelude to this historic encounter on a winter evening in December 1979, when the two teams reached the last-ever final of BBC Two's Floodlit Trophy. A record crowd of 18,500 wondered if Rovers could hoist the trophy for the second time in three years, or if Hull could break their duck after three semi-final defeats? In a hard-fought contest the 'Airlie Birds', whose achievements in that momentous 1979/80 season included third place in the league behind Bradford and Widnes, took the initiative and won by thirteen points to three. Game on!

Hull had begun the cup campaign with a 33–10 win over amateur side Millom at the Boulevard ground and then went on to beat York in an 18–8 home victory. They narrowly disposed of Bradford Northern at Odsal and then got the better of cup favourites Widnes by ten points to five in a fiercely contested match at Swinton in the semi-finals. In their cup run, Rovers won at Wigan 18–3 and then had two fairly comfortable home victories: over Castleford by 28–3, and Warrington by 23–11 before beating Halifax 20–7 in the first of the semi-finals at Headingley. The whole city of Hull was now abuzz with anticipation especially after a fast and furious league game – dubbed 'the final rehearsal' – between the two clubs on 4 April ended in victory for Rovers by twenty-nine points to fourteen. The 'Robins' were now favourites to win the Challenge Cup. But could Hull pull it off? They had last won the cup in the 1913/14 season and they had been runners up on seven occasions since then. Was this to be their golden year?

Local newspapers were full of articles about the rival teams, and the *Hull Daily Mail* published a souvenir edition of the paper on 26 April. The *Mail* also ran a competition to find the most topical or humorous message for both clubs, offering colour photographs of the respective teams to the winners. Mr Ron Goldspink was awarded the Hull photograph for this offering:

> Forget about winning the cup Rovers
> Forget the base or lid
> You'll have more chance while you're down south
> Of catching Hissing Sid.

Miss W. Dalby responded for Rovers with this winning entry:

> Thirteen big fat Airlie Birds
> Sat on Wembley Tower,
> Along came Red Robin
> And devoured 'em in an hour.

There were also radio interviews galore and the impending clash of the titans was the one topic of conversation in every pub in the city. Tickets for the game were as valuable as diamonds and they changed hands for vastly inflated prices. Flags, rosettes and photographs of the key players were draped in shop windows. As the excitement built, British Rail organised a mass exodus from the city by scheduling an incredible twenty-eight additional trains and reorganising the timetable. Hotel rooms were booked in the capital, and thousands of fans organised long weekends that left some local employers fuming.

With the respective teams training hard and discussing tactics, many colourful stories began to circulate about so-called secret weapons. Hull FC finally admitted that a change in their post-training diet had resulted in a change of fortune. Sandwiches had been ditched in favour of meat pies and mushy peas, and this secret ambrosia had ensured twenty-one wins out of twenty-two games played! Across the city, Rovers had a secret of their own. An unnamed West Yorkshire brewery had promised the club a free barrel of beer for every try scored.

As the day of reckoning approached, the respective fans performed their rituals. Among the rival supporters, there has always been great affinity with the respective liveries of the two teams; Hull Football Club sport black-and-white striped shirts, Hull Kingston Rovers wear contrasting red-and-white versions. So, no Hull fan could possibly eat red-and-white bacon rashers on cup-final day and, for the opposition, a good stomping on the local zebra-crossing to 'push the black and whites under' was an essential preparation.

With the prayers recited, the first contingent of fans left Hull's Paragon Station on Friday 2 May in two trains. Twenty-four trainloads of fans, carrying an estimated 20,000 passengers, followed on the Saturday. The carriages resembled mobile breweries, with luggage racks, aisles and freight vans bursting with crates of beer and lager. Before the engines had whistled in salute and left the platforms, some supporters were already well oiled.

The capital nervously braced itself to meet the Yorkshire invasion as the trains sped south. But Londoners had no need to worry. The two groups of rival supporters mingled freely, and toasted each others' health to choruses of 'Old Faithful' and 'Red, Red Robin'. 'We're not a soccer crowd', one fan soberly explained. 'We're just going to see the game – the best game there is. Everyone on these trains loves rugby, not punch-ups.' The exodus spilled out onto the platforms, and the Metropolitan Police marvelled at the good nature of the crowds. 'I don't really know what we're doing here' chirped one bobby. 'But I suppose someone might cut themselves on a beer can.' Some rival supporters linked arms and, before long, all roads to Wembley were awash in a sea of colour. Many ladies in the respective camps wore the appropriate clothing right down to matching pairs of socks and knickers! Fans unfurled home-made banners, and the legend on one particularly eye-catching length of bed linen read: 'Steve Norton stops more people than Humberside Police.'

Many fans made the pilgrimage to Wembley in fleets of buses, others arrived with scarves fluttering from open windows in cars. One contingent of Hull supporters hired a white Mercedes and stuck black-and-white tape all over the bonnet. The enthusiasm of supporters knew no bounds; one disabled fan even struggled to London in a wheelchair, 'I came by taxi,' he said triumphantly, 'It cost me £70 and I've practically blown my holiday money. But it's only once in a lifetime, so I couldn't miss it could I?'

As the fans swarmed onto the terraces, the strictly neutral Hull dignitaries took their seats. Councillors Pat Doyle and Louis Pearlman and Town Clerk Basil Wood waved to the crowd and joined in the community singing. The official delegation also included keen rugby fan Sir Leo Shultz. 'I shall be shouting for the city of Hull' he observed, diplomatically trying to hide a smile. 'I've been a follower of rugby for seventy years and I'm very happy that two Hull teams are at Wembley. It's nice to see rival supporters getting on so well, despite the friendly dissension about the better side.'

As the kick-off drew near, the two teams ran out onto the pitch and 95,000 supporters shouted themselves hoarse. Meanwhile, back in Hull, there was deadly silence. Many shops were shut and the streets were deserted. The vast majority of those left in the city stayed indoors glued to their televisions and radios. The teams lined up as follows. Hull Football Club: P. Woods, G. Bray, G. Walters, T. Wilby, P. Prendiville, J. Newlove, C. Pickerill, K. Tindall, R. Wileman, C. Stone, C. Birdsall, G. (Sammy) Lloyd, S. Norton. Hull Kingston Rovers: D. Hall, S. Hubbard, M. Smith, S. Hartley, C. Sullivan, R. Millward, A. Agar, R. Holdstock, D. Watkinson, B. Lockwood, P. Lowe, P. Rose, L. Casey.

Hull had a nightmare in the opening fifteen minutes. They conceded a try and two penalties and this would ultimately cost them the match. During early pressure, Millward of Rovers found touch in the ninth minute, thirty-five yards from the Hull line. From the tap, Watkinson, Holdstock and Agar worked a good move. Then an excellent pass to Lockwood allowed him to feed Hubbard who rounded Pickerill and beat off the close attentions of Bray and Woods to score a deserved opening try and make the score 3–0. In opening Rovers' account, Hubbard was fouled in a late and unnecessary challenge by Woods, with Bray throwing a punch for good measure. After consulting his touch judges, referee Lindop had no alternative but to award a penalty under the posts. Hubbard converted making the score 5–0 to Rovers. Hull tried to rally but Wileman was cautioned for a dangerous tackle off the ball on the influential Millward who, although he didn't realise it at the time, sustained a broken jaw. From the resultant penalty Stone was penalised for punching, and Hubbard converted the kick to make it 7–0.

The heads of the Hull fans dropped but they got behind their team and, in the twenty-eighth minute, they got their reward. Wileman heeled the ball to Pickerill, who fed Newlove. Racing round the blind side, he drew Smith and sent Wilby racing for the line. He crashed over, shrugging off desperate tackles by Casey and Hubbard to make it 7–3. The score remained the same after a disappointing attempt at a conversion by Lloyd. With half time approaching, Millward dropped a goal for Rovers with his famous left foot to make the score 8–3. With only five points separating the teams at the hooter, Hull fans had high hopes for the second period.

The contest resumed in lively fashion. Arguably the most crucial incident in the whole match erupted in the ninth minute when a lively move by Hull, involving sweet passing between Wileman, Pickerill, Stone, Birdsall, Tindall and Walters with a final throw to Bray, resulted in wild celebration. But the ecstasy of the fans lasted only a few seconds. Referee Lindop blew and disallowed the try for obstruction by Lloyd on Hall. Undaunted, Hull continued to attack. A penalty two minutes later, awarded after Agar had been penalised for feeding, allowed Lloyd to cut the deficit to 8–5. Bellowing loudly, the Hull fans lived in hope as their players surged forward. Apart from a penalty by Hubbard – awarded after Lloyd was found guilty of obstruction – to make the score 10–5 for the 'Robins' it was one-way traffic. But Rovers put up the shutters and, although they fought like tigers, Hull never succeeded in breaking down a stalwart Rovers defence. But they came close, and only a magnificent touchline tackle by the legendary Clive Sullivan in the closing stages of the game prevented a try by Bray. To the final whistle, the inspirational Norton kept Hull's hopes alive but, ruing the decisions that saw three tries disallowed, they finally succumbed and Rovers hoisted the cup for the first time and ran out winners by ten points to five. The Lance Todd Trophy winner that day was Lockwood, and he became the first 'Robins' player to receive it. Norton, who had a superb match for Hull, narrowly missed out on an accolade that, in the history of the game, has been awarded to few players on the losing side.

The final hooter was met by a cacophony of chants and cheers, and the supporters went off either to toast success or to drown their sorrows. There was much celebration and staring into glum pints that night but, amazingly, the Metropolitan Police's tally of misdemeanours for the day was just four arrests for drunkenness.

The fans returned to Hull almost as excited as when they left. The group of Hull supporters in their black-and-white striped Mercedes hooted their way back home. But they broke down at Watford motorway services and a low-loader had to be called. Far from being dispirited, the lads opened a bottle of champagne and began chanting 'We lost the cup' to the amazement of all around. 'They didn't understand the Hull FC humour' explained driver Kevin Horsley. 'But the final memories of the night are still of that big Merc being towed up the M1 on the back of a lorry and, when we got back to Hull, the sign that covered the fish shop on Boothferry Road. It read: "Will the last one out please turn off the lights." '

The greatest sporting day Hull has ever known brought great credit to the city. On the Sunday after the match, Rovers triumphantly returned to Hull and paraded their trophy from the top of an open bus. Large, cheering crowds lined the route. The vanquished Hull side also hired a bus to applaud their own supporters. Afterwards, both teams appeared on a balcony at the City Hall where thousands of fans applauded their heroes. At a civic reception for the two teams in the Guildhall, the deputy Lord

Mayor, Councillor Alex Clarke, said proudly: 'It is an honour to pay tribute to the game and its supporters for their behaviour at Wembley. What a contrast to the Scottish Cup Final [between Celtic and Rangers] and the speech the Provost of Glasgow had to make following the invasion of the pitch. More than 60,000 people from the city of Hull were at Wembley and they provided not one moment of trouble for either the stadium officials or the police.' Many of the players who had the fortune to play in that epic – described by David Bond in his book *Rivals Across The River* as 'the mother, father and Great Uncle Bulgaria of all derbies' – have since become household names. One of the most charismatic players on that day was Clive Sullivan of Rovers. He was a dignified and popular man on, and off, the field. Despite his roots in Cardiff, the Hull public took him to their hearts. He played for both clubs and scored a record seven tries for Hull in one match against Doncaster in 1968. In the history of Hull rugby, he is the only player who has scored 100 tries for both clubs. While on the wider stage he was awarded the England captaincy and an MBE, that winner's medal in the 1980 final was perhaps his greatest achievement. Tragically he died at the age of 42, in October 1985. But he has a lasting legacy. The A63 trunk road into Hull – Clive Sullivan Way – is named in his memory. Sullivan's team-mate that day, Len Casey, another 'Robin' who 'crossed the river' after playing for rivals Hull prior to 1970, also achieved national recognition. He won nine of his fourteen caps while with the 'Robins'. However, an unfortunate incident four years after the final blighted his career. In April 1984 he was playing for the 'Robins' in a league clash with Hull when he was sent off following a set-to with Hull hooker Neil Puckering. What happened next is still the topic of conversation in Hull pubs. On his way to the line, Casey was involved in an ugly scuffle with the 'Airlie Birds' scrum-half Fred Ah Kuoi. Worse was to follow as Casey reacted angrily to a remark and pushed a touch judge. His petulance, at a time when the held the Great Britain captaincy, cost him a six-months suspension, a Premiership winner's medal and an international place on the summer tour to Australia. Alongside Casey on that unforgettable day in 1980 was the talented Paul Rose, a former pupil at Hull's Jervis High School. He set the all-time record as the youngest professional player to pull on a 'Robin's' shirt, at the age of 16 years and 9 months. He also became the first man to be capped for Great Britain as both a Hull and a Rovers player. After that greatest of all finals, Rose divulged a Craven Park secret. 'We used to do it for all the big games, especially the derbies', he explained. 'The forwards were expected to take a sip of sherry before going out because alcohol is supposed to be good for adrenalin.' Players like Rose learnt much of their craft from Rovers immensely gifted player-manager, Roger Millward. Signed as a young stand-off from Castleford for £6,000, he was probably the best investment the 'Robins' ever made. His exceptional coaching skills brought on a succession of local players, making Hull KR one of the top four sides in the country by 1977. He will be forever remembered for bravely soldiering on with a fracture jawbone in that epic final.

On the 'Airlie Birds' side, a number of talented players stand out from that day. There was the charismatic Steve Norton, known affectionately by his many friends as 'Knocker', who was signed for a record fee of £25,000 from Castleford in 1978. A mesmerising player possessing magical skills, he could waltz round opponents with great balance and pace. He was a key player and helped Hull achieve success in the 1980s. Another stalwart was Charlie Stone who, like his opponent Millward from across the river, came originally from a mining background. A former Featherstone miner, who was regarded as one of the toughest forwards in the game, Stone would start work in the pit at five in the morning so that he could work a full eight-hour shift before driving to Hull to play a game of rugby! He was a great leader of the pack, an inspiration to many younger team-mates and held in awe by thousands of fans. Second-row forward Sammy Lloyd was another star buy from Castleford. A goals and points record holder for Hull in the 1978/79 season, he once kicked seventeen goals for Castleford and equalled the record with fourteen in one game for Hull. He became the league's leading goal-kicker with a magnificent tally of 172, including two vital goals in the semi-final win over Widnes. The name of full back Paul Woods also sticks in the memory. A product of Welsh Rugby Union, he was originally recruited by Widnes. He proved to be a real bargain and was, without doubt, one of the most aggressive players ever to don a black-and white-shirt. And we must mention Graham Walters who joined Hull in October 1979 from Kidwelly Rugby Union in Wales after scoring two tries as a trialist. A real hard man, he was a judo expert, former amateur boxer and soldier. But, on that magical cup final day, not all the players hailed from 'foreign' parts. Following in the footsteps of his father, who also played for Hull, prop Keith Tindall was a local lad who came through the ranks at the Boulevard and made the position his own.

All the players who fought out the Challenge Cup final in 1980 are, over two decades on, still the subject of fierce debate in what is undoubtedly the most rugby-crazed city in the world. Every available ticket for the game was eagerly snapped up by fans, and many changed hands at extortionate prices. The city of Hull could have filled Wembley twice over that day. Strange and annoying then that, in September 1988, eight years after the event, a number of unused tickets in mint condition came to light. They were sold for charity by the Wakefield branch of the mental health charity MIND and were quickly snapped up by souvenir hunters anxious to remember what was described in 1980 by Rugby League secretary Sumner Baxendale as 'the greatest Wembley final of them all'.

21

THE RAILWAY COMES TO TOWN

The flesh falls from our bones as we cling on to an illusion of permanence. We find our hallowed plot and try to fend the world off as it hurtles through space. We particularly resist technological change, complaining about everything from the art of making fire to the science of the human genome. It was always the case, and the proposals to link Hull with the growing rail network in the nineteenth century aroused more resistance than most.

Imagine a world without railways and imagine a coach journey from Hull to York in the depths of winter. In the mail coach in December 1787, you would have set out 'about half-past three in the afternoon' from the Cross Keys in Market Place, Hull 'with a guard, well armed'. The fare was ten shillings and sixpence 'inside' or, God forbid, five shillings and three pence 'outside'. Your money would, if you were lucky enough to avoid highwaymen and broken axles, have given you six hours of pelvic pounding. The late start ensured that meals were well digested lest they reappear along the way in Beverley or Market Weighton. Even in good weather, the dust-choked passengers on the outside would be expected to get out and push on the return journey up Arras Hill, near Market Weighton. And, if the wind blew, as it did on 7 January 1839 even first-class muscle would be press-ganged into action: 'For an hour and a half the mail-coach horses could not contend against the wind. The inside passengers of the Beverley coach had to get out and support the vehicle from being overturned.'

In 1832, a fleet of stagecoaches – the *Rockingham, Rodney, Trafalgar, Wellington, True Briton, Express, Telegraph, King William* and the *Queen Adelaide* – all ran from Hull. Their romantic names and the picturesque images of the old 'flyers' on Christmas cards distorted the reality of a transport system that was archaic, unreliable and dangerous. Indeed some passengers were, on occasion, frozen to death in theirs seats. But by 1832, there were unstoppable forces at work to end the domination of the horse. A new beast had been forged when George Stephenson's iron horse first took to the tracks seven years before, in 1825. The age of the locomotive had begun and, with the opening of the Leeds–Selby Railway in 1834, there were calls for Hull to join the race for modernity. Predictably, however, there were dissenting voices, and the objections of wealthy landowner Robert Raikes of Welton typified the attitudes of those who wanted to protect the status quo. The railway, observed Raikes, would be 'a very real nuisance forever destroying all the present advantages of scenery and rural and picturesque privacy.' But there were other, more compelling reasons for resisting change.

When the Hull–Selby line was first mooted, both towns were already served by efficient steam-packets that operated along the Humber and the Ouse. The vested interests of the owners of these vessels, and the speculative nature of the newly opened railways, generated a mood of caution. With so many businessmen in positions of influence in local politics, Hull aldermen had earlier decided not to support the Leeds–Selby project and they were suspicious of the ultimate extension of the line to Hull. The impetus for change had therefore to come from private quarters.

Undeterred by the sceptics, Hull customs officer John Exley initiated a campaign for a new railway. In an enthusiastic open letter published in the *Rockingham* newspaper in December 1833, he addressed the bankers and merchants of the town, writing, 'on the necessity for, the utility of and benefit to be derived from a rail road from this town to Selby.' The most persuasive part of his argument was that investors in the project were likely to enjoy a 10 per cent dividend on their investment. Supported by articles that suggested a railway needed to be built to counter the economic threat from the burgeoning port of Goole, the idea took root and prospered. In a few years railway mania would lead to a dash to invest in the new technology. The fear of missing out on the benefits of the transport revolution prompted Hull's Guardian Society for the Protection of Trade to recognise the threat of inertia. In February 1834, it issued its own battle cry: 'if immediate steps are taken to bring about so desirable an object, it will probably put an end to the projected railways from Scarborough and Bridlington which if carried into effect will no doubt prove highly injurious to the port.'

The commercial argument was won. The painful moment of truth had arrived when all Yorkshiremen had to take a great intake of air and dig deep. Two local bankers, George Liddell and James Henwood, raised an initial sum of £20,000 to facilitate survey work and the process of seeking parliamentary approval. At the same time, a number of directors were recruited. Most of these were local men, although it is interesting to note that the famous Leeds entrepreneurs, Benjamin Gott and John Marshall, also joined the board. Belatedly, Hull Corporation, with one hand clinging nervously to its corporate wallet, committed £30 to the scheme! Within a few months of the prospectus being released, £100,000 of working capital had been secured and preparations were advanced to obtain parliamentary approval and to identify the preferred route and the location of stations. The consequences of what happened next are still being felt today.

A casual glance at the modern map shows that the Hull–Selby line was built in the wrong place! From Howden, it gets a sniff of the estuary and hares off to the middle of nowhere. Logic suggests that, en route to Hull, the line should have served the settlements of North and South Cave and Welton. Although the railway engineers came to a similar conclusion, it had to be built elsewhere to satisfy the complaints of Robert Raikes and another local landowner, Mr J. R. Pease of Hesslewood House. Raikes and Pease had their way, and Raikes even received compensation of £10,000 together with an assurance that no station would be built on his land. The sensible route was duly abandoned in favour of a line along the foreshore. And there was still the religious lobby to contend with.

A petition was raised against the railway by the Hull clergy, its magistrates and merchants. These citizens were outraged that the trains would violate the sabbath and they insisted that a clause be inserted in the bill prohibiting Sunday travel except under special circumstances. The grievance was given due consideration, but common sense prevailed. The petition was rejected and, in June 1836, the bill passed into law. Hull would have its railway.

During the next four years the line, which was thirty-one miles long, would boldly link Hull with Manchester and the port of Liverpool. The construction process was relatively straight-forward. Including the cost of rolling stock, total expenditure was some £700,000. The Hull terminus was sited in Kingston Street, west of Humber Dock. Upon completion it was described by Henry Broadley, the chairman of the Hull and Selby Railway Company, in glowing terms. Broadley went onto declare that: 'the stations on the line are at Hessle, four miles from Hull; Ferriby, seven; Brough, ten; Staddlethorpe, sixteen; Eastrington, nineteen; Howden and Bubwith, twenty-two and Cliffe, twenty-eight.'

The great day of opening was fixed for 1 July 1840. Preparations for the event went on for weeks in the hope of organising one of the biggest carnivals in the town's history. Fate, however, brought a deep depression from the Atlantic, and incessant rain considerably dampened proceedings. Nevertheless, shops were closed throughout Hull for the occasion and many places of business were shut up as almost the entire population, controlled by a large contingent of policemen, joined in the fun. Would-be passengers gawped at the incredible accomplishments of science and perused the first timetable as bands played and the directors of the company entertained their guests in style. According to a newspaper report, a 'cold collation was spread over fifteen tables . . . seven hundred and sixty dishes, exclusive of vegetables, were laid and included every delicacy of the season.'

Henry Broadley waxed lyrical about the advantages of his new railway. However, at one juncture he spoke of the difficulties encountered along the way: 'at one time, their magnitude was so great', he confided, 'that it came under the consideration of some of the directors whether it might not be better to abandon it altogether.' A succession of distinguished guests then joined him in toasting the new railway. There were so many toasts in fact – there was even one to 'The Ladies of Hull' – that none of the guests could possibly have remained standing!

The Revd H. Bromby, of Holy Trinity church, did manage to struggle to his feet. He then affirmed, to loud cheers, that as far as running trains on the sabbath was concerned, for his part, 'he did not consider it sinful to go into the county on Sunday to enjoy the fresh air and the society of friends.' Other speakers included Thomas Wilson – the father of Charles Henry and Arthur who went on to develop one of the most successful shipping companies in the world. Wilson suggested prophetically that the Hull–Selby Railway would be 'a keystone to future prosperity'. Also in attendance was another man of destiny – George Hudson, who would later become known as the 'Railway King'.

Away from the back-slapping, the real business of the day went off without a hitch. The sparkling locomotive *Prince* (the other engines were *Kingston*, *Exley*, *Andrew Marvell* and *Selby*) left the station just after midday, taking just two hours to reach Selby. She covered the thirty-one miles of the return leg in an astonishing sixty-five minutes. The travelling public was well pleased, so much so that 4,526 passengers forked out for a ticket in the first week alone. Five weeks after opening, a derailment at Wressle caused five fatalities but this was a minor setback and the railway went from strength to strength, with new lines being opened in quick succession.

Within a few short years, the commercial merits of network expansion convinced even the sceptics to stand aside, and Hull soon had direct links with Doncaster, Barnsley, Hornsea, Bridlington and Scarborough and Holderness. The intricate network of lines linked the port with every major town in the country, and myriad little stations across the East Riding and elsewhere. The coming of the railways boosted the local economy and enabled Hull to become not only the biggest deep-sea fishing centre in Britain, but also the third largest port. Its eleven docks and twelve miles of quays were served by around three hundred miles of standard-gauge railway line and scores of engines. Indeed, such was the sheer volume of rail traffic using the docks in their heyday that a queuing system had to be introduced. Hull Wagon Control organised the flow of empty trains and the marshalling of loaded wagons in the vast assembly-yards west of the city. In 1935, these yards were greatly improved and equipped with wagon retarders, floodlights and a control tower, and thirty sidings provided space for around three thousand wagons.

Take a map of Hull and environs from the early days and be

amazed at the spider's web of lines that connected the outlying villages with the port. Imagine now a great Thompson Class B1 engine thundering, with smoke belching, through the leafy suburbs of Willerby and Kirkella. Stand for a moment beneath the serene spire of the 'Queen of Holderness' (Patrington Church) to recall a Stanier Black Five as it steamed with carriages filled with excited holidaymakers on their way to Withernsea for a summer break. Closer to home, you will identify stations at Botanic Gardens, Stepney, Wilmington, Southcoates, Marfleet and Cannon Street. Each of these had a spick-and-span ticket office, a station-master complete with uniform, luggage porters, a lamp man and a roaring fire in the waiting room during winter!

You may also notice on the map the position of four locomotive sheds. Botanic Gardens and Dairycotes – at one time, the latter was the largest engine shed in the north-east of England with six turntables – served the North Eastern Railway. Springhead and Alexandra Dock were allied to the Hull and Barnsley Railway. In 1914, this railway company alone employed 3,500 men. The Botanic Gardens shed mainly catered for passenger locomotives. Dairycotes, which was closer to the marshalling yards, was primarily a freight-engine facility. All four sheds combined could accommodate over three hundred engines.

Springhead was built on agricultural land near the waterworks, and early photographs show boys proudly posing on the running plates of engines they had just cleaned. In 1912, 16-year-old apprentices were paid ten shillings for a fifty-three hour week. At the age of 22, they could expect to earn a whole pound. Interestingly enough, a similar photograph taken during the period of the Great War in 1918 shows a party of female polishers in similar mode dressed in mob-caps, coat overalls and trousers.

The impact of the railways on the economy and character of Hull was immense. The railways brought thousands of jobs to the city and kept the mines and machines of the industrial West Riding running. Millions of tons of coal were exported, and woollen imports came in from Australia and New Zealand for the Yorkshire textile industry. Timber and grain were also important commodities. Fish of course left the port by the trainload, and St

Andrew's Dock in the 1950s bulged with fish trains that could reach their destinations in under twenty-four hours from the time the trawlers landed. It seems to be prodigal now but, in the fifties, there was an endless supply of fish of every variety, and Hull's eight fish trains served an amazing one thousand stations and in the region of four thousand distribution points. At every hour of the day and night, trains rattled by. Noise and vibration, soot and smoke, and the visual and nasal impact of ten-ton wagons loaded with fish became an integral part of Hull life as the infrastructure of the network imprinted itself upon the architecture of the city. At every corner, there were viaducts, embankments and cuttings and, within the city boundaries alone, there were thirty-five high-level bridges. It was even claimed that the layout of the railways deterred crime. Such was the proliferation of level crossings guarding all the main arterial routes into Hull – on the instructions of the police, these could be quickly closed in the event of a major crime – that no sensible criminal would, it was said, dare operate in the city.

For a while, it seemed that the universal march of the railways was unstoppable. Then along came a little man with a red flag. The age of the internal-combustion engine had dawned. At one time, everyone and everything was transported by rail but, between the 1920s and 1930s, the railway companies began to close their loss-making stations and to curtail some services. All thoughts of retrenchment receded, however, during the Second World War when the value of the railways had to be exploited to the full. With peace came the prospect of a bright new dawn. Nationalisation promised much but ultimately delivered little. Poor management, a lack of long-term investment and the absence of a strategic plan, coupled with increasing competition from road transport, led to the publication of the infamous Beeching Report in March 1963. The report recommended the closure of a third of the national network and the consequential axing of around 300,000 jobs.

The deed was done and Hull lost part of its heritage. Opened in May 1853, the three-mile long Victoria Dock Line finally closed in 1968 and the six level-crossings at Spring Bank, Park Road, Beverley Road, Dansom Lane, Bankside and Holderness Lane were removed much to the relief of harassed motorists. Victoria Dock itself closed in February 1970 and has since been filled in and occupied by a housing estate. As for the rest of the network, it survives in skeletal form. A glance at a modern map of the Hull area reveals just two remaining lines: one to Selby and Leeds, and the other to Bridlington and Scarborough. Even the latter was threatened with closure – but reprieved – in 1969 following the biggest protest of its kind ever mounted. In a year, the line was estimated to chalk up some 2,300,000 passenger journeys covering around forty-four million miles.

Today, you can still take a train from Paragon Street Station but the general advice of passenger groups and regular commuters is to leave plenty of time for your journey. In 1885, the Hull, Barnsley & West Riding Junction Railway issued the following timetable announcement: 'Greenwich time is kept at all stations'. What a pity its modern successors cannot say the same.

22

HE HATH EATEN SOME HULL CHEESE

There are bars in every port in the world. Alcoholic beverages seem to have an uncanny affinity with salt air and seamen. Hull is no different and the story of its seafaring tradition and public houses are inextricably linked. In Hull, brewing and ale drinking are as old as the town itself. Ale was a favourite of the Anglo-Saxons and the Danes well before the establishment of the port and the introduction of Christianity. In the Middle Ages, ale and bread appear to have been considered necessities. By the thirteenth century, statutes had been enacted fixing the price and quality of a drink brewed in great quantities by the owners of large estates and the inmates of religious houses. No self-respecting abbot would produce an unpalatable pint. Indeed his head brewer had to swear four times to God on the purity of his ale, and to mark his barrels with four crosses. Wyke, the settlement that would ultimately become the new King's Town on Hull had, of course, a number of monastic establishments. Their expertise, following the Dissolution of the Monasteries in 1536, passed into the hands of lay brewers who had already established a lively trade in the town.

Drunkenness and debauchery were major problems in Hull during the sixteenth century. The authorities, who were anxious to improve public morals, attempted to reduce ale consumption and decrease its strength. In 1560, mariner George Shaw – a former sheriff – was convicted of keeping an unlicensed alehouse and imprisoned for three days as an example to others who flouted the draconian regulations. These prescribed that all strangers to Hull were to be provided with good, value-for-money lodgings, and stipulated that inns were to be reserved for travellers on horseback. Taverns were to be kept for those arriving on foot. Both inns and alehouses were to have a minimum of two beds although, interestingly, they were allowed to 'accommodate as many as could sleep there'. A curfew bell was to be rung in both types of establishment at eight o'clock in the evening and no new visitors were to be admitted after that time. Every inn and alehouse had to display a suitable sign. No drinks were to be served except at mealtimes and servants were to be denied entry unless they were engaged on their masters' business. Provided they had a minimum stock of ale of four gallons, alehouses were required to serve all customers and they were deemed to be in breach of the code if they refused to proved overnight accommodation. Hull landlord Anthony Winter was fined heavily in 1603 for refusing to accommodate 'poor maimed soldiers'. He was further chastised for allowing his customers to play backgammon! As far as the actual brewing was concerned, proprietors were allowed to brew beer but not ale. If this beverage was requested by guests, it had to be bought in from the 'tonners'.

By 1574, Hull had twenty-one licensed brewers, ten inns and twenty-nine alehouses. This plethora of establishments led to condemnation by the authorities of the attendant drunkenness and public disorder 'which do abound by reason of the great number of alehouses, the unreasonable and excessive strong ale by brewers there brewed and the continual and disorderly repair of people to these lewd houses.' In that year, the bench demanded even stricter adherence to its codes, encouraging a reduction in the brewing of beer and ale to address both the moral concerns and the need to conserve stocks of malt and fuel squandered by the brew houses. In 1593, aldermen were empowered to inspect each ward in the town and weed out those licensees who were unfit to follow an honest trade. Brewers were prohibited from purchasing their malting corn in the local market, especially after a bad harvest, and made to travel to the country for supplies. Then, in 1597, alehouses were closed to all but genuine travellers in an attempt to conserve grain stocks. Any beer or ale drinker who was apprehended in an alehouse was punished, having the choice between a fine of three shillings or a week in prison! But the number of offending houses increased; such was the depressed state of the local economy that some people could only support themselves by brewing. By 1630, there were forty-two alehouses in Hull, and new premises also sprang up on the outskirts of the town in Hessle, Anlaby, Ferriby and Kirkella.

By the middle of the seventeenth century, High Street, which was Hull's main thoroughfare, had no less than twenty-five taverns (some later records show a tally of fifty) along the few hundred yards of its length. Drinkers embarked on the ultimate pub crawl to visit the George and Dragon, Dog and Duck, Brotherton Tavern, White Swan, Lincoln Arms, Old English Tavern, Old Harbour, Sheffield Arms, Knaggs Head, Abercrombie, Edinburgh Castle, Square and Compass, Yarmouth Arms, Globe, Prince George, Hammer-in-Hand, Anchor, Unicorn, Fleece, Tigress, Doncaster Arms, Regatta and Black Boy. Adjacent to the river, which was the only mooring point until the construction of the first dock in 1778, the narrow High Street attracted a large and disparate clientele of seafaring men, merchants and ne'er-do-wells. The cramped taverns acted as lodging houses, drinking dens and dubious places of business. Unsanitary and verminous, they were nevertheless perversely attractive places, much like the dockside Spy Glass in *Treasure Island*.

The beetling premises in High Street, with their intimate little rooms, dark-raftered ceilings and inglenooks, must have heard enough conversations to fill a hundred novels. And one of its still surviving taverns, the Black Boy, provided more inspiration than most. The infamous Black Boy first mentioned in 1331. In its seven centuries, it has variously served as a tavern, a private residence, a corn-merchant's warehouse, a coffee shop, a brothel and a tobacco-and-snuff shop. During the early part of the eighteenth century its cock-pit, discreetly located to the rear of the premises, attracted large crowds. It was also well known at this time as the haunt of smugglers. A tunnel was reputedly dug under High Street to connect its cellars with the riverside wharves, and another subterranean passage – excavated during the Civil War – led to the parish church. The tavern's distinctive name, though, was only coined at the end of the seventeenth century when the building was converted to sell tobacco and snuff, staples in every alehouse in the land. In order to promote his business, the enterprising new owner placed a full-sized figure of a high-caste Mohammedan in the doorway of his shop. And he installed another attraction, a black Moroccan slave, who acted as an eye-catching door boy. The Black Boy also has another attraction. It is said to be haunted by an ethereal figure dressed in a top hat and white pantaloons.

Not far from the Black Boy, in the Land of Green Ginger, is the establishment reputed to be the oldest, continually licensed pub in Hull, probably dating from 1449. The George also has another claim to fame. It has what is regarded as the smallest window in Hull; no bigger than a shaving mirror, it is in fact a spy-hole through which the night porter could watch for the arrival of coaches.

Away from the riverside dens, a peculiar type of drinking establishment known as the mug-house developed in Hull. These sprang up during the eighteenth century when up to 15,000 troops were deployed in the town to counter the threat of an invasion by the French. The number of licensed premises in Hull between 1740 and 1794 rose from 103 to 187. The mug-house took its name from the practice of hanging personally owned mugs and tankards on hooks, either over the bar, in windows or even on rails outside. These establishments were a favourite resort of political candidates and their supporters, although they achieved a certain notoriety leading to criticism from the Tory party during the election of 1713. One contemporary record describes the Whig Mug House in Whitefriargate with its 'signe-borde of a Quart Mug over th' Doorsteade'. It goes on to refer to others such places as 'Nests', 'Dens' and 'Free an' Easy clubs' giving their locations as Trinity House Lane, Low Gate and Sewerside. The ale sold in these mug houses was invariably brewed on the premises – John Ward established a commercial brewery, the forerunner of the Hull Brewery Company, to supply multiple outlets in Dagger Lane in 1765 – and Hull developed a reputation for the strength of its brews. In its intoxicating history, Hull can record some eighty or so breweries with names like the Globe, the Imperial, the Golden Gallon, the Popular and the Neptune. John Taylor, the well-known poet who knew a thing or two about good ale, visited Hull in the early seventeenth century, paying tribute to his hosts at the Kings Head in verse:

Thanks to my host and hostess Pease,
There at mine inn each night I took mine ease;
And there I got a cantle* of Hull cheese.'

*a small piece or segment

The treacly, honey-rich brews concocted by the landlords at the Kings Arms and other neighbouring inns, put 'hairs on your chest' to quote the local vernacular. Taylor described the ale thus: 'Hull cheese is much like a loaf out of a brewer's basket – it is composed of two simples, mault and water, in one compound, and is cousin germane to the mightiest ale in England.'

Such were the intoxicating properties of this brew that the phrase – 'He hath eaten some Hull cheese' – became a common euphemism for describing drunkenness. Indeed, the overwhelming strength of the ale contributed to the widespread reputation of all Yorkshire beers, which were collectively known as 'Yorkshire Stingo'. Hull's contribution to the county's brewing hall-of-fame was so celebrated that it was feted in a poem; the ditty, 'In Praise of Hull Ale', was regularly aired at the King's Head to the strains of 'Greensleeves'.

For centuries, the local alehouse was a sanctuary for working men who drank hard and were oblivious to the strength of 'Hull Cheese'. Dry, warm and commodious, these establishments offered convivial company away from the squalor and overcrowding of the nearby court housing. Men often escaped the misery of dingy rooms filled with complaining wives and bawling children (the ladies had nowhere to go!) to spend a mind-numbing hour or two with their friends. Publicans offered further temptation by installing back doors that offered immediate access from the slums. Some employers also directly encouraged patronage by paying out weekly wages in bars. Such was the popularity of the drinking house in Hull that it was reckoned that the town had one of these so-called 'Tom and Jerry' or 'Swankey Houses' for every twenty homes.

Along with gin, 'Hull cheese' was always popular in the town. Its sales received a further boost when the social evils of drinking gin – the so-called 'mother's ruin' – were recognised by Parliament. Such was the polluted state of the town's water, that gin was the preferred tipple of much of the local population including children.

Gin production was actively encouraged by landowners as it consumed vast quantities of corn. In addition the spirit was so ridiculously cheap – it was hardly worth smuggling – that at the height of the gin era between 1740 and 1742, it has been estimated that, in some inner-city areas, it accounted for twice as many deaths as births. The government decided to do something and an Act of Parliament in 1751 greatly increased the tax on spirits. The Beerhouse Act of 1830 further reduced the demand in favour of beer by halving the duty on beer and actively encouraging any person of good character to apply for a beerhouse licence costing two guineas. Within twelve weeks of it becoming law 25,000 licences had been granted in England and Wales, and the walking distance between the taverns on High Street became even shorter.

Some of the more enterprising of the Hull publicans had a dual role, selling not only beer but also their skills as cobblers, blacksmiths and carpenters. The symbols of their professions naturally found their way onto tavern signs. At a time when window glass was prohibitively expensive, signs were the only way of declaring to the world that there was drink inside. Hull boasted a galaxy of brightly coloured boards that offered, to the footloose person who refused to get his lips wet, a potted social history of the town. There was, at the corner of Chariot Street and Waterworks Street, a ramshackle inn called The Sweeps whose board declared beyond a doubt that you could have soot with your cheese. The inn was kept by two chimney-sweeping brothers, and the sign of their calling showed a sweep with his brushes followed by his apprentice son. Some wag wrote underneath the board the words 'The March of Intellect' and the inn subsequently adopted this name. In Fetter Lane was the Marrowbone and Cleaver, its sign referring to an ancient Hull custom of serenading newly married couples. Local butcher boys would annoy the lovers by banging together shank bones and meat cleavers under the marital window until they were bribed to leave.

Heroics on the battlefield were widely trumpeted on scores of pub signs. The Vittoria, built on land reclaimed from the Humber near the pier, saluted the famous victory of the Duke of Wellington in northern Spain. The Lion and Key – the sign showed a lion with a large key in its paw – recalled another of his conquests at Ciudad Roderigo which was also known as the 'Key of Spain'. There were, of course, plenty of hostelries with allusions to the sea. What old salt could fail to feel at home in the Mermaid or the Lugger Tavern. There is also the extant Bonny Boat on Trinity House Lane. This pub with the intriguing name recalls an incident involving the rescue of a canoe. The tiny vessel – with the emaciated body of a sailor inside – was found floating in 1613 by Captain Andrew Barker, a brethren of Trinity House who was engaged in the Greenland whale fishery. The original 'bonny boat' (it was originally christened by the distinguished traveller Celia Fiennes in 1697) with the dummy figure of a seaman inside, is exhibited in the nearby mansion belonging to Trinity House.

On Salthouse Lane was another interesting and attractive tavern – the Cup and Ball, which had a distinctive sign inviting customers to enjoy the old bar-top game with their mugs. Likewise with the nearby Corner Pin, which had a ninepin court in the rear yard (the corner pin was the most difficult to knock over). In addition, there was a host of other pubs with splendid names. The Jack-on-a-Cruise, the Splaw Bone, the Blue Dumpling, the B Sharp and the Town and Trade of Hull, to name but a few.

The most interesting inn in Hull though is one with an ordinary name, but an extraordinary history. The Ye Olde White Harte, located down a narrow alley between Bowlalley Lane and Silver Street, has been filling mugs since the middle of the sixteenth century. A timeless and atmospheric place, miraculously untainted by modern 'improvements', it holds a unique place in the history of Hull and indeed in the history of the nation. In the climate of animosity between King Charles I and his Parliament in 1642, it was the residence of the Governor of Hull, Sir John Hotham. Given the news that King Charles was approaching the city with a troop of about three hundred men, Hotham ordered that the city gates be closed. The King, who was sorely grieved at the humiliation, prophetically said: 'This disobedience of yours will probably bring many miseries to the kingdom; and its consequence may cause much loss of blood'.

The aptly named 'Plotting Parlour' where Sir John made his

momentous decision to exclude the King, is still preserved and its Jacobean carving is in excellent condition. The inn has a number of other fascinating treasures including a well-preserved skull. This is thought to be the remains of a youth, and a slight fracture-mark in the bone proves that the poor lad was bludgeoned to death with a pistol butt. The murderer was a sea captain stirred to violence by French brandy. Hidden beneath a staircase, the body remained undiscovered for generations until it was uncovered by a fire sometime during the nineteenth century. Inevitably, a ghost stalks the ancient corridors of the Ye Olde White Harte. Some landlords have experienced shivers down the spine and an eerie chill blowing down the corridors when they shouted 'time'. After the inn was damaged by fire, it became a private house until it was first licensed after major alterations in 1881. During the alterations, the builders made an exciting discovery. Two seventeenth-century maritime cutlasses were found. These are now displayed above the fireplace in the Plotting Parlour.

Near Hull, there were other notable inns. Six miles east of the town in Paull, a riverside village whose gun batteries guarded its important neighbour, was the Humber Tavern. The landlord's duties in 1836 included those of lighthouse keeper. Nearby Hedon – which in its early days eclipsed Hull as a trading port – had several inns frequented by the Haven Commissioners. During their official meetings in the bars, they imbibed punch made from a secret recipe. Contemporary accounts suggest such was the potency of their tipple that, after the conclusion of business, some of the gentlemen had to be transported home by their servants in wheelbarrows!

But it is the powerful 'Hull cheese' that has left such an abiding legacy on the area. Only in recent years, with the demise of the deep-sea trawling industry, has the pernicious link between seafaring and intoxicating liquor been broken. By all accounts there was only modest drinking on Hull trawlers although Jeremy Tunstall in his definitive book on the Hull trawling industry – *The Fishermen: the sociology of an extreme occupation* – recounts a tale told to him by a crewman who witnessed a drowning:

It was all hushed up like. Everybody on board was drunk except the skipper and the watch on the bridge. I was leaning out of a porthole back aft. Something flew by into the sea. I thought it was the cook throwing garbage away. Then I saw it was a body. I ran up to the bridge. Another bastard was so drunk he shouted out: 'Tell me what the water's like, maybe I'll take a swim too.' When I got to the bridge and told the skipper he turned the ship round, but we didn't find the body. It was washed up at Flamborough Head a week later. Some of the lads were so pissed up when we got back to Hull a few hours later, they didn't even know this man had been lost over.

Incidents such as this were comparatively rare at sea but it was a different story once ships had docked. Many fishermen – sometimes referred to as 'three-day millionaires' – gravitated to their favourite pubs for 'session' drinking. Not all fishermen were persistent drinkers but those that were created a stereotypical image of the drunken salt that was hard to shake off. Tunstall points out that, in many cases, they only consumed average amounts of alcohol but it was the concentration of the drinking during the short periods between voyages that strengthened the impression of being 'constantly on the piss'. Fishermen themselves offered another explanation. 'Of course fishermen get drunk,' they would say. 'Anybody who does what we do has to get drunk to stay sane.'

Fishermen used the dockside pubs but they also were particularly fond of another cultural institution – the Working Men's Club. Eight of these were to be found in the Hessle Road area where many of them lived. Such was the outlay of hard-earned money on liquor that wives would often 'confiscate' the proceeds of a voyage, and hand back small sums to fund modest bouts of drinking. But come the last day before the next fishing trip, moderation 'went up against the piss-house wall'. There was an abiding custom among fisherman that it was unlucky to return to sea with any money from the previous trip. So the old soaks spent it. They either bought extra rounds for the road or gave whatever money they had left to grateful children.

Today, attitudes to alcohol have changed everywhere. The modern seamen in Hull adopt a more sensible approach to social drinking.

The majority of their old taverns, including several gems such as the Leicester Hotel in Mytongate (dating from 1791, it was refused listed-building status and demolished in 1979) and the Sculcoates Arms on Charles Street were senselessly swept away. The 'Scully', or 'Smokey Joes' (after the landlord), was reckoned by some to have the most attractive façades in Hull. Its intricate ceramic tile-work swags, stylised panels and leaded windows were matched internally by white-glazed tiling in the bar which, incidentally, was off-limits for women. This gem of a pub had an internal gaslight for smokers and a corner stove with a complimentary pan of peas perennially warming. Sadly, after a long fight, the 'Scully' was knocked down in 1983. Scores of old redoubts have long gone but irreplaceable establishments like the Black Boy, the Bonny Boat and the Ye Olde White Harte remain. And to this list one can add the White Hart in Alfred Gelder Street, The George in the Land of Green Ginger and the Minerva on Victoria Pier. The latter, built on land reclaimed from the Humber in 1809, operated as a cosmopolitan hotel in 1830, and its trilingual staff served English, French and German visitors. Fittingly today, it has its own brewery at the rear. One of its heady products is the excellent 'Pilots' Pride'. Say cheese.

23

ALL THE FUN OF THE FAIR

Will anybody out there admit to paying good money to see Christina the Tattooed Princess, The Tiniest Lady in Existence Shown Here Live, George – Scotland's Tallest Living Man or Barney and Joy – The World's Heaviest Married Couple? Europe's largest, and certainly one of its oldest travelling fairs has been stuffed with such nonsensical extravaganzas for centuries. But how did it all start? Blame it all on religion my son. The Abbot of Meaux – who was granted a royal charter by King Edward I in 1279 for 'a weekly market on Thursday and a yearly fair on the vigil, the feast and the morrow of Holy Trinity and the twelve days following' – has a lot to answer for.

The first fair, in what was then Wyke-upon-Hull, was held between 9 and 23 March 1279 in the grounds of Holy Trinity Church amidst the gravestones. There was nothing unusual in that. On feast days, congregations spilled out into the churchyards to participate, as they had done in heathen times, in games, dancing and other amusements. Large numbers of people with money in their pouches attracted hawkers and traders who set up stalls, and cassocked Arthur Daleys like the Abbot of Meaux seized the opportunity of making a little offertory money with the formal blessing of the King. Wyke's inaugural fair, however, backfired somewhat. The tumult of the occasion, which was no doubt fuelled by libations of wine and old sack, caused the priests to fluff their recitations and complaints were made. So much so that, in 1282, a law was passed making it illegal to hold fairs in church grounds. A new venue had to be found for Wyke Fair.

Never one to let his priests have all the fun, Edward I acquired the town of Wyke-on-Hull from the Abbot of Meaux in 1293. The bargain-basement price of £78 14s 8d allowed him to give it his own name and to bestow on the town the status of a free borough. Along with the new royal privileges, the King allowed the burgesses: 'one fair in every year, to continue for thirty days, namely on the day of St Augustine after Easter, and for twenty-nine days following.'

The fairs of the day were held in the Market Place, although a profusion of stalls also clogged up the adjacent thoroughfares of Lowgate and Whitefriargate. An essential conduit of trade, this fair offered local producers an outlet for their goods. And when the bargaining was done how about a little entertainment? Even in this early period, there was no shortage of amusements on offer. You could despatch your servants homeward with the cart – 'tell your mistress I'll return in a few days' – and do a little quaffing and wenching. And, when you'd grown bored with that, there were always the musicians, acrobats, the street players and the dancing bears to keep you occupied. 'And how about a little something for the weekend sir?'

Wherever humans congregate, you will find in their midst sundry rogues, conmen and quack physicians. They offered, in their secret elixirs, all manner of cures and aphrodisiacs. You could also buy redemption for the soul. The purveyor of this purgative was a trickster called a 'pardoner'. He professed to have the authority of the Pope to pardon sins in return, of course, for a little remuneration. To prove his veracity, he produced a portfolio of genuine-looking parchments from his Holiness. These were duly impressed with the papal seal. What could be more convincing?

During the fairs of the fourteenth century, the normal trading restrictions imposed by the all-powerful city guilds were suspended to allow outsiders to sell their goods without hindrance for the duration of the fairs. An Act passed in 1331 ordered that 'every Lord at the Beginning of his Fair shall proclaim how long the fair shall endure', and fixed penalties were imposed on any trader who sold goods beyond the end of the fair. Otherwise, fairs were unregulated and largely uncontrolled, with not a public convenience in sight. The Hull Fairs of that time must, as a consequence, have been unhygienic, even without the dreaded pestilence. According to the records, some of the fair's attractions were just as bad as the pestilential streets themselves. Measures were taken to counter the 'divers idle and lewd persons, players or setters-out of plays and interludes that frequented the town'. Fines of up to twenty shillings were imposed on offenders, and one contemporary bishop joined in the chorus of disapproval in his denunciation of the 'vile and indecorous games which tempt unseemliness.' The fair also attracted an inordinate number of beggars.

Before the suppression of the monasteries, it was the custom in Hull for the local monks to offer sustenance to the poor and needy at the time of the annual fair. One year, as the monks were busy preparing food for the paupers' feast, a dog surreptitiously crept into the buttery and made off with a choice joint of meat. Running into the street with its prize, the animal was pursued by a braying mob incensed at the loss of dinner. The dog was summarily despatched and for decades afterwards, the entire canine species was barred from Hull Fair.

By the sixteenth century, the fair had been given yet another royal charter. The new venue of 1598 extended to Northgates, Chapel Lane, Sewerside along Denton Lane to Bishop Lane and Salthouse Lane. By this date every manner of trade was represented, and exhibitions of exotic animals and satirical plays added even more variety to the occasion. In the seventeenth century, Hull – the chief garrison town of the north of England – flourished on its whaling and fishing industries, although its fair was again diminished by both plague and war. In 1637, the fair was cancelled following an epidemic that claimed the lives of seven hundred inhabitants of the town, and a law was imposed, banning the assembly of groups of 'more than eight people'. As the disease was still rampant a year later, an embargo was placed on the unloading of fair goods. The gradual provision in later years of brick-built housing and improved water supplies helped improve the health of the town. The fair grew in size and popularity year on year. In 1661, it was granted a new charter stipulating that it would begin on 29 September. The date was changed again following the re-adjustment of the calendar in 1751.

Hull Fair existed on its trade and peripheral entertainment for an amazing five hundred years to the dawn of the Industrial

Revolution. But mass production and the introduction of modern retailing undermined its core purpose. With the availability of local shops selling the widest range of consumer goods, old-fashioned fairs, like those in Topcliffe, Boroughbridge and Hull, seemed redundant and many predicted their demise. By the middle of the nineteenth century, travelling showmen had become an essential fixture in the fair calendar and their livelihoods were threatened. One pessimist suggested that, 'the last showman will soon be as great a curiosity as the dodo'. Herein lies the seed of the fair's survival.

Curiosity and the dodo. With the need gone to stock up on cartloads of victuals, what could possibility entice customers to attend Hull Fair? 'Ah! We need to keep them intrigued and inquisitive. We need to provide them with fun, with novel and exciting experiences and with a touch of the exotic. How's about a peep-show and a menagerie of lions, tigers, bears, wolves, hyenas, leopards and elephants? That should do the trick.' In 1815, Hull Fair presented perhaps the most novel exhibit in its long life. 'William Bradley of Market Weighton, the famous Yorkshire giant was a great attraction,' reported an old chronicle. 'He was on exhibition (admission 1 shilling) at 1 Queen Street. Bradley had the honour of being presented to King George IV, who gave him a massive gold chain as a souvenir. He was seven feet nine inches high, and weighed twenty-seven stones, and the sight of him never failed to give universal gratification to his beholders.'

Successive years after 1815 witnessed the gradual displacement of the fair from its traditional venue in the Old Town. Dock expansion and the needs of commerce caused the fair to be re-sited, and the crowded stalls at various times occupied Market Place, Wellington Street, Humber Street, Mytongate, Dock Green, Queen Street and Nelson Street. One of the great draws of the period was Alger's Dancing Saloon. Measuring an impressive 110 feet by 55 feet, this emporium was brought from London by steamship, taking its place alongside Springthorpe's Waxworks, Wild's Picture Gallery and a host of other entertainments. In the absence of motive power, the proprietors of these amusements had to rely on children – who they frequently whipped – to keep their machines turning. Within a few years, the fair lost its town centre sites for good. It first relocated to Brown Cow Field on Anlaby Road then, in 1861, it went to Argyle Street. A further move to Corporation Field in Park Street in 1865 said much about the perception of an event that was regarded in some quarters as a 'disgrace to the town'. But the punters enjoyed it, and the fair of 1865 was described as a 'huge success'. For the price of a bob, children a tanner, there was Mander's Menagerie displaying performing lions, Bengal tigers and ostriches. Alternatively there was Steven's Royal Menagerie, which boasted a 6-year-old Infant Lion Tamer. Then there was a bearded lady, 'accompanied by Professor W. Crowther on the Dulcimer', Tanner's Troupe of Performing Dogs, an exhibition of undersea monsters, a boy giant, Calver's Marionettes and roundabouts and steam-powered high-flyers galore. That's entertainment!

The fairs attracted large crowds. The thousands of feet transformed the showground, especially in wet weather, into a quagmire. There was mounting opposition to the fair from residents and the council. One prominent figure added to the controversy by suggesting that parts of Hull had been, 'transformed into a very Bedlam with roundabouts, swings, shooting galleries, travelling menageries, circuses, sea serpents, double-headed oxen, jugglers, in fact anything likely to cause circulation of the coin in the well-filled pockets of the visitors'. The local press further fanned the fires of dissent. One reporter wrote, 'there has been the usual disgusting amount of fat females exhibited and the customary peep-show with its pictures bordering so close to obscenity.' Local residents were equally disgusted. 'They have been annoyed to boiling point of rage', trumpeted an article in another publication, 'and the quantity of catarrh caused by the sloppy condition of the fairground is unlimited.' It was time to act.

In a pivotal debate in the council chamber on 3 May 1888, Councillor Cohen suggested that the fair should be abolished altogether. Thankfully, the council chose an alternative course and voted for yet another relocation. Many of the councillors hoped that a tactical banishment to 'the dismal wilds of Newington' and Walton Street would see the fair's demise. But it continued to flourish despite early setbacks and some mediocre crowds.

The 1896 extravaganza brought moving pictures to the town and massive crowds were once again in evidence. Extra trains, ferries and wagonettes brought in thousands of customers beguiled by Pedley's Fine Art Show, a tableau that offered eye-popping spectacles of ladies in various stages of undress. There were also the usual rides, whose gyrations were set to music provided by the electrically operated Gavioliphone. With the provision of the Anlaby Road extension to the municipal tramway in 1899, access to the fair became easier, and the growing throng of people encouraged the showmen to introduce new stalls and novelties. By 1906, the event was being described as 'England's largest fair', and the doubling of the show area from six to twelve acres in 1908 proved the claim beyond doubt.

After the suspension of the fair during the war years, the festivities returned in 1919. Subsequent fairs witnessed the arrival of bigger machines designed to scare the pants off any customer who dared to take up the challenge. The arrival of these leviathans – the Racing Porkers, the Waltzing Balloons, the Figure-of-Eight Railway, the Monkey Speedway and the Water Dodgem – made the ground shudder. In fact, homeowners in Spring Bank West complained about the 'violent trembling and cracking of walls.' Later on, there were the Farrar's Mont Blanc, offering 'all the excitement of mountaineering from an armchair without any of the dangers', and Marshall's Hey Day which promised to 'shake you nicely and make you feel ready to fight Carnera'.

The spoilsport Germans again brought a temporary halt to the proceedings during the Second World War. But, by 1945, the fair had returned in all its pre-war splendour. Since then, it has continued to sparkle and entertain, keeping its Walton Street site in the midst of rumours of redevelopment and yet another relocation. And Hull Fair remains as cussedly popular as ever. But why has it remained so? The challenge throughout the last two centuries of the fair's existence has been to maintain its excitement and novelty. The hard work, ingenuity and investment of the travelling folk have achieved this. Their commitment to providing better fairground rides, with the emphasis firmly on 'heart-in-the-mouth' fun for all ages, has encouraged visitors to make the annual pilgrimage to Hull from all over Yorkshire and beyond. This innovative approach, however, can be only part of the explanation for the fair's popularity, especially in the twenty-first century. So why do visitors continue to come when they have such a choice of alternative entertainment? Hull Fair and its ilk can no longer claim to have a monopoly on the white-knuckle rides that were once the backbone of the fairground business. Now, sophisticated theme-parks with their multi-million pound machines make the old carousels and gallopers seem like children's toys. So why do they still come to play 'Hook-A-Duck' and win a goldfish when there are state-of-the-art pleasures elsewhere?

They come because Hull Fair has an atmosphere of its very own. They come for the bright lights and the bustling crowds. They come for Westlers hot dogs, candyfloss and Carver's famous fish-and-chips. They come for the thrills of the many rides and the roller-coasters that have a timeless fascination for young and old and they come because they've always come, for Hull Fair is part of a happy heritage that many people want to share with their own children. But I think they come for another reason.

In this cynical, predictable and corporate-controlled world, I believe that people come to Hull Fair for its spontaneity, variety and its fizzing, here-today-gone-tomorrow appeal. The timeless draw of the showmen with their wit and happy invitations to relieve you of your money simply add to the sense of theatre. Throw in the opportunity, just for a few hours, to play the court jester, to let your hair down and to throw coconuts and inhibitions to the wind, and you have a delectable cocktail that is hard to resist. And at heart, I suggest we come because we have a soft spot for the hard working, loveable rogues who make it all possible.

24

FROM HULL THE GOOD LORD PRESERVE US

In the beauty stakes, most people regard Hull as a spiky Yorkshire rose rather than a violet. The rigours of making a living in dirty, and frequently dangerous, industries have given the port a gritty if somewhat dour appearance. But age does betray a lovely youth. The infant Hull, at a time when its population was no more than two thousand souls, was as fair as any settlement in the county. The monks of Meaux and their contemporaries made it so. The religious houses of the Black friars, the White friars and the Carthusians, 'charmed with their quaint architecture the stranger who visited the picturesque old town of Hull'. Their extensive pastures, allotments and herb gardens imbued the place with a rustic feel. While it might appear at first glance that all vestiges of the city's monastic past have disappeared this is simply not the case.

Some years ago when I was engaged in research for another book, I happened to visit a garden in Welton, a village a short distance to the west of Hull. There, to my amazement, I discovered a link to Hull's monastic past; a fifteenth century carved and fluted font that had miraculously survived the dissolution of the monasteries. I was told that for many years, the receptacle – it had been suitably drilled for the purpose – had been used as a urinal in the town's Tiger Inn. Other fragments from the monastic past were put to a more sinister use.

After the rapacious Henry VIII had dissolved the nation's monasteries, he set in train a systematic process of acquisition. The fabric of the religious houses, together with their treasures, were appropriated by the state. On 1 October 1540, the King visited Hull to inspect its fortifications. At the time, the town was well defended on the northern, western and southern sides, although the eastern boundary was vulnerable to attack. Henry was aware that the town had fallen into the hands of rebel forces in both 1536 and 1537 during the doomed Pilgrimage of Grace. He also realised that the wealth of Hull, concentrated as it was in High Street with its prosperous merchants' dwellings, bulging warehouses and crowded quays, was temptingly exposed. Noting the problems, the king immediately issued orders for the erection of bulwarks east of and running parallel with the river Hull on its left bank (on a line from the present Drypool Bridge to the Deep). The works were to consist of a central castle, linked to two stout blockhouses north and south. Henry was heavily involved in drawing up plans for the project, and several royal alterations in the work specifications attest to his personal interest in the scheme. He paid for the work from the royal exchequer, the sum of around £23,000 coming from the vast fortune he had amassed through the dissolution of the monasteries and the confiscation of their goods. The former monasteries also provided stone and land for the works. In fact, the construction site was appropriated from the holdings of local priories and Thornton Abbey.

The work started on 2 February 1541, with some building materials coming from St Mary's Church, Lowgate. Its poor foundations had caused the church to collapse in 1518. Additional materials were brought from other convenient sources: Hull's demolished Black and White Friaries and its Carthusian Priory and the Cistercian Priory in Swine provided hundreds of tons of stone. Every figured yard was ruthlessly hacked out, and the masons mutilated capitals, carvings and sumptuous tracery to convert the stone for a much baser role. Even the grave covers of the monks were not immune from this desecration. When the new bulwarks were constructed, the memorials on the incorporated tombstones could still be read. It was said that you could turn a dungeon corner and be confronted with inscriptions such as: 'Hic jacet quondam XXX a domo M.CCCCLIII, Amen', 'FRATER' and 'TERCIUS'. These and dozens of other faded and indecipherable marks added to the melancholy of that awful place. There's an old saying in Yorkshire: 'You never own stone; you only borrow it.'

The old religion was gone and the erection of Hull Castle marked the beginning of a more ruthless epoch. It was built midway between the blockhouses. A moat and an embattled wall, that extended north of the Humber along the line of the river Hull for about three-quarters of a mile, protected the entire fortification. The castle had inner and outer buildings. The inner was sixty-six feet in length and fifty-feet wide and it had three storeys. There were two dungeons on each floor with walls eight inches thick. The outer building was 174 feet square with two storeys and two projecting dungeons on the east and west sides. A vaulted corridor encircled this structure within the thickness of walls that were nineteen feet thick. The only entrance was a doorway measuring just five feet six inches high on the south side. The blockhouses were of a trefoil shape, resembling the outline of the club on a playing card. Built around an open courtyard thirty-seven feet square, they rose to two storeys and incorporated three projecting dungeons reached by circular staircases. The walls were fifteen feet thick. The castle and its blockhouses were designed to be an impregnable platform for an array of heavy guns mounted in bastions and splayed embrasures, both capable of withering, enfiladed fire.

This then was the new external face of Hull, the belligerent countenance that for three centuries would change the character and reputation of the town. Gone forever were the softly intoned words, 'Angelus Domini nuntiavit Mariae', to be replaced with martial cries and, for several decades, moans of anguish. Indeed, anyone who reads the story of Hull cannot fail to encounter the following well-known expression: 'From Hull, Hell and Halifax, the good Lord preserve us.' The reputation of Halifax, where petty pilferers had their heads removed, needs no further explanation. The reasons for the inclusion of Hull in the adage, though, have always been less certain. Historians have advanced a number of theories down the years. But a study of the history of Hull Castle provides the true explanation. In terms of protecting the town, Henry VIII's new fortifications were a towering success. The imposing castle and its blockhouses presented a deterrent to the world. The defences were used for military purposes but it was their function as vile prisons that, I am convinced, inspired the recitation that is still part of Yorkshire folklore to this day.

From the time of Henry, for a century and a half, except for a short respite in the reign of Queen Mary, Catholics were subjected to progressively more draconian persecution. Year on year, new laws inflicted further punishments on anybody who followed the faith of Rome. In his book – *The History of Kingston-upon-Hull* – Hadley suggests that Henry left 'behind a memorial of perfidy, bigotry, rapacity, profusion of cruelty, contradiction and lust' when he died in 1547. The events that took place within the confines of Hull Castle and its blockhouses merely served to underline these evils. The history of these prisons brings to mind a work of fiction – *A Tale of Two Cities* by Charles Dickens, which vividly describes another gaol in another time. How strange that the dreaded Bastille with its inmate Alexander Manette is better known than its counterpart in Hull. Is not Dickens's description of the French prison equally relevant to the English gaol? 'Through the gloomy vaults where the light of day had never shone, past hideous doors of dark dens and cages, down cavernous flights of steps, and again up steep rugged ascents of stone and brick, more like dry waterfalls than staircases.'

The reality of the conditions in Hull Castle and its blockhouses was much worse. Dickens described unglazed windows and the luxury of warming fires. The prisons in Hull had little light, no ventilation and few hearths. And at the time of the spring tides, many of the lower dungeons were flooded. Contemporary records speak volumes about the appalling treatment of prisoners. They were often held in solitary confinement for years on end in cold and unsanitary conditions. The prison regime was presided over by ruthless characters named in the records as Hawick, Bisbie, Alcoke and Hubert. These keepers charged rent for cells and levied extortionate rates on the supply of even the basic commodities. Those unfortunate prisoners who could not afford to pay were beaten and went hungry. Many inmates, such as priests who had been caught in the act of saying mass, were incarcerated in the prison for decades.

Hull Castle did not execute its own condemned men. York had the dubious distinction of erecting the gallows tree. Among the first Catholics to be sentenced in Hull were two Carthusian monks,

John Rochester and James Wannert. Both men were hung in York in 1537. Other Papists suffered a far worse fate.

There was no more barbarous form of punishment than hanging, drawing and quartering. Eye-witness accounts described the enormous barbarity and cruelty. Priests were hung by the neck until they were half-dead before being cut down choking and led away by a rope for ritual disembowelling and dismembering. The executioner would reach into the bloody torso to pluck out the still-beating heart, casting the organ, together with the entrails, into a fire. Then he would cut off the victim's head and hold it aloft with the exclamation: 'Behold the head of a traitor!' The final horror saw the priest's quartered body tossed into a cauldron for boiling before it was disposed of in a dunghill. Dozens of men who left Hull were subjected to this gruesome end. Others were more fortunate and were released on licence although many inmates died in prison as a consequence of the appalling conditions.

All Catholics were the subject of intense scrutiny. Spies and professional priest-hunters rooted out the miscreants with an amazing zeal fuelled by a system of rewards. In the 1580s a man called Henry Hastings, the Earl of Huntingdon and President of the North, controlled the apparatus of terror. One description painted him as a 'bloody and heretical tyrant with an insatiable thirst for the lives and destruction of all good men.' Hastings had a number of professional informants called 'searchers' working in and around the town of Hull and he also had the loyalty of the mayor. His agents scored Hull's taverns, alehouses and inns for Catholics.

The traitorous words of one Hull citizen – a man called Horsley – were reported to the authorities and he was arrested on suspicion of being a Catholic. After interrogation in York, he was sent to Hull Castle where he was monstrously abused. Thrown into a filthy dungeon called the Hall, he had his ears cut off and was systematically starved. Only meagre crusts, tossed in through his cell window, eased his hunger. After weeks of sustained barbarity, he died. His corpse lay mouldering for weeks, and swarms of rats gnawed away at his unrecognisable face and other parts of his body. The evidence of such cruelty is well documented, and documents from the period survive in the archives of the English College in Rome.

The persecution of the so-called recusants took place in an atmosphere of fear and paranoia. The threat of invasion from Spain, and a suspected fifth-column uprising by disaffected English Catholics, caused the utmost suspicion and a fevered state of readiness. The fortifications demanded constant repair. Premature reports of the embarkation of a Spanish fleet in early 1585 led to the urgent digging of additional ditches. Defeated by bad weather, adverse tides and the might of the English navy, the Armada floundered in 1588 but, in 1597, rumours of a second invasion force, led the Privy Council to order the removal of all Catholic prisoners from the blockhouses as a security measure. In the reign of James I, Catholics continued to be incarcerated in Hull prison and, in 1613, four recusants, who were arrested for refusing to swear an oath of allegiance to the king, were ordered to be removed to the flood-prone south blockhouse for 'their better ease and conveniency'.

Gradually, religious persecution waned and the Hull bastions reverted to their original role as defenders of this increasingly important city. The defences were severely battered during the Civil War, suffering particularly badly in 1643 when an explosion in the northernmost blockhouse and damage by garrison soldiers necessitated substantial repairs. In the following decades more repairs were needed but, by 1660, the work was much neglected. And then, in the reign of Charles II, as part of a national strategy to upgrade the defensive capabilities of the nation, a decision was taken to strengthen the fortress of Hull. A new bulwark would be at the heart of its defence. This would be known as the Citadel.

Twenty-nine acres of land were purchased adjacent to the original fortifications and work began on the new project in 1681. Designed as a massive, triangular-shaped artillery fort, the Citadel incorporated, on its north-west side, the south blockhouse and the castle Its massive bastions at all three corners, and improved weaponry, enabled fire to be trained on attackers approaching from any direction. During its construction, which lasted some nine years, an army of craftsmen was employed, with local entrepreneur John Fitches becoming one of the project's main contractors. Scores of masons, bricklayers, carpenters, sod-layers, plasterers, coopers, gunsmiths, painters and 'raff' merchants who supplied the wooden scaffolding were joined by hosts of day labourers. Deployed in their hundreds, these men were recruited from the countryside to help with moat and ditch digging, earth moving and rampart construction. At times, the military also helped. In 1687, troops of Colonel Cornwall's regiment, who were billeted in the town, assisted in the raising of the earthworks.

Barracks were built in the Citadel and a garrison was installed there. The fortress later served as a billet for troops deployed to counter the threat of invasion during the Revolutionary and Napoleonic Wars with France. Between 1799 and 1800, Hull's defences were again used as a prison. Assisted by its new Russian allies, Britain attacked Napoleon's forces in Holland, and the Citadel served as accommodation for wounded Russian soldiers and French prisoners of war. During their internment, some of the captives carved model ships from bone. Some of these are currently displayed in Hull's Town Docks Museum. In 1801 the northern blockhouse was taken down, and the demolition of the southern blockhouse followed in 1803. A prime function of the Citadel was as an arsenal, and its walls held tons of gunpowder and hundreds of guns. Some idea of its strategic importance can be gauged by its role in fitting out the 1807 expedition to Copenhagen, when the armoury provided supplies for 35,000 men and stores for six ships of the line and twelve frigates.

In the decades following the allied victory at Waterloo the Citadel was occupied by various regiments of the militia, and one particular Regiment of Foot made more impression on the local inhabitants than most. Between 1820 and 1821, twenty-one of its soldiers married local girls! Two detachments of the Queen's Dragoon Guards followed, and the novelty of equestrian troopers exercising on the parade ground opposite the Neptune Inn drew many admiring spectators.

During the peace, the garrison was occasionally summoned to quell civil disorders. A wage riot by seamen was quashed, and a disturbance incited by the agitator James Acland, who demanded that the elections to the Corporation of Hull be held on a Sunday, was put down by a detachment of infantry and cavalry. But the garrison did bring some levity to the town. The 53rd Regiment of

Foot began an annual prank that long continued in the town. For some reason, they took to stealing door knockers during autumn, and nineteen pieces of this important ironmongery disappeared during one week in 1836. The military also played cricket, with notable matches between the garrison and Hull taking place between 1852 and 1856.

Gradually, however, the strategic function of the Citadel diminished and the commercial pressures of the burgeoning port signalled its demise. The Citadel buildings were razed in 1863–4 and, during the period between August 1940 and May 1942, the site was devastated by German bombing. This important part of Hull's heritage was thought lost forever until archaeological excavations in 1987 unearthed half of the original foundations and some of the clay ramparts intact. These discoveries provided an indelible footprint of Hull's often-bloody past.

The Citadel stone was used in other construction works in the town, notably in the building of the docks. Former ecclesiastical shafts and piers, and some of the tombstones of the old priests scratched with the names of prisoners of conscience, no doubt prop up local buildings and roadways. One timeworn manuscript suggests that a number of friary grave covers from the original castle eventually found their way into a church in Sculcoates Lane. They may be uncovered in the fullness of time. As the saying goes, 'You never own stone; you only borrow it.'

25

THE HOLY TRINITIES

One building, immovable and indomitable, stands like a giant oak casting its benevolent shadow over the history of Hull. In the centre of the city it has seen the epochs fly and great men come and go. It has witnessed pestilence, famine, insurrection, war and bombing. It has gazed down, generation after generation, on a city that grew up around its walls. Risen from the clay, this structure is the oldest brick-built church in Britain. Organically and spiritually, Holy Trinity is at the very heart of Hull. In the British Museum archives is a manuscript of 1285 that notes: 'the High Church dedicated to the Holy Trinitie was at first founded as a Chapell by one James Helward'. This was probably built before 1160 and destroyed in 1204. After this date, the displaced congregation had to trudge all the way to Hessle to practice their faith. Nothing, of course, remains of that original chapel – it was referred to in the *Chronicle of the Monastery of Meaux* as Myton Chapel – and the erection of the present Holy Trinity began at the dawn of the fourteenth century.

Profits from the wool trade ensured that Holy Trinity would be the grandest of edifices. At 285 feet long and 90 feet wide, with a crossing tower rising to 150 feet, it is, according to the *Guinness Book of Records*, the largest non-collegiate parish church in England. Fashioned from weather-resilient local bricks, it stands like Beverley's North Bar as a testament to the brick-maker's art. Built on a geologically insubstantial site composed mainly of alluvial clay, the new church had to be a light structure. Architecturally, it is cruciform in shape, consisting of an eight-bay nave, a five-bay chancel and short transepts.

It's worth pausing here to remember the faith that raised such a noble church at a time when people 'lived in hovels and worshipped in houses'. In the fourteenth century, Christianity was as fundamental to living as the air itself. Worshippers were passionate about a religion that regulated their entire lives and they firmly believed in the concepts of prayer, self-sacrifice and redemption. The essence of love has always been defined in the single word 'giving', and the people of the Middle Ages gave generously. The widow's mite and the prince's fortune all helped to endow an institution that grew to be one of the most powerful in the land. Cynicism, of course, went hand in hand with selflessness, and the richest men attempted to buy shares in the celestial kingdom right here on earth. The result of all this, at a time when the average worshipper lived in abject poverty, was a status-symbol that was a symbolic contrast between God and man.

In the great period of prosperity between 1400 and 1490, people generally had an unshakeable belief in the efficacy of prayer, and chantry priests were installed in the many side chapels and side altars built into the fabric of Holy Trinity to pray for the dead. The wealthiest men would install their own priests, while poor men had to join a sort of prayer union, in which a guild chaplain sang for their corporate souls. At one time, there were at least twelve chantry chapels in the church, predominantly on the south side of the chancel. One contemporary observer decried their proliferation: 'by the gradual addition of Chapel after Chapel, the plan . . . lost all likeness to its original state and seems at first sight to be a collection of buildings heaped together without much method.' The rich and powerful De la Pole family had its own sumptuously fitted chapel. This is now known as the Broadley Chapel in honour of its restorer.

At the time of its completion, when it served a population of 4,000 people, Holy Trinity would have stood alone on its site as a beacon of God's majesty. Its pinnacles, carvings and stained glass, which gave an illiterate population a lesson of the scriptures in pictures, all added to the sense of awe. Internally, the church was not furnished with pews, and had only a scattering of rushes and a few stone or wooden seats at the bases of the pillars or against the nave wall. But the daily congregations came in their hundreds, and probably as many as twenty priests held services 'at all hours of the day from cockcrow'. These priests lived in a purpose-built residence near the church at the spot where the old markets were once held.

Holy Trinity played a vital role in both the religious and secular life of Hull over the succeeding years. By the time of the Reformation though, this life of service and harmony was coming to an abrupt close. There was some indication of the problems ahead in 1522 when, under edict, the doors and windows of the church were barricaded with briars and thorns. In addition, the surrounding pavements were torn up, its bells were silenced and all services ceased. Before the door was sealed, the vicar of North Cave preached an inflammatory sermon from its pulpit. An arrest followed, and the priest had to recant his heresy and endure a public penance that compelled him to walk round the church on Sundays and market days dressed only in a shirt, carrying a large faggot in his hand. By 1534 the church was in such a poor state of repair that the mayor and corporation decide to sell some of the silver plate to raise funds for emergency works.

Just five years later, Hull's Whitefriary and its Blackfriary and Carthusian Monastery were dissolved, and the avaricious Henry VIII paid a visit to the city in 1540. Would Holy Trinity be next on his list for destruction? Around the walls, some of the displaced monks were reduced to begging in the streets and, although the fabric of the church survived, an assault was made on its ancient chantries. In 1545, church commissioners were appointed to carry out an inventory and survey of the chantries. Incumbent priests were displaced and their possessions were appropriated to the Crown.

Henry VIII rampaged through the religious life of the nation and changed it forever but Holy Trinity survived to another era. It was again in the forefront of momentous events when, on 21 April 1642, the Governor of Hull, Sir John Hotham, precipitated the English Civil War by refusing to allow Charles I to enter the city. It is fascinating to consider that, if hostilities had broken out that day, Holy Trinity might have been in the thick of the action. Hull at the time was widely regarded as the arsenal of the north, and old church records reveal the following entry: 'In the Powder house in the Holy Trinity Church barrels of gunpowder, 2.'

Just eight years later with the King dead and new codes of

religious conduct imposed by Parliament, the church was again the scene of dissent. The military centre of Hull was garrisoned by a large contingent of soldiers who, in terms of religion, were of the Independent, or Congregational, persuasion. Holy Trinity itself was by now a Presbyterian church. The soldiers pressed for their own place of worship and, when no suitable building could be found, their general came up with the novel idea of partitioning the church. Despite the protests of local worshippers, the military got its way and a dividing wall was erected. This would have been bearable for the devout brethren of Holy Trinity had the interlopers shown even a measure of decorum. In reality, the new occupants of the chancel were an uncouth lot. They further disfigured the old chantry-chapels, ripped out brass plaques and kept their horses in church! And the clergy of both factions insisted on holding their services at the same time on Sundays, and even the dense partition did little to muffle the discordant homilies. By 1660, when Charles II assumed the throne, equilibrium was restored and the dividing wall was taken down. The life of Holy Trinity Church returned to something like normality. And so it served on, while Hull expanded and crowded in on its sacred edifice.

When the great and good of Hull died the interior of the church recorded their passing in plaques and monuments. There is a tribute to Sir William de la Pole the Elder and his wife. There is another to Thomas Ferres who ran away way to sea and made a fortune, returning to his native Glaisdale to build the delightful 'Beggar's Bridge'. Then there is a bust of Thomas Whincop who was Master of Charterhouse, and an eagle lectern made to commemorate former vicar John Bromby who preached in Holy Trinity for seventy years.

And what of the strangely truncated form of the painting of the Last Supper dating from 1711? Like all the treasures in this fascinating place, it tells a story. But surely there were thirteen figures at the table? This large picture was originally given to the church in Hessle. Its sheer size, however, prevented it from going through the doors. Enter a man with a saw! Although he surgically removed one of the apostles it was still jammed, and another apostle was sent for an early bath. The picture was still too big and, not wanting to leave Christ dining on his own, the saw man desisted and the picture was given to Holy Trinity.

In every age Holy Trinity has been a proud symbol of the fortitude of the people. In every age it has been a source of succour, leading its people through the plague, the Civil War and conflicts with the Germans. Writing about the Zeppelin raids on the city in 1915 and 1916, a past vicar of the parish noted: 'Bombs fell on all sides of the old building, making holes and awakening the spirits of the past who hover there. North, south, east and west the missiles fell, but the church of the ages stood out dignified amid the storm; the ages looked heavenward and smiled.' The Germans, of course, carried out more concentrated and sophisticated bombing missions during the Second World War . . . but thankfully, they still missed!

*

'For the relief of decayed seaman.' This simple dedication flaps like a masthead pennant, and announces a chapter in Hull's history that deals with what is undoubtedly the port's finest institution. Over the years, it has done as much for Hull as all the churches and hospitals combined. Founded in 1369, it is known the world over as Trinity House of Kingston-upon-Hull. The organisation was originally a scion of Holy Trinity Church and was formed by a group of forty-nine men and women as the Guild of Holy Trinity. The group had its own chantry chapel located within the church and adopted a strict code of conduct to safeguard the moral and physical welfare of its members. They paid two shillings per year by way of subscription. Used until 1461, the original chantry-chapel was probably bricked up in 1548 and then uncovered again during alterations in 1869. The stone carvings on the east and west jambs that depict kneeling figures and ships with masts and high prows show something of the chapel's opulence.

By 1457, all the associates of Trinity House were master mariners and pilots. Its constitution, which has hardly changed since it was first drafted in 1581, provided for two wardens, ten elder brethren and six assistants, supported by a number of younger brethren and several honorary brethren. The eighteen-strong governing body is responsible for every aspect of the organisation's business. The constitution also imposes a strict dress code on the brethren, who must wear a naval cap, frock coat and trousers, white shirt and black tie.

Under a charter issued by Henry VIII in 1541, the guild was able to become a corporation. This important privilege allowed it to levy fees on all cargoes coming into, and going out of, the port of Hull. The levy was termed 'primage', and was imposed at a rate of 3d per ton of cargo. The penalties for non-payment of this tax were severe. Goods could be confiscated, and reluctant captains also risked the threat of imprisonment. The money raised funded the maintenance of Trinity House and its chapel and also contributed to the relief of thirteen poor brethren. Subsequent charters gave the guild the power to govern, regulate and set standards for the occupation of seamen, to licence masters and pilots and to maintain buoys and beacons in the Humber. The guild had wide-ranging control over almost every aspect of the port's activities. It managed the movement and docking of ships and the employment of seamen, and it even had authority to intervene with a system of punitive fines in situations where foreign vessels were used to carry cargoes when English ships were available. Over the years, the organisation grew rich and powerful and further expanded its nautical interests.

By 1461, the guild had vacated its chantry chapel in Holy Trinity Church and moved to purpose-built accommodation on the site of its present headquarters. Occupied by thirteen 'decayed seamen' and their widows, the adjacent almshouses were also completed during this period. Gradually, the guild enlarged its charitable works. The poor of Hull, the port in general and even deserving causes from outside the town received aid. Fees and port taxes formed the bulk of the relief fund, but poor-box fines imposed on brethren, mariners and merchants for relatively minor offences were also earmarked for the purpose. The guild-records were kept fastidiously and reveal some very interesting donations:

1569 'To mariners who had their ship taken from them by the Irishmen – 2s.'
1585 'To a poor lame man – 12d.'
1587 'Given to a mariner of Denmark shipbroken – 3s.'

1597 'To a poor mariner, his wife and two children who were robbed with Dunkirkers and had their house burned – 4s. 8d.'

1613 'To a boy for a shirt – 4d.'

1614 'Given to a Fleming whose ship was taken in Humber by a pirate – 15s.'

1628 'To three Dutchmen what had been long in York Castle upon suspicion of piracy – 2s 6d.'

1685 'To Mary Swanfleet to look to a blind woman – 6d.'

Other records show that, in 1689, the brethren bought a consignment of beef for distribution among the poor of Hull. In 1781, they gave £200 for the building of an infirmary and promised to contribute towards its running costs. In 1830, after a devastating storm had ravaged Filey, they donated £30 to help re-equip the fleet. From time to time the guild also advanced monies to help pay for town defences. Such humanitarian and civic works were funded, of course, from the guild's enterprises, which in no small measure contributed to one of the best-organised ports in the country.

Trinity House was charged with installing a system of beacons and buoys to aid navigation in the notoriously difficult channels of the Humber. Originally these were limited in number and of poor construction. They consisted of little more than ships' masts, timber bracing and hooped barrels filled with stones placed at strategic locations near shallows and sandbanks. Over time, the quality of these hazard markers improved, and accounts show the purchase of a professionally made buoy from Holland in 1621 for £11 9s 4d. As primitive as they were, these devices must have saved countless lives. The brethren also embarked on another scheme for the benefit of seafarers that positively makes the heart swell. And hearts come no bigger than that belonging to the legendary Henry Greathead.

This pioneer of the lifeboat service had established his boat at South Shields at the beginning of the nineteenth century, and news of his amazing invention came to the attention of Hull's local newspaper. In 1802, Greathead wrote to Trinity House offering to build a boat to be stationed at Spurn. Of revolutionary design, his craft dispensed with the traditional stern allowing it to be rowed either way. It was offered in two versions – an eight-oar boat for £130 and a ten-oar boat for £150. After deliberating for some years, the brethren allocated fifty guineas for the purchase of a ten-oar boat – both the Corporation of Hull and Lloyds of London gave £50 – and they launched a subscription fund to defray the rest of the cost. The order was duly placed, and the brethren appointed Robert Richardson as the first-ever master of the Spurn lifeboat, which was delivered by Greathead in 1810. Trinity House was charged thereafter with selecting new masters, organising the operational functions of the lifeboat and settling salvage claims. Interestingly enough, Richardson was expected to obtain his living by managing a specially established Spurn tavern. Was the selling of intoxicating liquor an incitement to shipwreck? In addition to grog, he sold poultry, vegetables and provisions to the sailors whose five hundred or so vessels stopped at the promontory each year to collect ballast. Just a month after the new vessel was commissioned she was thrust into action, saving the crew of the *John and Charlotte* from the perils of Trinity Sand. Following the suggestion of the brethren, cottages were built at Spurn to house the lifeboat's crew and, in later years, new lifeboats were purchased. Hundreds of rescued seafarers praised Trinity House and the other benefactors of Hull for their deliverance. It was not altogether altruistic, however. The brethren usually claimed the right of salvage from the unfortunate ship-owners, and the resultant dividends went to the poor box for investment in other charitable works.

In 1787, Trinity House expanded its sphere of operations by opening a Navigation School on Trinity House Lane north of the house for thirty-six pupils. Each member of the board nominated two pupils who would be 'clothed and educated for sea service'. Maritime studies and religious education featured prominently in the curriculum. Entrant boys of between 10 and 11 years of age – they had to be literate – undertook a three-year course underwritten by their parents who had to 'engage in the penalty of five pounds and two sureties of ten pounds for the due observance of the rules in general.' Dressed uniformly in a garb consisting of 'a dress coat of blue cloth with long tails, lined with white, a stand-up collar of white cloth, brass buttons and trousers of white duck or blue cloth,' the pupils were a familiar sight in the old town of Hull, especially when they truanted during class time. According to the attendance books of the eighteenth and early nineteenth centuries, absenteeism was not uncommon, and excuses such as 'I was waylaid by the press gang, sir,' regularly caused the teachers to break out their canes. Reviewing the arcane rules and rituals which are still associated with the school to this very day, it seems to have been a regular Hogwarts, and two examples of its traditions remind me of Harry Potter. On what is known as 'Dinner Day', an annual celebration to commemorate the founding of the school, boys are required after their meal to reach out behind them to pick two oranges unseen from a fruit basket. Not to be outdone, the Warden takes onto his finger a golden ring called the 'Cameo Ring'.

Hull rapidly expanded its maritime facilities during the early part of the nineteenth century and, to reflect the growing demand for places, the school altered its entrance qualifications in 1834. After that date, only boys who were the sons of seamen or carpenters affiliated to the port of Hull were eligible for entry. In 1842, the accommodation was enlarged to cater for an increased school complement and shortly afterwards a Lower School was established for forty boys between 9 and 10 years of age. In 1854, it was agreed that teachers familiar with the nautical arts should be recruited to educate pupils in the use of navigational instruments and maps and charts. The wonderfully named Zebedee Scraping – J. K. Rowling never came up with anything as imaginative as this – took over responsibility for the upper school, with William R. Salmon assuming a similar role in the Lower School.

In 1873, the two schools merged. The core curriculum encompassed reading, writing, arithmetic, English, geography, nautical astronomy, navigation, the magnetism of iron ships and the usage of navigational instruments, maps and charts. The burgeoning port of Hull, with its worldwide reputation for maritime trade, offered wonderful opportunities for pupils. But the standards at Trinity House were high, and only the best pupils obtained an apprenticeship upon matriculation at the age of 14.

Throughout its history, Trinity House has always had the highest financial standing. Sound investments have reaped rich rewards and allowed it to divert large sums of money into educational and charitable works. It has also used its finances in other ways. In 1783, it bought its own vessel for use in the 'Buoyage and Beaconage Department'. The *Humber* was the first in a line of vessels named *Zephyr, Ariel, Dream, Duke of Edinburgh* and *Queen*. In addition, the organisation built its own rest homes, houses and shops, and its investments even extended to the erection of an inn – the Neptune – that was opened in Whitefriargate in 1796.

The most obvious sign of the institution's unique place in the life of the city, though, is Trinity House itself. This resplendent Georgian building of 1753 announces itself to the world in a confident entrance façade, crowned by a pediment richly carved with a coat of arms and reclining figures of Neptune and Britannia. Nearby is the former almshouse and the chapel. Profits from fees and levies helped pay for these buildings, and monies were also allocated for the procurement of works of art. Behind the grand entrance, Trinity House is arranged around a courtyard, and small rooms that once housed pensioners have now taken on the more utilitarian function of offices. The nucleus of the house is its council chamber, where brethren continue to meet around a substantial table matched with thirty-four magnificent Chippendale chairs. Honouring tradition, its polished floorboards are still strewn with rushes. Elsewhere in the building are many other treasures. These include marine paintings, a superb Spode dessert set of eighty pieces, collections of silver and old pewter, model ships, the harbourmaster's axe which was used in the eighteenth century to sever the cables of ships whose masters refused to comply with berthing regulations or failed to pay their dues, and relics brought back by Captain James Cook from the South Seas. Another notable attraction is the 'bonny boat', referred to elsewhere in this book in the chapter on Hull's old inns.

In 1908, Trinity House passed over its responsibilities for buoys and beacons to the Humber Conservancy Board, and concentrated its efforts on educational and charitable works. Significantly it still maintains it age-old ties. The brethren continue to worship in Holy Trinity Church, which is a mentor and inspiration. It could be argued that many institutions like Trinity House, however laudable their original intentions, become bloated and corrupt as a consequence of so much power and influence. Therefore, it says much for the exacting Christian ethics of the brethren that the organisation has survived these four hundred years with its credentials intact. In the new millennium, a range of educational and charitable works underline the integrity of Hull's finest institution.

26

HAUNTED HULL

York, it is claimed, is the 'ghost capital' of England. Tour operators, street entertainers and publicans all milk the city's spiritual fecundity with commercial fervour. There are haunted inns, churches with phantoms and creepy ruins. The nightly tours introduce eager, fee-paying visitors to headless wonders, vapoured villains, chain-rattling prisoners, wailing maidens and cherubic babes in arms. But such entertainment makes any self-respecting spectre vanish on sight! Despite hundreds of nocturnal visitations, I know of not a single verifiable sighting in that esteemed city. Ghosts in York then are not readily recruited to the ranks of Equity. By contrast, those in Hull may be experienced by the bewildered few.

If you are an unbeliever, I challenge you to run the gauntlet alone by walking through the Old Town some cold and foggy winter's night. Fortify yourself and wrap up warm and begin at precisely twenty minutes to eight outside the Old Grammar School in Trinity Square. But this itinerary comes with a health warning. Be advised that if you look up towards the first-storey windows of the school at this time you are likely to see, fluttering across the panes, the robed apparition of Revd Yates, a nineteenth-century vicar of St. Mary's Lowgate. The appearance of this cleric is, you must understand, a portent of ill. After one visitation, a fire erupted at the rear of the school and, after another, a terrified watcher fell off his bike and damaged his knee. Onward then, passing Holy Trinity Church and over Trinity Square which was, 150 years ago, Hull's main graveyard. Near the church was another property with an intriguing reputation. Oddly, it was renowned for the mystery of its disappearing wristwatches, and one tenant lost timepiece after timepiece upon retiring to bed. After the eighth consecutive loss, the watches mysteriously started re-appearing and vanishing again in sequence, in a repetitive eight-watch cycle. The phenomenon lasted, it is said, for several years.

Your next spooky port-of-call can be the famous Ye Olde White Harte pub in the eternally crepuscular alley between Bowlalley Lane and Silver Street. Inside, you will discover a rather daunting ornament named Freda, a preserved skull that suggests mysterious death and haunting. Some observers believe it was discovered during renovations carried out in 1881, and conclude that it belonged to a servant girl who was murdered and sealed up. Other people take the view that it is the remains of a youth who was beaten about the head with a pistol by a drunken sea-captain, and that the lad's body was concealed under a staircase until it was revealed by a fire in the nineteenth century. Whatever the truth, this inn has a widespread reputation as a haunted house, and many of its landlords and customers have experienced an eerie presence and cold chills. Linger awhile and take something to gird you for the road ahead.

You can follow in the footsteps of the old monks along Whitefriargate next, past the Town Docks Museum. On its public-address system during the day, as a background lament, it plays the hypnotic and utterly haunting sonar calls of long-dead whales. But animals too have ghosts. Is the tape mysteriously playing now?

On to Jameson Street, where once stood the Francis Ladies Hairdressing Salon. In 1959, this was the scene of a bizarre event that scared the living daylights out of a 15-year-old apprentice called Angela. Angela's dark adventure began prosaically enough one sunny afternoon when, as usual, she was called upon to make tea in an upper-storey staff room. Idly engaged in practising her skills on a wig block as the kettle boiled, she suddenly became aware that her back was frozen. Concerned that the emerging steam was responsible, she spun round and was astonished to see a large man's-handkerchief hanging in the air. Terrified, she bolted from the room, descending two stairs at a time to be greeted by laughter and incredulity. Only one lady was sympathetic, and she soberly suggested that it must have been 'the Old Man knocking about with his bits and pieces'. Angela later found out that someone else had experienced a similar occurrence in the room years before.

Leaving Jameson Street, walk the short distance to the modern Prospect Centre on Prospect Street. It's gaudy and glitzy, and you may smile at any notion of ghostly happenings here, until you realise that the shopping centre now occupies what was once the site of the old Hull Royal Infirmary. Opened on 1 September 1784, it had a life span of 183 years, and scores of patients ended their days in great agony on its operating tables. It was claimed that the hospital was haunted by the ghost of a porter who committed suicide in his lodge house, and that his spirit stalked the wards thereafter eager for conversation. At the time demolition of the hospital was mooted, many Hull residents voiced concern that development of the site would bring nothing but heartache. Sure enough, when the bulldozers moved in, one contractor reported seeing a ghostly visitor. And when the new centre was opened in the mid-seventies, some cleaners and staff, particularly those who worked late, complained of feeling uneasy. To mark the occasion of the official opening, all staff were asked to pose for a communal photograph. When the memento was printed, however, everybody was amazed to see an uninvited and unidentified person! Since then, there have been multiple reports of strange happenings. Waste bins, kitchen utensils and shop products have been scattered round work and storerooms. When retrieved, they have been cold to the touch. There have been reports of ethereal children's voices and multiple sightings of mysterious, shadowy figures dressed as nurses or hospital porters from a previous age. One store manager complained of feeling uncomfortable late one night. Emerging from his office, he saw a hook in a display board spinning round at great speed. And in recent years, early-morning cleaners at one retail outlet were shocked to find, on four consecutive Saturdays, trails of muddy footprints leading from the door of a shop, past the display stands to the rear of the premises. There were no signs of a break-in and, strangely, one footprint was equidistant either side of the front door, which was kept locked. The footprints were measured at between two-and-a-half and three feet apart, and the shop manager concluded that the intruder was a tall person. Quite naturally, he instructed his cleaners to remove the prints but they proved stubborn to conventional cleaning methods, and faded away without any interference from human hand around midday.

Pulling up your collar against the chill of the river mists that spiral in from the Humber you can, if you dare, leave the modernity of Prospect Street and venture into the eerie sunken-oasis that once strained to the mooring ropes of a thousand ships. Flit quickly across Queens Gardens and pretend that the creaking sounds of old timbers and the twinkling chimeras of masthead lights are figments of your imagination and present yourself at the head of High Street, the most haunted thoroughfare in all Hull. What nefarious deeds this old street has witnessed. Proceed cautiously, for thousands of tortured souls have gone before you on this same route, and your footsteps raise the dust of men and women who died horribly in the nearby Hull Castle and aboard the ships that once crowded in on Hull side. You will pass, on your left, Wilberforce House, a benign pile associated with the emancipation of slaves, hearing the exultant but eerie crack of chains as you go. Then you will arrive at perhaps the most haunted house in the city. The ancient and sinister Black Boy pub at the end of High Street has witnessed dozens of apparitions by a rather dapper ghost wearing white pantaloons and a top hat. Other scary moments include spirit bottles that have inexplicably dropped from the bar shelves and spectral, disembodied hands sprouting from the wainscoting. Hold on to your glass and take a comforting dram in the Black Boy before steadfastly completing the ghost tour and visiting the Humber bank where, like others before you, you may walk in the company of a band of phantom monks swinging bells.

Back home, suitably shaken and stirred, you may read before you sleep yet more amazing stories from Hull's arcane past. One of the best authenticated of all the town's psychic encounters dates from the Victorian period. The story begins just before midnight on 26 August 1867 when two lovers, Robert D'Onston and a girl named Louise met on a bridge over a watercourse for the last time. Grasping the opportunity to make something of his life, D'Onston had decided to end his affair with the beautiful Louise and get engaged to a prominent North-country heiress with exceptional prospects. It was understood that, on the date of his marriage, he would take the lady's name and stand as a prospective Liberal MP. D'Onston had broken the news to the devoted but distraught

Louise weeks earlier, and a few minutes before a distant clock struck the hour on that balmy August night, they kissed tenderly for the last time. The lady aptly recited the opening lines to Longfellow's poem, 'Bridge', which begins, 'I stood on the bridge at midnight'. But, before the pair said goodbye forever, Louise hesitated and accosted D'Onston with a final plea. 'Grant me one last favour', she implored, 'the only one I will ever ask you on this earth. Promise to meet me here twelve months from now at this same hour.' D'Onston was reluctant to enter into the bargain but, afraid to upset Louise, he relented with the words: 'Well, I'll come if I'm alive.' 'Say alive or dead' responded Louise. 'Very well then,' he promised, 'we'll meet alive or dead!'

On the anniversary of the pact, and true to his word, the newly married D'Onston was there on the bridge at the appointed hour. A year on, with a new wife to impress, he regretted agreeing to the arrangement but took the view that it was 'of too solemn a nature to be put aside.' Louise also arrived as promised and she persuaded D'Onston against his better judgement to meet again in 1869. Then they repeated the strange mantra: 'Alive or dead.'

In the summer of the following year, D'Onston was off the Yorkshire coast aboard a ten-ton yawl belonging to Thomas Piles of Hull, a celebrated fisherman and smuggler, when he was accidentally shot in the thigh by Piles. The accounts of the incident make no reference to what Piles was doing with a loaded gun aboard his vessel but it seems reasonable to assume – as the yawl was sailing north of Bridlington – that his party was engaged in shooting sea birds at the Bempton Cliffs colony. Carried ashore at Bridlington, D'Onston was treated by a surgeon in the port's Black Lion Hotel. From there, he returned home to Hull where his wounds were treated by Dr Kelburne King. By 26 August 1869 he was still crippled from his injuries, and only crutches and a Bath chair enabled him to travel any distance. He was a man of honour though and, on that special day, he presented himself on the bridge. A faithful retainer called Old Bob – he also knew Louise – pushed him to the appointed spot. Leaving him on the bridge with his crutches, the retainer removed the Bath chair to a discreet distance and left his master alone twenty minutes before midnight under a starlit sky.

Leaning against the top rail of the bridge, D'Onston reflectively lit a pipe and steeled himself to tell Louise that their yearly vigils must end. Presently, at around a quarter to the hour, he heard a distinctive noise. It was the instantly recognisable tapping of Louise's brass-heeled shoes on the flagged footpath. Instinctively, he turned to greet her and watched as her silhouette passed a series of gas lamps, coming ever closer. As she reached the wooden bridge, the timbers dulled the resonance of her stride. After his former lover had passed the last of the gas lamps, D'Onston noticed that she was wearing only an evening dress. The night was warm, but the lack of a cape or hat suggested that she had taken a cab to the far end of the footpath, left her outer garments with the cabman and elected elegantly to walk the short distance to the bridge. D'Onston was strangely captivated now and, as Louise came within touching distance, his old passion welled up and he reached out tenderly to embrace her. But she passed straight through his arms, mouthing the words, 'Alive or dead'. Many years later, D'Onston recounted the terror of that unique moment: 'I even heard the words, but not with my outward ears, with something else, some other sense – what, I do not know. I felt startled, surprised, but not afraid, until a moment afterwards, when I felt but could not see, some other presence following her. I could feel, though I could not hear, the heavy clumsy thud of the feet following her; and my blood turned to ice!'

Regaining his senses, D'Onston shouted out to Old Bob who had been ensconced in the Bath chair at the side of the footpath, commanding a full view of its length. 'Bob', he asked insistently, 'who passed you just now?' 'Ne'er a one passed me, sir' he answered. The next day, bewildered and frightened, D'Onston called on Louise's family to enquire about her whereabouts. Solemnly, they told him that poor Louise had died three months before in Liverpool. They recounted how, in her death throes, she had constantly repeated a most perplexing phrase: 'Alive or dead. Shall I be there?'

Before you blow out the candle, I will recount the details of one final ghostly Hull mystery guaranteed to infuse your sleep with wild dreams. This time, we must go back to the afternoon of 12

October 1658, when perhaps the weirdest and most widely experienced paranormal incident ever to afflict Yorkshire stunned the entire area. With Oliver Cromwell recently dead, and his son Richard in the chair of state, England was at peace. So why on that otherwise quiet, sunny afternoon were there sounds of battle in the air? Three distinctive discharges of heavy cannon from the north-east quarter were heard in sequence by hundreds of people in the Hull, Hedon and Holderness areas. This celestial barrage preceded the massed firing of muskets that lasted a full fifteen minutes, and was accompanied by the incessant banging of drums. With plumes of smoke rising over Hull and blotting out the sun, bewildered people in the countryside assumed that the city was repelling a concerted attack from a large and heavily armoured force. And yet there were no troops in the area. Struck with wonder and terror, people across the east of the county are said to have abandoned work and retreated to their homesteads to await an attacker who never came.